Jennifer Lauck has won two Society of Professional Journalists awards for her work in television news; she also founded a public relations company that represents non-fiction authors. She now lives in Portland, Oregon, with her husband and son. *Still Waters*, the sequel to *Blackbird*, is now available in paperback.

'I doubt you will read a better book this year . . . it is not the astonishing story that makes this book extraordinary. It is the way its author tugs Jenny's skin down over your head like a balaclava and makes you look out through her bruised eyes' *Scotland on Sunday*

'It is a small miracle that Lauck actually survived to tell her sad story. Although the scars will surely be with her forever, she has written a memoir that may reassure other victims of childhood neglect and abuse that the human spirit does rise above adversity and is, ultimately, indestructible' Val Hennessy, Critic's choice, *Daily Mail*

'Lauck has constructed a riveting narrative from the awful mess of her life. That she has managed to do so fills me with admiration for which I cannot find words. The best I can do is to suggest that you read this book and be humbled, as I was, by the story of this lovely child, and her ultimate triumph over events and experiences that seem impossible to overcome' *The Times*

Blackbird

A Childhood Lost and Found

Jennifer Lauck

An *Abacus* Book

First published in Great Britain in 2000
by Little, Brown and Company
This edition published by Abacus in 2002

A CIP catalogue record for this book is
available from the British Library.

ISBN 0 349 11468 4

Printed and bound in Great Britain by
Clays Ltd, St Ives plc

Abacus
An imprint of
Time Warner Books UK
Brettenham House
Lancaster Place
London WC2E 7EN

www.TimeWarnerBooks.co.uk

For Janet Lee Ferrel Lauck and Joseph Edward Lauck

Blackbird singing in the dead of night
Take these broken wings and learn to fly

—from "Blackbird," The Beatles (1968)

ACKNOWLEDGMENTS

All thanks begin and end with my husband and best friend, Steve, who said he knew I could tell this story and that he would provide the funds and space and support for as long as I needed.

From this circle, I found my teachers: Hannelore Hahn and all the lovely writers of the International Women's Writing Guild; Suzan Hall and the writers who meet at her table; Diana Abu Jaber and PSU's writing program; Tom Spanbauer and his Dangerous Writers; and, of course, Remedial Readers and you too, Howard Waskow.

Then I was blessed with three graces. Kimberly Kanner at Pocket Books, who proved time and time again that there is truly good in a cynical world. Rita Rosenkranz, who stepped in with wise and tempered advice and then, in the final hour, a third gift from the gods, Molly Friedrich, whose vision of the future surpassed my own. Thank you Kim, Rita, and Molly.

The circle closes with final thanks to the one person who has really made the telling of this story possible: my son, Spencer. Thank you, Spencer, for leading me back to the joy of unconditional love; I thought I'd never know it again.

UCLA MEDICAL AND CLINICS
Death Summary: Lauck, Janet L.
Admitted: August 25, 1971
Expired: September 19, 1971

PRESENT ILLNESS: This is the sixth UCLA Hospital admission for this thirty-three-year-old white female. The patient presented to the Emergency Room with a five-to-seven day history of weakness, fatigue, cough, and left anterior chest pain. Her significant past medical history began in 1961 with removal of a benign tumor; she had a recurrence of the benign tumor in 1968 with another neurosurgical procedure. She then developed paraplegia, neurogenic bladder, and recurrent urinary tract infections. She was hospitalized in February 1970 for an overdose and again in February 1971 because of a duodenal ulcer. She was again hospitalized in May 1971 for septic shock secondary to a left pneumonia and an empyema of the urinary bladder.

HOSPITAL COURSE: This patient was admitted with numerous medical problems: bilateral pneumonia, sepsis, and severe metabolic acidosis and severe hypokalemia. The patient had a catheter placed in the left subclavian vein; by her first night in the hospital she rapidly went into respiratory arrest and was resuscitated with intubation. Chest film taken after resuscitation reveals a large left-sided pneumothorax. A left-sided chest tube was placed with reexpansion of the lung. The patient seemed to be improving; however, she rapidly deteriorated pulmonary-wise with the development of what was felt to be the adult respiratory distress syndrome. The patient had a tracheostomy performed and seemed to improve on this regimen, however continued to have difficulty with the left-sided pneumothorax, with repeated malfunction and replacement of chest tubes. The patient died suddenly in the morning on 9/19/71. The immediate cause of death was felt to be respiratory arrest; however, arrhythmia could not be ruled out.

Edited Dictation and Transcription,
Resident of Medicine, UCLA Hospital

part one
Carson City, Nevada
1969

one

The only house I'll ever call home is the one on Mary Street.

Mary Street is in Carson City, Nevada, and Carson City is flat valley to soft hills. Past the hills are the Sierra Nevada Mountains. When you look up, the sky is deep blue, forever blue, and there are almost never any clouds up there. The clouds that do come gather on top of the Sierras and they look like wadded-up tissue paper. Every now and then, a piece of cloud will tear away and float across the forever-blue sky.

There's one main street right down the middle of the city and it's called Carson Street. The state capital building is on Carson Street and the dome of the capital is painted silver since Nevada is the silver state. Over the silver dome, two flags kick the wind, one blue for Nevada, one red, white, and blue for America.

The Golden Nugget is on Carson Street too, but everyone just calls it the Nugget.

From the Nugget, you go a couple blocks and you can see the house where Auntie Carol and Uncle Bob live with the pack of my wild cousins. There's Steven, Bobbie Lou, Andy,

Mark, Tracy, and Faith Ann. Auntie Carol is Daddy's oldest sister, and the only time I go to that house is for holidays or if Momma has to see a special doctor.

West of Auntie Carol's house, you go Iris Street, Angus Street, and then it's Mary Street and our house is the one with the white fence and the big willow tree.

When you come in the front door, there's three ways you can go. Straight ahead is the living room, right is the kitchen, and left is a long hallway to bedrooms and bathrooms. The first bedroom is B.J.'s, then it's the bathroom, and then it's my room. Momma and Daddy's room is at the end of the hall, and out their window you can see the big willow tree. If the sun is just right, the shadow of the tree comes into their room and lies right over the middle of the California King. Momma says the bed is called that because it's not as wide as a regular king, and just a little longer, like the state.

Next to the California King is a pair of silver crutches, the kind you adjust tall or short by pushing in a little silver bead. Momma can stand up without the crutches and can even take a couple of steps. She still has to use the crutches when she walks to the bathroom or when she goes to any other part of our house.

There was a time when Momma walked just like everyone else, when she was only in bed at night, when she drove her car and talked on the telephone and had lots of ladies over for card games and coffee and thick slices of banana nut bread. I remember when Momma was strong enough to lift me off my feet, toss me in the air, and catch me again.

There's never been a time when I haven't been home with Momma. Daddy works, B.J. goes to school, and it's just Momma and me all day, everyday.

In the morning, I sit outside her door and listen.

That's the rule.

Moshe and Diana wait too. Moshe is one of those fast-moving crazy cats. Diana is all liquid and wait. I pet Diana's soft, sand-colored tummy and lay my head against the wall. Moshe sits apart from us, his brown head held high, blue eyes half closed.

The rule is, no cats, no kids, not until the toilet flushes.

When the toilet finally flushes, Moshe runs to the door, Diana rolls away from my hand, and I get off the floor and walk to the kitchen.

The kitchen is eighteen steps from Momma's bedroom door.

I drag a chair from the kitchen table to the counter, climb up, and lift the coffeepot with both hands so I don't spill. Daddy makes the coffee before he leaves for work and he sets out Momma's special cup so I can fill it. The cup is white and the lightest color of yellow, garlands of tiny purple and red flowers painted around the outside, a line of gold around the inside. The cup and saucer are part of our china kept in the hutch for special occasions. Momma says she likes coffee in special china, says it makes her feel pampered.

Four slices of bread in the toaster and I press the TOAST button down.

I cut off four squares of real butter, put them on the side of the plate.

The toast hops up and I stack the four slices, cut diagonal with a butter knife, and put the toast next to the butter.

Momma says presentation is everything.

I spoon into a jar of marmalade, thin orange slices swimming in the jam, one, two, three spoons next to the toast and butter. Momma says the marmalade is from Carmel, California, which is her most favorite place in the whole world.

I put the plate on a tray with the cup of coffee in the special china.

One foot in front of the other, I walk extra slow so I don't spill.

When I get to her room, Moshe and Diana are up on the California King, cat bodies around and around and Momma pets with both hands.

"Good morning, Sunshine," Momma says.

The best part of seeing Momma is how she always calls me Sunshine and how there's that look in her dark brown eyes. It's one of those special looks for special people. Momma has that special look for Daddy too, but I mostly see it when she looks at me, and when she looks at me that way, I know I can do just about anything.

After toast and coffee, Momma lets me brush her dark curly hair and it's fine and soft between my fingers.

One time she showed me a photo of Mrs. Kennedy in *Life* magazine. Momma calls her Jackie, says the former First Lady is bursting with style. She wants her hair just like in the magazine and I make the part on the side, brush all her curls into one curl just under her chin.

"Does Mrs. Kennedy have curly hair too?" I say.

"That's a very good question," Momma says. "I don't think so."

Momma holds the mirror and watches me pat the last curl in place.

"Ready?" Momma says.

I cover my eyes and hold my breath.

"Ready," I say.

Momma sprays a cloud of Aqua Net and it's the smell of hairspray and that sticky mist on my hands and legs. The hairspray makes Moshe shake his head and that's when he jumps off the bed and disappears until tomorrow morning. Diana doesn't care about hairspray, rolls over on her back, and takes up the sunbeam Moshe left behind.

"Getting put together is more than hair," Momma says.

She always says "getting put together," like she fell apart overnight. Momma leans over, opens the top drawer of the nightstand, and she takes out the black and white zip-up cosmetic bag.

Momma dumps her makeup out on her lap and lines the cosmetics in order: compact powder, a tube of rouge, eyeliner, and lipstick. She picks up the powder compact, snaps open the lid, and inside is a soft round pad. Momma rubs the pad over the pressed powder and moves the pad under her eyes, over her nose, up her cheeks, and down her chin. Momma touches her face so light, it's almost like she doesn't touch at all.

"Just a whisper of powder does the trick," Momma says. "Too much and you look like a clown."

Momma taps the pad of powder to my nose and that always makes me laugh. When I laugh, Momma laughs too, and the sound is better than music.

After the powder, Momma taps rouge high on her cheekbones and rubs the color until it's the lightest shade of pink.

"Rouge is like a trick on Mother Nature," Momma says, "it gives that flushed fresh look, even when you're not."

The best part of getting put together is when she does her eyes. Momma has the kind of eyes that are so dark they take in light and make it dark too. Momma says eyes never lie and if you know how to look just right, you can always find the truth in another person by watching their eyes. When I look at Momma, I mostly see that special look like she's happy I'm here. I know there are other things going on inside that she doesn't say, but I'm still learning how to look just right.

Momma takes the tube of eyeliner, shakes it like a thermometer, and pulls out the long wand. Her hand is steady and she makes a thin line to the outside of one eye and then the other. After the eyeliner is dry, Momma looks me dead on and her eyes are even darker, which doesn't seem possible.

"Nice?" Momma says.

"Perfect," I say.

The finishing touch is lipstick and I always get to put it on. Momma gives me the tube of lipstick and I take a deep breath, hold my hand steady, and fill in her lips with the red color.

When I'm done, I let out my breath again and hand back the tube of lipstick. Momma pulls two tissues from the box on the nightstand, folds the tissues in half and then half again. She presses her mouth around the tissues and some of the red comes off in the shape of her mouth.

"Nice?" Momma says.

"Perfect," I say.

If it's a bad day, Momma puts her cosmetics away and stays in bed.

If it's a good day, she pushes her covers back and puts her feet on the floor.

Today is a good day.

"Can you get my robe, Sunshine?" Momma says.

Momma wears matching nightgowns and robes called peignoir sets and they are all different colors of yellow, pink, and peach. Today it's a creamy yellow lemon meringue and I hold her robe in my hands, the silk like water in my fingers.

One arm, the other arm, twist, shrug, and then Momma stands up so she can pull the robe around her legs. Momma shimmies a little under her own weight and I move close, help tug the silk so the robe falls right around her feet. She sits down heavy on the end of the bed and takes a deep breath.

When something's wrong, really wrong, my skin knows first. It's a prickly feeling at the back of my neck, over the top of my head, down my forehead, and into my nose. Feels like a nosebleed coming on.

"You okay?" I say.

Momma sits up tall, shoulders straight, chin tucked. She calls sitting that way the posture of a lady.

"I'm fine," she says, "just a little dizzy."

I look past her words and into her truth and I know it's not such a good day after all.

Momma clears her throat and blinks the truth away. She crosses her legs at the knee, adjusts her robe.

"Okay now," Momma says, "take a few steps back and see the big picture."

Momma sits on the edge of the California King and she's silky lemon meringue, Mrs. Kennedy, dark eyes wide open, with that special look she gets when I'm around.

"Good?" Momma says.

"Perfect!"

"Pretty?"

"You're bursting with style."

Momma laughs when I say "bursting with style" and it's music in her room.

There is no special time for taking pills, Momma opens and closes bottles all day. Mostly aspirin, but there are others too, yellow pills, red pills. Her pills are in brown bottles with white lids and there are labels on the front. Momma lifts the bottles and reads the labels, squinting and moving her lips without speaking out loud.

Next to her pills is a water glass and it's my job to keep her glass rinsed and full of fresh water.

Momma opens bottles, tips out pills, closes bottles. She holds all the pills in her palm, makes a fist around them, but I make her open her hand so I can see. I point to the five matching pills, each one with a red *A* in the middle of white.

"What are those pills for?" I say.

"For the pain in my back," she says.

"What kind of pain?"

"An aching kind of pain."

"What's the pain from?"

"The operation."

"The operation for B.J.?" I say, "the one for him being born?"

"The one after," she says, "for the cancer that's not a cancer. You know, I told you before."

"The operation for the tumor as long as my arm?"

"That was operation number two."

"The operation for the tumor that grew back because stupid doctors didn't get it right the first time?"

She smiles when I say "stupid doctors." She holds up her empty hand, holds up three fingers.

"Operation number three," she says, "that's right, honey."

"If the tumor is really all gone now," I say, "how come you have pain?"

She takes a deep breath, lips together, air back out through her nose.

"You always ask the same questions."

"I know," I say, "but how come?"

"The pain is from nerve damage," she says, "from the operation where they took out the tumor but cut some nerves to my legs and my tummy. That's why it's hard to walk. Okay?"

Momma's hand tries to close on the pills, but I keep her fingers open, point to the purple pill with the white line around the middle.

"What's purple for?" I say.

"For the infection where I pee."

"Will the pill make you better?"

"We'll see," she says, "I hope so."

Momma always says that, says she hopes she's going to get better.

"What are those ones for?" I point to the red pills, smaller than all the others.

She takes a deep breath and closes her hand around her pills. I let go of her fingers.

"They are a laxative."

"What's a laxative?"

"Your questions are making me tired," she says. "Go get dressed in your play clothes now and we'll go out to the living room."

Momma takes all of the pills in one swallow, wrinkles her nose, and closes her eyes, like closing her eyes will make the pills go down easier.

You have to step down into the living room and Momma says a step down means the room is sunken. In the sunken living room is a new color television and Daddy's brown leather chair positioned right in front. His chair leans back, opens up, and lets him sit with his feet off the carpet. When Daddy's not here, I climb up on his chair and lift the headrest cushion up over my face. The smell is fabric and leather and Daddy and I love how it's always the same.

Across from the chair is a long green sofa and a wood coffee table. On top of the coffee table is a big bunch of fake grapes made from hard plastic and next to the grapes is a bowl of rock candy, where each piece looks like a rock you would find outside.

The only other furniture is a round sofa that Momma calls a lounger. I call it the big purple grape since it's a perfect round shape and the color of purple grape juice. The big purple grape is arranged near the sliding glass doors that lead to the backyard, and from there, it's the best view of the swing set on the grass, our big trees, and the roses and mint plants that grow near the patio.

After getting put together and morning pills, Momma uses her crutches to come into the living room and sit for a while on the big purple grape.

I run out back and swing on the swing set, pick dandelions, rub the soft part of the mint leaves so I can smell mint on my fingers. All I have to do is take one step to see Momma on the big purple grape, where she flips through a fashion magazine. She smiles when I do that, when I come to make sure she's still there. Momma smiles and squints, her hand up over her eyes like I'm a long ways off even though I'm right there in the backyard.

No one comes to visit until after ten in the morning.

That's the rule.

Momma says visitors before ten is uncivilized.

Most days, Momma's not up to visitors anyway, but that morning, just after ten, it's Aunt Georgia, Carrie Sue, and Jeff. Both Carrie Sue and Jeff are blond kids, white blond, and it's okay to play with them, except Carrie Sue is a tattletale.

I don't like to be too far from Momma when there are visitors since she gets tired and might need something. I come in from the backyard, stand next to the big purple grape, and wave at my cousins, at Aunt Georgia.

Aunt Georgia is thin, thin, bird thin, and she wears navy blue shorts and a blue and white striped tank top. Momma says Aunt Georgia dresses sportswear mix-and-match.

"I need more than a wave, little girl," Aunt Georgia says. "Come give me a big hug."

Momma laughs and Aunt Georgia puts her tanned arms wide. Aunt Georgia always gives me a hug when she comes to visit and I like that about her, like how she smells like soap and toothpaste and the same kind of almond lotion that Momma uses.

She sets me back from her then and looks at my face, really looks.

"That's better," Aunt Georgia says.

Aunt Georgia gets a cup of coffee for herself and sits on the long green sofa. I get out my crayons and color books and sit on the floor with Carrie Sue. Jeff crawls up on Aunt Georgia's lap the way little kids do and puts his thumb in his mouth.

Carrie Sue lies on her stomach, takes a brown crayon out of my crayon box, and colors inside the lines of a horse. I don't feel like coloring, just sit on the floor with my back against the big purple grape, where I can watch Carrie Sue, watch Momma, watch Aunt Georgia.

"You look thin, Janet," Aunt Georgia says.

Aunt Georgia snaps open her cigarette case, pulls out a cigarette, and offers it to Momma.

Momma takes the cigarette.

"You think so?" Momma says.

Aunt Georgia takes out another cigarette, puts it between her lips, and nods.

"You've lost more weight," Aunt Georgia says.

Aunt Georgia lights her cigarette with one hand and then passes the lighter to Momma. Momma uses both hands to light her cigarette and then she passes the lighter back.

"Maybe, I don't know," Momma says, "I don't think so."

Jeff climbs off Aunt Georgia's lap, gets on the floor with Carrie Sue, takes a blue crayon, and breaks it in half.

"Yes, you do look thin," Aunt Georgia says. "Maybe a little too thin."

Momma smokes and her cheeks suck in and in and then she blows the smoke up to the ceiling. She clears her throat and smiles.

"Can you be too thin?" Momma says.

Aunt Georgia smiles too and then the two of them laugh at some joke only they understand.

Aunt Georgia is married to Uncle Charles, except she calls him Chuck and he calls her George. Uncle Charles is Momma's favorite brother and out of all my uncles, he's probably my favorite too. He talks in a deep, loud voice and his eyes are the best color of blue and they look like they have a light shining from the inside out.

Momma and Aunt Georgia talk grown-up. Aunt Georgia asks if Momma and Daddy are going to take any trips to Carmel and Momma says no, not right now. Momma says she'd like to take a day and go up to Lake Tahoe and Aunt Georgia says she's been too busy for the lake and doesn't want to spend the money since they want to save up and get a house.

After a while, Aunt Georgia does all the talking and Momma is quiet like something might be wrong. Momma smiles and nods like everything is fine, but her eyes are tired.

Carrie Sue drops the brown crayon, just half a crayon now, and Jeff takes it, makes zigzags over his page.

"Let's go play in your room," Carrie Sue says.

"I want to stay here," I say.

"Momma," Carrie Sue says.

"I don't want to play in my room," I say.

Aunt Georgia clears her throat, snuffs out her cigarette in the ashtray.

Momma's cigarette is a long ash and it's burned almost all the way down. I slide the ashtray closer and Momma jumps a little. The long ash falls off in the ashtray and Momma looks at me, smiles a tired smile.

Aunt Georgia clears her throat again and I know she finally sees what I see.

"Are you all right, Janet?" Aunt Georgia says.

Momma coughs a little cough, shakes her head, and smiles.

"Just a little tired," Momma says.

It's quiet, quiet in the living room. Carrie Sue bites her fingernail and watches Jeff tear the paper off the brown crayon. Aunt Georgia looks at me, at Momma, at me again.

Aunt Georgia has eyes that know about things I don't understand yet. Her eyes move fast, but they have a quiet deep inside, like something in her hurts and it's from a long, long time ago.

Aunt Georgia squints and reaches her hand to Momma.

"It's none of my business, Janet," Aunt Georgia says, "but do you think you might need to see a different doctor? Have you thought about going to see those doctors in Palo Alto?"

Momma clears her throat, tilts her head, and cuts me a quick look. That look means this is grown-up talk and kids shouldn't be around, that look means I might get sent out of the room, that look means I should go outside and play.

Carrie Sue, Jeff, and me go out the sliding glass doors. Carrie Sue and Jeff run to the swings and laugh and yell.

I stop at the edge of the patio where the cement meets the grass, stand between the house and the swing set.

I can't hear them talk, but Momma shakes her head and Aunt Georgia goes over and sits close, puts an arm around Momma's shoulders. The two of them that close and I see how Momma is thin and small even compared to Aunt Georgia. Too thin, too small.

Carrie Sue pushes Jeff's swing and Jeff says "underdog, underdog," and then Carrie Sue runs under Jeff's swing so he goes even higher.

Overhead, the sky is forever blue, not a cloud in sight, and the only sound is Jeff's happy laugh.

After Aunt Georgia, Carrie Sue, and Jeff leave, Momma takes a nap and I watch the shadows come through the windows. I like how the shapes move around, how in the morning they're mostly along the front of the house, how by noon they shrink away and almost disappear, how when Dora comes the shadows are back again, long and lazy through the back of the house.

Dora cooks and cleans, wears a pink dress with a white apron tied tight around her middle. Dora is a brown woman from the reservation. Momma says she is Paiute and I learn how to say "Paiute" by breaking it up into two words, *pie* and *flute*.

The thing about Dora is how she moves quiet and talks quiet. Dora is so quiet, it's almost like she's not there at all. Another thing about Dora is how her eyes are like black still water. No matter how hard I look at Dora, I can't see what's in her eyes, can't see her truth.

If it's a good day, Momma cooks both lunch and dinner. Dora cleans.

If it's a bad day, Momma tells Dora what to cook for dinner.

Nowadays most days are bad days, so when Momma goes to her room and closes the door, I stay with Dora.

When it's just Dora and me, the house stays quiet until B.J. comes home.

Momma says B.J. is an All-American boy and that must mean boys are noisy. When B.J. walks home from school, you can hear him from Angus Street. B.J. yells and whistles and when he gets to our house, he stomps his feet on the floor mat and shoves the back door open with his shoulder.

"I'm home," B.J. yells, even though Dora and me are right there in the kitchen.

B.J.'s arms are full of stuff: books and papers and his Mario Andretti lunch box. B.J. throws everything on the kitchen table.

B.J. is crew cut hair so you can see his whole forehead and in the middle of his face are his dark brown eyes. The other thing about B.J. is this little black dot over his top lip. Momma says it's a beauty mark. Daddy says it's a birthmark. B.J. calls it a mole.

"Ssh," Dora says, "Momma sleep."

When Dora says to be quiet, B.J.'s face gets bright red the way it does when he's mad. He slams the door hard and tilts his chin like he can hide his angry even though there's no way to hide when your face is all red like that.

B.J. shoves himself into a chair and nods at me, just a nod, and then he puts his arm over the back of the chair. The red on his face slips away and that's when you know the angry has gone somewhere else, at least for now.

Dora takes out a box of graham crackers, tears open the brown paper, sets a pile on a plate.

"No cookies?" B.J. says.

"No," Dora says, "crackers."

"Mom always has cookies," he says.

Dora shakes her head on something she won't say, looks at me, and nods a sit-down nod. I pull out one of the chairs opposite B.J.

Dora sets the plate down between us and I take a cracker off the top of the pile and lay it on the table. I push the tip of my finger up and down until the cracker is all broken in tiny pieces and then I put one piece into my mouth.

B.J. half sits, half stands, his hand around the glass of milk. He takes two graham crackers off the pile, breaks them in half, chews on a corner, and looks around the kitchen.

B.J. is eight years old, three years older than me, and he knows everything since he's in third grade. Momma always asks B.J. about school, what he learned, did he eat all his lunch, stuff like that. Clearing my throat, I push my hands under my legs again.

"What'd you learn today?" I say.

B.J.'s face is still, no kind of expression, and he looks at me for a long time. Just like that, B.J. blinks his dark eyes and shrugs his shoulders.

"Not much," B.J. says, "stuff about astronauts and outer space."

"Outer space?" I say.

"You know, the moon," B.J. says, "flying in a spaceship."

B.J. moves his graham cracker around like an airplane, crashes it into his milk. He's a dipper. Graham crackers, Oreos, chocolate chip cookies, it doesn't matter, and when he dips, his milk ends up full of crumbs. I hate stuff floating in my milk. I never dip.

B.J. pushes the rest of his cracker into his milk, his fingers dip too, milk over the side and down in a puddle on the table. I don't think B.J. likes me very much since he acts like I'm not here, even though I'm right here.

Dora makes a click sound and wipes up B.J.'s mess. She taps her finger on B.J.'s glass of milk and he drinks, one, two, three swallows, a bunch of mashed-up graham cracker stuck in the bottom.

He puts the glass down with a bang and pushes away from the kitchen table.

"I'm going out to play," B.J. says.

Dora's quiet dark eyes stop on me and she tilts her head.

"Outside too?" Dora says. "Outside play?"

When it's just B.J. and me, it's trouble. B.J.'s always looking for a dare. Dares you to drink a lid full of red stuff he says is catsup but turns out to be hot sauce. Dares you to jump off the carport to see if you can fly like a bird. Dares you to pet that big black dog next door even though that dog bit you in the face and you had to go to the hospital to get stitches. I've had enough of being alone with B.J.

I eat another piece of my graham cracker real slow and shake my head side to side so my ponytail slaps at my face.

"See ya," B.J. says. He slams the door, the hard sound through the walls of the kitchen, into the quiet of the house.

Dora's face moves like the sound of the door slam is in her body too, and she wipes up the rest of B.J.'s milk mess.

I finish my cracker and drink half the milk, no good now since it's warm. Off my chair, I take the glass to the sink, pour it out. Dora comes to the sink, rinses her dishcloth off under the faucet. I rinse out the glass and she takes it, washes it out with the washcloth. I wipe my hands on my shirt.

"I'm going into the dining room," I say.

"Play quiet," Dora says.

"I will," I say.

Dora nods and her face moves again, maybe a smile, maybe not. I can't tell.

Through the kitchen is the dining room, and after Momma's room, the dining room is the best place.

Our table is wood and the ends are the kind you can slide in or out so the table gets smaller or bigger. Momma says the ends are called "leaves," which seems just right since the leaves of the table have leaves painted on. The painted leaves wind up around tulips painted red and vines painted brown. The same painting is on the back of each chair, six chairs, and there is more painting on the buffet and the hutch, all the leaves and the tulips and the vines making our dining room a garden.

Under the table, I lie long, look at the underbelly, see how our table is held together. There are wood pegs and flat bands of iron hammered in with iron nails, everything together like roots.

Another thing about under the table is the smell. Dora uses lemon furniture polish so there is the smell of lemons and wood.

Diana walks to where I sit and rubs against my leg, lies her cat body in a triangle of sunshine. Under the table, I pet Diana between her ears, over her soft creamy-colored tummy, and watch afternoon shadows spread wide over the carpet.

When the shadows are almost gone, when you can see dust float in the low angle of the sun, when Diana pushes under the drapes to catch the last bit of warm light, that's when I know everything in the house on Mary Street is going to change from shadows and quiet to light and sound.

First is the sound of a car in the driveway, the engine all sputter and spit. Then there is B.J., who yells out "Dad," and the sound of Daddy, who yells for B.J. to come in the house. Last is the kitchen door, a squeak on the hinge, and the sound of Daddy's voice when he says hello to Dora.

I crawl from under the table, run into the kitchen, and jump. Daddy always catches me, swings me up in a circle, and my stomach is full of caught butterflies.

Daddy settles me against his chest and I fit just right in the crook of his arm. This close he smells like tobacco and coffee and That Man cologne and I can see how his eyes are lots of different colors of brown, like spices all ground up.

"Did you miss me?" Daddy says.

"I did," I say. "I missed you a lot."

Momma says Daddy is the best kind of good-looking, boy next door mixed with drop-dead handsome. My favorite thing about Daddy is his smile, a big happy smile that makes you feel good about everything.

B.J. pushes into the door and his face is red around the cheeks from being outside.

"Dad!" B.J. says.

"Hey, buddy," Daddy says.

Daddy puts his hand on B.J.'s crew cut hair and B.J. smiles the kind of smile that's all the way into his eyes.

The kitchen is full of thick dinner smells and Dora says it's dinnertime in thirty minutes.

"Why don't you get cleaned up for dinner, son," Daddy says.

"Okay," B.J. says, out of breath.

B.J. slams the door and runs down the hall to the bathroom.

Daddy carries me into the dining room and turns on the light.

"How is your Mom today?" Daddy says.

Daddy carries me into the sunken living room and turns on another light.

"It's a good day and a bad day," I say.

Daddy reaches his hand to the lamp next to his big leather chair, turns the switch from off to on, and now the room is all light, no shadows.

"What's that mean?" Daddy says.

I bite my bottom lip and hold my arms around his neck, the warm from his body against my hands.

"She got up for a while," I say, "but then she was tired."

Daddy has the kind of eyes that tell you exactly what he thinks even when he won't say it. Most of the time, he thinks about work and money and important things I don't know about. The way he looks now, I know bad days make him nervous and restless, make him look like a trapped animal.

Daddy coughs a little cough, rubs his hand over his five o'clock shadow, and makes his face smile.

"Well, let's go see for ourselves," Daddy says. "Maybe she is all rested and ready to go."

In their room, Momma sits up in the California King and she has her pillows behind her back. When she sees Daddy, her dark eyes are full of that special look and Daddy leans down, kisses her on the lips. They talk to each other, voices low, hi's and how are you's and stuff like that. I hear Daddy ask how she feels and Momma says she's just fine.

When Daddy is home and all of us are in their bedroom,

that's when I know something is wrong. It's the sound of Momma's voice, high like a hostess who says one thing but means another. It's the way Daddy holds his breath back and gets that pinched-up skin between his eyes when he thinks too hard. It's how B.J. hits his fist into his open hand, over and over and over. I don't know what's wrong, but all over my arms and legs, I get a bad feeling.

Daddy takes his wallet, keys, and extra change out of his pants pocket, winds his watch, loosens his tie, and the whole time he talks about work and being busy and investments he wants to make, says how he is either going to be broke or rich by tomorrow.

Momma watches him move around and she just listens.

B.J. sits on the end of the bed, pushes his finger into Diana's side, and he talks about school and astronauts and what kind of bug he caught outside.

Momma smiles a hostess kind of smile and listens.

Daddy takes out a pack of Marlboros, lights his cigarette with a match, lights a cigarette for Momma, and then he and B.J. talk to each other about homework and tests and grades.

Momma smokes her cigarette and listens.

Maybe it's being tired, maybe it's not feeling so good, maybe it's how she's hungry for dinner. All you have to do is really look to know something else is going on inside Momma's head. When she looks that way, I sit as close to her side as I can and she smiles a real smile and blinks her secret thoughts away.

Momma says dinner in the dining room makes it special and that's where we always eat, at least when we are all together.

B.J. does the plates and glasses. Milk glasses for us, wine-glasses for Momma and Daddy. I do napkins and silverware, fold the paper napkins in triangles and then set the fork on top, knife and spoon on the other side.

Presentation is everything.

Dora puts the food on the table and there's mashed potatoes, meat loaf, a bowl of green beans, and a bowl of applesauce. She puts them on one side of the table, closest to where Momma sits. Dora pours B.J. and me a glass of milk, fills Daddy's wineglass just halfway, and then makes a pot of coffee for after dinner.

After everything is ready, Dora puts on her coat and leaves out the back door, so quiet you don't even know she has left.

Daddy helps Momma out of their room, her arm on his arm, and she's all dressed like it's a good day. Momma wears a pair of light pink pants and a pink and green sweater set, the top button of the sweater done up. Daddy pulls out her chair, the one right next to him at the head of the table, and she sits down slow and careful, her face with that smile like everything is just fine. Daddy helps her scoot her chair in and she takes her napkin, unfolds it, and lays it in her lap.

B.J. sits across from Momma and I sit next to her. B.J. and me unfold our napkins, lay them on our laps. That's the rule.

Daddy sits down in the big chair at the end of the table, unfolds his napkin too.

"Hand me your plate, son," Momma says.

B.J. lifts his plate with both hands and Momma puts B.J.'s plate on her plate.

"Are you hungry?" she says.

"I'm starved," B.J. says.

Momma cuts two pieces of meat loaf, lays them on B.J.'s plate, three big spoons of mashed potatoes with a cut of butter pushed in the middle.

"Not too many beans," B.J. says.

B.J. never eats vegetables and Momma laughs when he says that. She puts one spoon of beans and three big spoons of applesauce on his plate, lifts the whole thing up, and reaches the plate to B.J. The plate wavers a little up there between them and Daddy reaches, steadies the plate to B.J.

Momma takes a deep breath and sits up tall in her chair, the posture of a lady. She looks at me, smiles, and puts her hand out for my plate.

"Are you hungry?" she says.

"I am," I say.

Momma cuts me one slice of meat loaf, puts one spoon of potatoes on, a little butter in the middle, two spoons of beans, and two spoons of applesauce.

"Enough?" she says.

Nodding my head, I stand up, reach with both hands so she doesn't have to lift.

Daddy hands over his plate and she doesn't have to ask if he's hungry. B.J. and Daddy are always hungry. She loads up his plate, lots of everything on, and he takes it from her hands.

Momma serves herself last, and even on the best days, she never takes much. Tonight it's half a slice of meat loaf, a spoon of potatoes, a few beans, and a spoon of applesauce. She pushes the applesauce bowl away and smiles at all of us, her hands in her lap.

The dining room is dinner smells, butter, and meat loaf, and I'm so hungry there's water in my mouth.

Daddy closes his eyes and puts his head on his hands.

Daddy says we're Catholics, except we never go to church, not unless it's Christmas or Easter, and that's why I don't understand about praying like we do every night. Daddy says it's not really prayer, it's just taking time to be thankful.

After prayers, Daddy tells a story about a man in his office and Momma tells about Aunt Georgia's visit. Daddy says the weather feels like fall and Momma says we should take a trip up to Lake Tahoe before the weather gets too cool.

When Momma says we should go to the lake, B.J. looks up from his dinner, looks at Daddy, at Momma. Daddy is quiet and he looks at Momma.

"Do you think you're up to it?" Daddy says.

"Up to it?" Momma says.

"What I mean is," Daddy says, "do you think this is the time?"

Momma sits up tall, posture of a lady.

"I'm not an invalid, Bud," Momma says.

The sound of Momma's voice is sharp in the dining room.

Daddy clears his throat and sets his fork down in the middle of his plate.

"I know you're not an invalid," Daddy says, "I just thought we would discuss going to Palo Alto before planning any other trips."

B.J. looks at me and I look at B.J.

Momma takes a sharp breath and sets her fork down next to her plate.

"This is not the time, Bud," Momma says.

Daddy looks at B.J., at me, and he rolls his lips together.

"All right," Daddy says.

Daddy picks up his fork again, takes a bite of mashed potatoes. Momma lets a breath out her nose, her shoulders down a little. She smiles at me and touches her hand to my head.

I wish kids could be heard instead of just seen, wish I could ask about Palo Alto and the special doctors, but I just sit still.

"So?" B.J. says. "Are we going to the lake?"

It's quiet in the dining room, the smell of food all around.

Daddy looks at B.J. for a long time and then he shrugs his wide shoulders.

"Why don't we wait and see," Daddy says.

Bedtime is eight o'clock, eight-thirty on weekends, that's the rule.

Every night, I go into the living room to say my prayers out loud for Momma. I kneel on the floor, put my elbows on the big purple grape, and press my hands together. Closing my eyes, I say the same prayer every night, how I'm giving my soul to God and how I hope I'll wake up in the morning. It's a creepy prayer, but that's the way it goes.

After the creepy prayer, I open my eyes and thank God for all the good things, from the beginning to the end, and after being thankful, I get to wish for what I want most in the world. Every night it's the same thing. I wish tomorrow will be a good day. Momma smiles when I say that, her hand on the side of my face.

After prayers, she kisses me good night and gives me a hug. It's the best kind of hug with our faces cheek to cheek and the smell of her almond lotion.

"And I'm most thankful for you," she whispers, "you're my extra special gift."

There's something about how she says she's most thankful for me, like I did something just by being born. It's the best thing being someone's extra special gift.

I hug her back as hard as I can without hurting and that's when Daddy carries me to bed.

two

D addy shaves every day, even on weekends.

When I wake up, the first thing I hear is water running in the bathroom down the hall and I know Daddy's in there.

The door is open and Daddy has white shaving cream on his face. His hands are under the flow of water and he rinses off extra lather.

"Hi, Juniper," he says, "you're an early riser."

"Hi, Daddy," I say, "you're an early riser too."

"That's us," Daddy says, "early birds."

I climb up on the toilet.

Daddy wears a white undershirt and his long arms are tan and full of muscley muscles. He wears a pair of baby blue boxer shorts and his legs are tan too, dark hairs all over his legs and feet, even on his toes.

"Whatcha doing?" I say.

"Shaving," he says. "What are you doing?"

"I guess I'm shaving too," I say.

Daddy smiles underneath the white on his face and slides the can of shaving cream across the counter, a red and white can with a push button on top.

"Well," Daddy says, "you'll need your shaving cream."

I cup my hand under, push the button, white foam with a smell that stings. I rub shaving cream up the side of my face, under my nose, over my chin, and down my neck. The foam is like soap, only more soapy, and the feel is soft against my skin. Daddy opens a drawer on the other side of the bathroom cabinet, pulls out the black comb, lays it on the counter between us.

"Here's your razor," he says.

I lean over the counter, pick up the comb, and put it under the running water. Daddy's razor is silver with a wide head and a narrow handle. He picks it up between his fingertips, runs the head under the water too. In the mirror it's Daddy and me with foamy faces and we look funny that way. I laugh and Daddy laughs and the sound is around the bathroom and in my head.

"Ready?" he says.

"Ready," I say.

Leaning his hips against the edge of the counter, Daddy leans close to the mirror and lays the razor on his face, pulls down, and it's his face again, just a strip as wide as the razor.

Leaning to the mirror, I ease the flat edge of the comb down my face, the edge flat and smooth. A big hunk of foam builds up, wobbles on the edge, and I ease it over to the sink and rinse it off.

It's like that, over and over, more and more of Daddy's face in view, more and more of my face too. When he's done, Daddy splashes water on his face, pats dry with a towel, and then he slaps That Man cologne on his cheeks. The smell is lemons and wood and spices and it's on his face all day long.

I cup my hands under the water, wash off all the foam, and Daddy gives me a towel.

Faces dry, we look in the mirror again and he moves one hand over his cheeks, under his chin. He bends at the waist, lets me rub my hand on his chin. I love the way his face feels after shaving.

"Very smooth," I say.

Daddy smiles his best smile and puts both hands on the side of my face.

"You're smooth too," he says.

I laugh when he says my face is smooth, like it was scratchy before.

"Will you do my hair?" I say.

"Barrettes or ponytail?" he says.

Daddy opens the side drawer, takes out the brush and starts brushing my hair.

"Depends on the day," I say. "Are you going to work today?"

I love how Daddy brushes my hair, how he touches so light it's almost like he isn't touching at all.

"Nope," he says, "we're going to the lake."

"All of us?" I say.

Daddy looks into the hallway, looks at me again.

"Maybe Mom too," Daddy says.

If we are going to the lake, it has to be ponytails, and Daddy makes them high so they look like rabbit ears. Most times Daddy has trouble with ponytails, makes them crooked. Today he gets them just right. Looking at me in the mirror, I tip my head side to side, get the ponytails to flick around.

"Nice," I say.

"Thanks," he says.

Moshe and Diana wait at Momma's door and they are curled around each other. Daddy opens the door and inside the air feels like sleep. Moshe and Diana run without noise, jump on the bed, and walk slow long cat steps up along Momma's body under the covers. Daddy's side of the California King is all messed-up covers and a bunched-up pillow.

"Honey?" Daddy says. "You awake?"

Momma moves in the bed and Daddy sits down on the edge of the mattress.

"Who?" Momma says. "What?"

"It's me and Jenny," Daddy says. "How are you feeling?"

Momma is a slow waker-upper and her face looks like sleep wants her back again. Daddy leans over the pillows, his hand on her hair.

"Do you want to sleep a little more?" he says.

Momma pushes up, her face off the pillow, and she starts to cough. Daddy lays his hand on her back, fingers spread wide. She coughs and coughs, the sound dry and hard, her body shifting like she wants to turn over. Daddy puts his hands on her bare shoulders, helps her turn so she sits up a little. She stops coughing, moves her hands over her face.

"Better?" Daddy says.

Momma nods, eyes not really awake yet. Daddy moves the pillows around her back and she leans to the side. The strap to her peach nightgown is half on, half off, and she pushes her fingers under, makes the strap right again.

"Okay?" Daddy says.

She clears her throat, nods, and then she shakes her head, face white, and she coughs so hard she puts a fist up to her mouth and her shoulders shake.

The cats jump off the bed, run out of the room, and Momma stops coughing, moves her fist off her mouth, and there's bright red blood on her fist.

Daddy stands up quick, sits down again, stands up.

"Jesus," Daddy says.

There is blood on her lips.

Daddy pulls tissues out of the box, one, two, three, and presses them into her hand. He looks around like searching, eyes wide on me.

"Jenny, get your mother some water."

Daddy hands me the empty glass and I run to the bathroom, turn on the tap. Momma says I should always let the water run for a minute, let it run cool, but it takes forever and I push the glass under.

In the room, she spits red into her tissue. Daddy pulls out more tissues, takes the glass of water.

"Here," he says, "take some water."

Momma shakes her head no, spits a little more, and then she nods, takes the glass. Her hand shakes too much to drink and Daddy helps.

"What should I do?" Daddy says. "Should I call a doctor?"

She waves her hand, the other hand wads pink tissue. Daddy pulls three more tissues and she presses them to her mouth, shakes her head.

"It's okay," she says, "I'm okay."

Momma's voice is rough and she takes a deep breath, the bones in her chest up and down.

"What's going on?" B.J. says.

B.J.'s at the door with that look like he just woke up. He's wearing his cowboy and Indian pajamas, crew cut mashed against his head.

From the door, I know B.J. can't see the blood.

"Kids?" Momma says. "B.J.?"

B.J. leans forward a little, not in the room, not out, and his dark eyes are wide open and round.

"Mom?" B.J. says.

"I'm okay," Momma says, "it's nothing, just a little cough."

Daddy stands up, looks at us, at Momma.

"Hell," Daddy says, "it's more than a cough."

Momma shakes her head, hand up to touch Daddy.

"No, no," she says, "I'm fine. Really. We're going to the lake."

"Janet," Daddy says. "This is just enough, for gods sake, let's get you some help. Now, I mean it."

"Bud," Momma says.

Daddy puts his hands on his hips, presses his lips in a line the way he does when he's mad and he clears his throat.

"You kids go get some breakfast," Daddy says, "let me talk to Mom."

I don't want to leave the room and I look at Daddy, at Momma, at Daddy again.

"I don't want breakfast," I say.

"Go," Daddy says.

"No, Bud," Momma says, "I'm fine."

"Close the door," Daddy says.

B.J. and me sit in the kitchen. Down the hall, it's yelling and then quiet, a little more yelling and then quiet. I can hear Momma cough and Daddy talk in a low, quiet voice. The telephone rings, stops quick, and I know one of them picked up in their room.

B.J. goes down the hall on his toes. He leans to their bedroom door, holds still. He tiptoes up the hall to the kitchen again, walks normal when he gets to the kitchen. I back up and sit down at the kitchen table.

"What?" I say.

"Dad is talking on the telephone and she's crying," B.J. says.

"Crying?" I say.

"No way we're going to the lake now." B.J. says.

B.J. stands at the kitchen window and his face is a low red color under his skin, the red up to his ears.

"Why is she crying?" I say.

B.J. tilts his chin to his chest, looks at me with his eyes all shadowed by his dark eyebrows, and he presses his mouth shut tight.

"Is it sad crying or hurt crying?" I say.

B.J. climbs on the kitchen countertop, opens one of the cabinets, takes out a box of frosted cornflakes.

"Maybe she's not really crying," I say.

B.J. jumps off the counter with the box against his chest and he takes a bowl and a spoon out of the rack of clean dishes, carries everything to the table. The red on B.J.'s face isn't so red and maybe he's not mad, not really.

"Maybe you didn't hear right," I say.

B.J. pours the milk and sets the carton on the table again.

"I heard right," B.J. says, "and I bet you they are going to California after all."

"California?" I say.

B.J. mixes his cornflakes and his milk.

"Don't you know anything?" B.J. says. "There are doctors there and they're supposed to see what's wrong with her."

B.J. spoons cereal and milk into his mouth.

"Who says that?" I say.

B.J. tips his head back the way you do when your mouth is full of food and you want to talk.

"Dad told me," B.J. says.

He swallows and wipes milk off his face with his pajama sleeve.

I hate how B.J. knows things I don't know, wish I was eight years old, wish I knew what was going on.

B.J. stays in the kitchen, eats frosted flakes all soggy in milk, and I go the eighteen steps down the hall. At their door, I lean against the wall and listen. There's coughing, Daddy's low voice, the toilet flushing. There is the sound of moving around, water running in the sink, and I bet she's taking some pills.

Diana winds herself around my legs, soft, soft fur and the sound of purring. I like how she purrs before you even touch her, her engine always on.

Squatting down, I lift Diana with both hands under her soft tummy. Standing up, I lean against the wall again and Diana curls warm and perfect against my chest.

∿

Momma doesn't want to go see the doctors in California. She doesn't have to say it, I see the truth in her eyes.

B.J. says they are going on Friday night and that morning, Friday morning, it's just Momma and me and getting put together. After getting put together she lets me do pretend dress-up in her daytime clothes.

Momma sits on the edge of the California King and she has on a white silk robe with the design of purple flowers all over. Momma smokes one of her white Parliament cigarettes and the smoke twists up to the ceiling.

"This is going to be great," I say.

In the walk-in closet where she can't see me, I pull my nightgown over my head and get myself dressed in her day-time clothes.

"Well, come on," Momma says, "I'm dying from the sus-pense."

"Close your eyes," I say.

Momma sits with her legs crossed, eyes squeezed shut, and I jump out of the closet.

"Ta da," I say.

I have on her white skirt with green leaves, big orange flowers in the material, and it comes past my knees. The blouse is chiffon, with ruffles around the collar and tiny orange flowers on see-through material. I always try to wear the chiffon shirt since it's my favorite.

Momma opens her dark eyes and then she laughs and laughs, her hand over her mouth.

"Well," Momma says, "you've got a lot going on there."

"Too much?" I say.

Momma puts her cigarette between her lips, smoke deep in her body. She squints her eyes like the smoke hurts and then blows smoke to the side.

"It could be too much," she says. "You've got a daytime skirt with a cocktail blouse, plus all those flowers."

"I love this shirt," I say.

Momma moves the ruffles on the collar and the chiffon fabric lifts and falls again.

"I love it too," Momma says.

She looks at the ceiling.

"I wore that shirt to a party at the Governor's mansion, let's see, it must have been six years ago," she says. "Your father loved those swanky parties, loved being around all the important people."

Momma's voice is full of memory and the look in her eyes is happy from a long time ago. She looks at me again.

"Seems like yesterday," Momma says. "Seems like an eternity."

"An eternity?" I say.

Momma tucks her hair behind her ears.

"A long time," she says. "Trust me, that shirt is pretty racy for 9 A.M.; besides, the rule of thumb is one print for effect and then look for a solid to set it off. Try the green sweater with that skirt."

Mademoiselle, Vogue, and *Ladies' Home Journal* are in a stack by the night table. Still holding her cigarette, Momma leans down, pulls up a magazine, and flips the pages while I go back to the closet.

"Listen to this," she says. *"Good fashion accents the woman, notice the woman not the clothes and you have successful fashion."*

Pulling the green sweater over my head, the wool scratches my skin and my hair flies up in all the static. Momma shuts her magazine and tosses it back on the carpet between us. She waves her hand for me to come closer to the California King.

"It doesn't matter so much about fashion," Momma says, "it's really a matter of style. If you have style, you're always in fashion."

She straightens the seams down the side of the sweater, adjusts the little buttons, each button a tiny green pearl.

"I never did look good in green," Momma says, "but it is your color."

"My color?" I say.

"Your color," she says. "It brings out the little green flecks in your brown eyes."

I lean close to the mirror, just me in there, and I wish I could see what she sees. I step away from the mirror and it's still just me.

Momma reaches long, lays her cigarette in the ashtray.

"Now, sit down," Momma says, "and I'll do your hair like a hip chick."

On the floor, I lean my back against the California King and Momma brushes my hair in long strokes.

It's quiet in her room and I move my fingers in the white carpet.

"Why do you have to go to California?" I say.

Momma stops moving the brush and then she starts up again.

"It's nothing you have to worry about, Sunshine," Momma says.

Momma pulls my hair through the rubber band, ponytail high in the back. The hair is so tight it pulls on my face.

"That's too tight," I say.

"Sorry," she says.

Momma moves her fingers in my hair, eases the ponytail back a little, and the hair gets loose around my face. I turn around on the carpet, sit on my heels.

"B.J. says you're going to see new doctors," I say.

Momma smiles, the dark in her eyes darker than usual.

"That's true," she says.

"Are they stupid doctors?" I say.

Momma laughs and stops fast. She tilts her head and touches her finger to my face from the cheek to the chin and her hand smells like almond lotion.

"Let's hope not," Momma says.

"Hope?" I say. "Don't you know?"

Momma drops her hand off my face and it's cool where she touched my skin. She takes up her cigarette and it's almost burned all the way down. Momma presses her lips on the filter, smokes the last bit of the cigarette, and holds her breath while she smashes the butt in the ashtray.

She blows the smoke up to the ceiling and clears her throat.

"Some things you can't really know," Momma says.

"Sometimes all you can do is try to believe, try to have faith."

"I don't understand," I say.

Momma presses her lips together the way she does when she thinks hard on something. Her room is so still and quiet, it's like we are the only people in the whole world, and then Momma clears her throat.

"Things happen to you," Momma says, "bad things, and no matter what you do to make them right, they don't seem to get better."

Momma looks me eye to eye, her dark eyes with the same truth as her words.

"I don't know why bad things happen," she says, "I don't understand them either, and when you can't make sense of things, you have to go inside and find what is real, what you can believe in, what matters."

I roll my lips between my teeth and look at her serious face.

"What do you believe in?" I say.

Momma smiles, but it's a sad smile and her dark eyes move around my face like she is searching for something.

"I believe in you," Momma says. "I knew when you came into this world that you were meant to be my daughter and I was meant to be your mother."

My hands are in my lap and it's nice to have someone believe in me the way she does.

"What do I believe?" I say.

Momma leans to me, her elbows on her knees, white silk robe around her feet.

"You have to wait," Momma says. "The thing we believe comes to us through our experiences. The thing you believe has to come through your heart."

The willow tree shadow is long over the California King and Diana sleeps half in the shadow, half in the sunbeam.

I close my eyes and push down to find what I believe, but all there is is a bad feeling about Momma and California.

"I wish you didn't have to go," I say.

I open my eyes and Momma smiles.

"I'll be back," Momma says, "don't worry so much."

I want to tell her about the bad feeling, I want to make her stay right here in the house on Mary Street where things are safe. My lips are dry and I lick them to make that tight feeling go away, but I don't say what I want.

"All right now," Momma says. "Stand up and let's see how you look."

I get up off the floor and turn a circle. In the long mirror, I see me in Momma's flowered skirt and green sweater, see the big ponytail on top of my head.

"Good?" I say.

"Perfect," she says.

"Pretty?" I say.

"A pair of green pumps and a matching handbag with that," Momma says, "and you're bursting with style."

Auntie Carol's big house is on the corner of Mussler and Minnesota Street and inside is every kind of room with every kind of rule. Downstairs is a living room where kids are not allowed, a family room with a television where kids are allowed, a dining room with glass doors where kids are not allowed, and a kitchen with a big picnic table where kids are allowed. Upstairs are the bedrooms, one for the girls and one for the boys, no mixing. There are two staircases, one up from the living room, the other up from the kitchen.

Auntie Carol is wide hips, thick legs, and great big boobs that look like they might launch right off her body. She dresses in nothing but black: black sweater with long sleeves, and black pants that make a swish sound when she walks.

Momma says Auntie Carol wears black because it's a slimming color.

I think Auntie Carol wears black because she's one of those people with magic powers who can tell your fortune by looking at your hand or by reading these cards she keeps hidden in a drawer in the grown-up dining room.

Auntie Carol never showed me the cards, but my cousin Tracy told me they were there and says lots of people come to Auntie Carol's house to get their fortunes told.

When Daddy drops us off, B.J. and me go straight upstairs. B.J. goes to the boys' room, I go to the girls' room.

As soon as I open the door to the girls' room, Tracy throws her doll on the floor and runs to meet me.

"Jenny," Tracy yells.

"Tracy," I yell.

Tracy hugs so hard I can't breathe, but it doesn't matter about air. Tracy is my most favorite cousin and we look almost exactly alike, dark hair, dark eyes. We are almost the same height too, except I'm stronger. I hug Tracy around her middle, lift her feet up off the floor, and she laughs when I do that.

"Me next," Faith Ann yells, "me!"

Faith Ann pushes between Tracy and me, pushes Tracy back, and puts her arms around my neck and her legs around my waist.

"Jenny, Jenny, Jenny, " Faith Ann yells.

Faith Ann is thin and tiny and she has clear blue eyes that

are happy all the time. Her favorite thing is to be carried and to spin.

I turn around and around and Faith Ann laughs a high-pitched laugh.

"Faster," she yells, "faster!"

"You're going to make her throw up," Bobbie Lou says.

Bobbie Lou is the oldest girl, almost a teenager, and she never plays since she's supposed to be in charge of us kids.

"Faster," Faith Ann yells.

"If she throws up," Bobbie Lou says, "you have to clean it up."

Faith Ann doesn't look like she is going to throw up.

I turn so fast, the room gets blurry, and just like that, I'm in the middle of a whole new world where all you do all day long is spin in circles, play with dolls, and laugh until your sides ache.

Tracy, Faith Ann, and me sit on the floor and cut out paper dolls.

Tracy gives me a pair of little scissors so I can cut out the evening gowns, Faith Ann cuts out shoes, and Tracy cuts out hats.

Bobbie Lou reads a book like we're not here at all, says paper dolls are kids' stuff.

Tracy holds up a grown-up lady paper doll wearing a white tank top with something like camping shorts and high-heel pink shoes.

"That's clashing," I say.

"Clashing?" Faith Ann says.

"Clash means it doesn't match," I say.

"I kind of like it," Tracy says, "it's different."

"Not very practical though," Bobbie Lou says, and lays her book in her lap.

"You're not playing," Tracy says.

"Try the sandals," I say, "trust me."

Tracy pulls off the pink shoes, takes the brown sandals, and folds the tabs. Tracy holds the doll at arm's length, looks at the big picture.

"Pretty boring," Tracy says.

"Very boring," Faith Ann says.

"Not if she's in Africa," Bobbie Lou says, "or the desert searching for a lost civilization."

"You're not even playing," Tracy says.

Bobbie Lou shrugs her shoulders and picks up her book again.

"I'm just trying to help you have some imagination," Bobbie Lou says.

"Why don't you go back to the pink pumps and find a party dress," I say, "get her out of the desert."

Tracy pulls off the shorts and shirt, finds a pink dress, puts the pink pumps back on her doll's feet.

"Nice?" Tracy says.

"Perfect," I say.

The best part of paper dolls is you forget about everything and just worry about what to wear next.

"Dinner," Auntie Carol yells.

Tracy and Faith Ann drop the paper dolls and run for the door. Bobbie Lou folds the edge of her page over and closes her book. I stay on the floor, a paper doll in my hands and all the clothes on the floor around my feet.

"Are you coming?" Bobbie Lou says.

"Yeah," I say, "I guess."

Bobbie Lou walks out of the girls' room and I can hear all my cousins yell, can smell the dinner up the stairs and into the hall, can hear Auntie Carol yell the rules about shoving and sharing.

Down the hall, down the stairs, and at the big table in the kitchen, I am with my cousins, but at the same time I feel like I am on the outside looking in.

Steven, Bobbie Lou, Andy, Mark, Tracy, and Faith Ann pull and reach and fight over food, and across the table, B.J. fights with them.

"Hey, stop pushing," Mark says.

"I'm not pushing," Andy says.

"You're in my way," B.J. says.

Steve grabs the macaroni and cheese bowl from Tracy, Tracy screams to let go, and they both drop the bowl in the middle of the table, where it tips and knocks Faith Ann's milk into her food. Faith Ann screams and Bobbie Lou tells her to hush and Mark points at food floating in milk and says how it looks like puke.

The swinging door between the kitchen and the dining room is closed, and on the other side, Auntie Carol and Uncle Bob eat dinner in the no kids allowed dining room where it's peace and quiet.

When you get them one by one, my cousins aren't so wild, but when you get them together, they are just crazy. Even though there is food on my plate, I can't eat, can't think, just watch them go crazy the way you watch a storm explode.

Mark calls Tracy a slob for dropping the bowl before he got any macaroni and cheese and Tracy yells how it was an accident. Andy picks up a handful of his macaroni and cheese and drops it on Mark's plate, says, "Here, have mine." Mark screams, "Food fight!" puts his hand into his food, and throws peas and carrots on Andy's plate.

Steven stands up, arms wide, yells, "No food fight," and B.J. shoots a spoon of peas and carrots over Steven's head.

Red and green fly over the table and land on my head, on Tracy's head, and both of us scream and laugh.

"Don't make me come in there," Auntie Carol yells.

"It's Mark's fault," Andy yells.

"It's Tracy's fault," Mark screams.

"I'm counting to ten," Auntie Carol yells.

Faith Ann gets up on her knees, reaches for her glass of milk, and tips it over. Milk runs down the table, into Mark's lap, and Mark jumps back, knocking Andy and B.J. off the bench. Faith Ann screams how her milk spilled again and Andy jumps up and punches Mark in the arm.

"Ten," Auntie Carol yells.

Auntie Carol pushes the swinging door open and her big wide body fills the kitchen.

For one second, just before the door swings closed, I see Uncle Bob at the head of the dining table. He doesn't look up, just sets his fork and knife down, lifts up the newspaper.

After dinner is bath time.

After bath time, it's pajama time.

After pajamas it's TV time, one half hour before bed.

That's the rule.

After TV time it's bedtime and Tracy and me share the big double bed.

I lie in bed on my back and out the big window are tree branches and black sky and a piece of the moon.

I'm tired and wide awake at the same time and I know Tracy is awake too, waiting until Faith Ann and Bobbie Lou breathe the deep breaths of sleep.

It's quiet like that for a long time and then Tracy pulls the covers over our heads.

"Come on," Tracy whispers.

She fumbles around under the sheets and flips a switch and then white light is between us, white and black points of light in my eyes.

I cover my eyes with my hand and blink my eyes used to the light.

"Where did you get that?" I say.

Tracy wiggles around so she sits cross-legged and puts her finger to her lips.

"You have to whisper," Tracy whispers, "or Momma will hear you."

"Where?" I whisper.

Tracy smiles, her dark eyes with cuts of white light and her face is full of secrets.

"The boys' room," Tracy whispers. "I've been hiding it for when you came over."

"Really?" I say. I twist around and sit up too.

"Whisper," Tracy whispers.

Tracy moves her hands over her face and pushes her long dark hair back.

"Now it is time," Tracy whispers, "for secret fortunes."

Tracy takes my hand in her hands, turns it so my palm is up, and she traces over the lines with her first finger. Her finger tickles and I bite my lip to keep from laughing.

"I see a long life," Tracy says, "with much travel."

"No, you don't," I whisper.

Tracy looks right at me, her dark eyes dead serious.

"Momma says this is a life line," Tracy whispers, "and the little lines off the life line are travel."

I look at all the lines across my palm, just lines. Tracy pokes her finger in the middle of my hand.

"These dents mean pain," Tracy whispers, "you have lots of little dents."

I hold my palm closer to my face.

"Like I'm going to fall and scrape my knee?" I whisper.

Tracy shrugs one shoulder and makes a frown. She opens her hand in the light and we look at her palm.

"I fall all the time," Tracy whispers. "I don't have those dents."

Tracy looks at me and I look at Tracy and it's a bad feeling on my skin, up my neck and into my nose.

There is a sound outside the covers and I pull my hand out of her hand and lie down flat. Tracy turns off the flashlight, black all around us under the sheets, and she pushes the covers off our head.

Tracy holds still. I hold still.

The house is quiet like sleep and I breathe out real slow, the idea of my hand and the pain and the long life around and around in my head.

Tracy rolls close to my body and I roll on my side too so we are nose to nose, knee to knee. I can't see Tracy's eyes in the dark, just see shadows where I know her eyes are.

"Do you think it's true?" I whisper.

"Momma says your hands never lie," Tracy whispers.

"I don't think it's true," I say.

Tracy puts her arm around my body and she squeezes like part of a hug.

"I wish you could stay here all the time," Tracy whispers.

I put my arm around Tracy's body and she feels warm and soft and safe. It's nice being close to Tracy, nice to have a favorite cousin and to know I'm her favorite too.

"Me too," I whisper.

three

Something bad happened in California. It's the way Daddy looks at Momma and then looks away fast. It's how Momma's voice is high and wrong.

When she comes home, no one talks about the bad thing and it's just like it always is. Daddy at work, B.J. at school, Momma and me together all day long.

I get her coffee in special china, make toast, carry the tray to her room, and she calls me Sunshine, just like always.

But her eyes don't have the special look.

Momma's dark eyes are busy on something else.

My stomach moves around and around the way it does when I'm hungry except I'm not hungry. I pet Diana's sand-colored fur in long strokes from her head to the black end of her tail.

Momma drinks her coffee in noisy sips and her dark eyes move back and forth like she lost something. Momma tips her cup all the way back and sets it down in her saucer.

"Enough is enough," Momma says.

"What's enough?" I say.

"Being in this house," Momma says, "this room, this bed. I've had it."

Momma's eyes are back and forth, stop-start.

"Momma?" I say.

Her dark eyes stop-start on me, she blinks slow one time, and then her eyes stop and hold steady.

"I need to see Dr. Smernoff," Momma says.

"Dr. Smernoff?" I say.

"Right," Momma says. "Dr. Smernoff is my friend, he'll tell me the truth, he'll get to the bottom of this."

"The bottom?" I say.

"Right," Momma says.

She presses her lips together and even with red lipstick they are the lightest shade of pink, a little blue too. Momma's eyes move quick, back and forth, stop-start, and she licks her lips.

"I need my black slacks," she says, "a sweater too. You pick."

"We're going all the way to Reno to see Dr. Smernoff?" I say.

"Right," she says.

My heart beats in my ears and I get off the California King. In the walk-in closet, sweaters are folded and stacked, green, blue, black, white, and red. I pick red since she looks perfect in that color.

Momma stands next to her bed and I can see her shape through her nightgown. Her legs sway under her weight and she puts a hand on the nightstand to steady herself.

"I'm fine," she says. "I'm fine."

I put the sweater on the bed and get down on my knees. Her crutches are on the floor under her bed and I slide them out, stand them up so she can reach.

"Thank you, sweetie," she says.

Momma takes a crutch, pushes her arm through the

armhole, and stands up straight. She breathes in and out like she can't catch enough air and sweat dots poke out on her top lip. Momma takes a deep breath, puts her hand over her chest.

"Here's the plan," she says. "You go get dressed. Pick something pretty, a dress, the white dress with the little red flowers."

"Maybe we should just stay here," I say.

"Wear your red tights too," she says.

"Maybe you shouldn't get out of bed yet," I say.

She wipes sweat off her top lip and shakes her head.

"It'll be perfect," Momma says, "we'll match."

Momma sways on her crutch and I reach my hand like I can help even though there's no way I can catch her if she falls. She gets her balance and sets her feet wide.

The look in Momma's eyes, the bedroom with the morning sun through the willow tree, Moshe and Diana still on the bed, and I just know we shouldn't leave the house on Mary Street.

Big Red and Baby Blue are sports cars and they are parked under the carport in front of the house. Red is Daddy's, Blue is Momma's.

In Baby Blue, the seats are made of white leather and there is that smell all around, the smell of a car sitting for a long time with the windows rolled up.

Momma wears her black slacks, her red sweater, and a black wrap-around coat. I have on my white dress with the red flowers and my red tights.

"Everything should be in the glove compartment," she says.

I reach forward, turn the black knob, and the glove compartment door flips open. Inside are the three things Momma needs for driving: the black scarf with the big red roses, her driving gloves, and her cat-eye sunglasses.

"Perfect," she says.

Momma flips the scarf open in a big square, folds the square into a triangle, and lays the whole thing over her hair. She takes the ends of the triangle under her chin and ties them together behind her neck.

The gloves are next and she puts on one, then the other, and snaps the snaps at each wrist.

The sunglasses are last and Momma opens them with both hands, lowers her face into the glasses, and then looks at me with a movie star smile on her face.

"Nice?" she says.

"Perfect," I say.

"Pretty?" she says.

"You're bursting with style," I say.

Momma's eyes are hidden behind her sunglasses, but she smiles so wide her cheeks are perfect and round. She laughs, head back, and pats her hand on my leg.

"It feels so good to get out," she says.

Momma starts Blue and the engine kicks in with a loud sputter spit. She presses her foot on the gas pedal over and over again.

Daddy says Baby Blue and Big Red are German sports cars with delicate engines. Daddy says you should never rev the engine, not ever.

Momma revs two more times and presses her foot on the other pedal, shifts Baby Blue into reverse.

"Here we go," she says.

The front yard is a wide stretch of grass, the willow tree, and there is a white rail fence around the whole thing.

Moshe runs under the rail of the fence and hides under a bush next to the front door.

We back out of the driveway and sunshine comes through the windshield. In the light, Momma is all wrong. She has too much powder around her chin and her lipstick is off its line.

She shifts the gears around and drives real slow down Mary Street. I turn around in my seat and watch the house out the back window. Momma makes a right turn and the house on Mary Street is gone.

"Turn around now, Sunshine," Momma says.

She stops at a stop sign and there is sweat on her lip and it lifts the powder off her skin. Momma looks at me, cat-eye sunglasses on her face, and I can't see her eyes at all.

"You should buckle your belt," she says.

"I never buckle," I say.

"I know," she says, "but why don't you do it this time, just for me."

Momma smiles and I can see a dot of red lipstick on her teeth. I rub my finger on my tooth.

"You've got a lipstick spot on your tooth," I say.

Momma tips her head back and looks at herself in the rearview mirror, wipes the lipstick off her tooth.

"Thanks, honey," she says. "Now buckle up."

I twist and pull the safety belt around, push it into the buckle on the other side of the seat, and the strap is tight over my middle.

A car honks behind us and Momma looks in the mirror again.

"Wait a damn minute," she says to the mirror.

She waves her black glove, puts her hand on the shifter, pulls into the intersection.

"Everyone is in such a hurry," she says.

When I'm buckled in, I sit so low in the seat, all I can see is the inside of the door and the glove box.

I can't see the car that hits us from the side and pushes us all the way to the other side of the street. All I see is Momma push on the brake pedal, turn the steering wheel hard to the right, and then jerk back so hard her head just snaps. A horn honks, then lots of horns honk, and I hear someone scream and scream and scream.

"Calm down, little girl," a policeman says, "you're fine, your mommy is fine, just calm down now."

The policeman is big hands, big arms, big chest. His nose is big too and his eyes are little points of dark under dark eyebrows. The policeman's big fingers are around my arms and he shakes me.

"Momma crashed," I yell. "She's not supposed to crash."

"She crashed all right," the big policeman says.

"What's your name?" the big policeman says. "Where do you live?"

Another policeman comes with Momma's purse and he's not so big. He opens her purse, his hand around in her stuff, and he takes out her thin black wallet.

"Lauck," he says, "the lady's name is Janet Lauck."

All of me shakes—my legs, my arms, up my back. I'm cold, cold and I cross my arms over my chest.

"We live on Mary Street," I say.

"Well, you didn't get far," the big policeman says.

"Where's Momma?" I say.

"She is going to the hospital," the big policeman says. "She has a bump on her head."

The little policeman takes a bottle of pills out of Momma's purse, shakes the bottle, and looks at the label.

"Is your mother sick?" he says.

There is a tear in my red tights just over my knee and my mouth hurts. I push my arm over my mouth, wet spit on my skin.

"It's a good day," I say, "I thought it was a good day."

"This label says Doctor Smernoff," the policeman says, "is that her doctor?"

I nod my head.

"We were going to see the doctor," I say.

"Well, that's something," the policeman says, "I'll get on the horn and find Dr. Smernoff."

Dr. Smernoff has an office with chairs lined up against the wall, a table with magazines piled up, and there is a desk for his nurse to sit and talk on the telephone. I used to come here for my baby shots, but I mostly remember getting a sucker after, sometimes lime, sometimes cherry. My favorite is lime.

Sitting in a chair, I look at a skeleton that hangs on a wire, don't remember any skeleton from before. The skeleton is all bones and some of the bones make circles and others are straight lines.

Dr. Smernoff is a little man and he talks with an accent so his *S*'s are all mixed up. He pushes his hands into his white coat, nods at the big policeman, the little policeman, them talking, him listening. They all look at me and Dr. Smernoff tilts his head and they move across the office. The nurse comes over and hands me a cherry sucker.

"Your father is coming to get you right now," the nurse says.

I pull the wax paper off the sucker, put it into my mouth, and it's a little sour, a little sweet.

Daddy opens the office door and his face is full of worry. I take the sucker out of my mouth and he kneels down by my chair.

"Hi, Daddy," I say.

Daddy laughs, but the sound is wrong, not like a laugh at all. He hugs me tight and then holds me back.

"Are you all right?" he says.

"I ruined my tights," I say.

Daddy puts his hand on my head, his other hand over the hole in my red tights.

"But you're all right?" Daddy says. "Nothing hurt?"

"I had my seat belt on," I say, shaking my head.

"Why the hell was she driving?" Daddy says.

"We were going out," I say, "she had to get out, had to see Dr. Smernoff."

Dr. Smernoff comes over and puts his hand on Daddy's arm. Daddy stands up and the policemen and Daddy and Dr. Smernoff talk the way grown-ups talk, all at the same time.

Daddy puts his hands up and the police ask him a couple more questions and then they close their notepads. The policemen leave and the big one waves at me.

I don't know what to do, wave, not wave, and I just smile and put the sucker back in my mouth.

Daddy and Dr. Smernoff stand close and talk in whispers. I know they talk about the bad thing that happened in California. Dr. Smernoff pats Daddy on the back and that's funny since Daddy is so big and Dr. Smernoff is so short.

"I have to do something," Daddy says, "she belongs in a hospital."

Daddy's voice is wrong, too loud.

Dr. Smernoff looks at me, pats Daddy again, but Daddy shrugs him off.

"Come on, Juniper," Daddy says.

"What about Momma?" I say.

Daddy presses his lips together, looks at Dr. Smernoff.

"You're making a mistake," Dr. Smernoff says. "She doesn't belong in an institution, Bud."

Daddy tugs me off the chair and I stumble to get my feet down on the floor.

"Bud, please," Dr. Smernoff says, "don't be hasty."

"Let's go," Daddy says.

Dr. Smernoff stands next to the skeleton of bones and he has his arms at his sides like he doesn't know what to do.

"Bye-bye, Dr. Smernoff," I say.

Dr. Smernoff puts his hand up, makes a slow wave.

"Bye-bye, Jennifer," he says.

❧

Tracy, Faith Ann, and me are cats all afternoon and it's a lot harder being a cat than it looks. A cat has to be on all fours and you can't talk. The only sound you're allowed to make is a mew or a growl, maybe some snarls too.

We crawl around the backyard, go under bushes, search for rats and birds to jump at. When we can't find birds or rats, we crawl the steps to the back porch and eat little hard pellets of Purina cat food right out of the bowl, just like the cats do. The cat food is hard and crunchy and it tastes a lot like paper tastes. After cat food, we lick our hand-paws and wipe them over our faces.

Faith Ann is the best cat of all, her skinny body jumps and springs and fits into the smallest places. She takes it the most serious too, never laughs, not even when she wipes spit on her face and in her hair.

"I'm done," I say, "my knees hurt."

"Me too," Tracy says.

"Meow, meow," Faith Ann says.

I lie out under the big tree in Auntie Carol's backyard and pieces of dry grass poke through my T-shirt, into my skin. Tracy stretches out so we are right next to each other except her feet are by my head and her head is by my feet. Tracy puts her hand in my hand, our fingers all together. She squeezes tight and I squeeze back and it's nice to be quiet and hold hands.

Faith Ann crawls over my legs, over Tracy's head. Tracy hits at Faith Ann.

"Knock it off, Faith," Tracy says.

"Meow," Faith Ann says.

Faith Ann crawls the other direction, over both our middles, face against my hand.

"I don't feel like being a cat anymore, Faith Ann," I say.

"MEOW," Faith Ann says.

"No more," Tracy says, "we're done."

Faith Ann puts her fingers up like claws, hisses, and scratches the air between her and Tracy.

"STOP," Tracy yells.

Faith Ann makes her nose scrunch like a cat, shakes her head like a cat, and crawls under a bush.

One day, two days, three days, and it's like forever that we're gone from the house on Mary Street.

Auntie Carol goes to our house, gets some clothes and toys. She says everything's fine, says Momma is in a special hospital, says Daddy has to work on a special project. Auntie Carol says I should just play with the girls and have a good time, except it's getting harder and harder to have a good time.

Without Momma, it's like being lost without a reason, and inside my body is an empty space that can't get filled up, even with Tracy.

Sunday morning, Auntie Carol, B.J., and me are in the no kids allowed living room and I sit on the floor between Auntie Carol's heavy legs. Auntie Carol brushes my hair and pulls it through a rubber band.

"You're making it too tight," I say, "that hurts."

"Quit fussing," Auntie Carol says. "It'll hold better."

I have on a pair of white tights and a red dress with a white ribbon around the middle. B.J. wears his best navy pants and a white button-up shirt with a checkered vest buttoned up too. He sits on the no kids allowed sofa with his chin tucked into his chest and he looks up with the shadows of his eyebrows over his eyes.

Auntie Carol pulls my hair through the rubber band one more time, and when she lets go, my face skin is pulled tight too.

"You look like a rat," B.J. says.

"She does not look like a rat." Auntie Carol says. She gets off the sofa, goes out of the adults only living room.

B.J. keeps his chin tucked, his eyes all shadow mad, and he presses his mouth in a line.

"You do," B.J. whispers, "you look just like a rat."

"MEOW," I say, claws in the air.

Auntie Carol comes back, a red ribbon in her hand.

"No fighting," Auntie Carol says, "sit still and be good."

Auntie Carol ties the ribbon around my ponytail.

There's a knock on the front door and all three of us look that way.

"That's your father," Auntie Carol says.

Daddy opens the door and just like that, all the mad in B.J. is gone. He runs through the living room, puts his arms around Daddy's neck. I try to get up too, but Auntie Carol keeps me down with her hands tying the ribbon.

"Hey, big guy," Daddy says, "what's this?"

Daddy holds B.J. away and looks at his face. I can't see B.J., but I bet he's crying and I wish I could see that. Daddy takes out his handkerchief, but B.J. shakes his head no.

"I missed you, Dad," B.J. says, his voice low and sad.

"I missed you too," Daddy says. "I missed both you kids."

Daddy is just like always except he has on weekend clothes, jeans and a T-shirt, a dark red V-neck sweater over. He stands up and roughs his hand over B.J.'s hair.

"Hi, Juniper-Girl," he says. "Don't you look pretty."

Auntie Carol clears her throat, her hands pressed hard on my shoulders.

"I thought you were taking them to church," Auntie Carol says.

"Not today," Daddy says.

I twist and turn, crawl on my knees to get away from Auntie Carol. Daddy bends down and picks me up, hugs me against his chest.

"There's my girl," he says.

"Do I look like a rat?" I say.

"Of course you don't look like a rat," Daddy says, "you look like a princess."

"I dressed them for church," Auntie Carol says.

"Not today, Carol," Daddy says, "we're going to breakfast."

Auntie Carol stands up, the brush in her hand, and she hits the handle against her palm.

"You should go to church, Bud," Auntie Carol says, "a time like this calls for prayer."

Daddy shakes his head and his brown eyes are tired. He sets me down, puts one hand on my shoulder, the other hand on B.J.'s crew-cut head.

"What's done is done," Daddy says, "prayer isn't going to change a damn thing."

B.J. bends his head back and his dark eyes are wide open.

"What's done?" B.J. says.

Auntie Carol stands wide, her hands on her hips, and she looks at Daddy with a long hard look.

Maybe Daddy doesn't know how Auntie Carol has special powers and I look up at his face, look at Auntie Carol. It's quiet between them, the air quiet too, and overhead I can hear my cousins' feet like they are jumping up there.

B.J.'s face gets a low pink red and he looks at Auntie Carol, at Daddy, at Auntie Carol again.

"What's going on, Dad?" B.J. says.

Daddy looks away from Auntie Carol, smiles at B.J.

"I'll tell you guys later," Daddy says. "Let's go."

Inside the Nugget, it's day turned to night and there's every kind of slot machine noise: money falling into metal trays, coins fed in one at a time, and the thump of slot machine arms pulled down.

Men and women sit on stools in front of the slot machines and their eyes watch cherries and apples and oranges and bananas spin and spin.

Momma says gambling is the worst kind of weakness, says she won't have a thing to do with casinos and making bets, says you never win playing another man's game.

Daddy stops at a slot, digs into his pocket, and pulls out a quarter.

"Let's try our luck," Daddy says.

B.J. and me stand back, watch him feed in a quarter and pull the long handle, let it go. B.J. stands up on tiptoe, watches the fruit spin. One, two, three, thump, thump, thump, and some coins fall into the tray.

"Wow," B.J. says, "you won!"

"Look at that," Daddy says, "struck a little luck today."

Daddy takes a quarter out of the tray, feeds it into the slot, pulls the handle.

B.J. steps up to Daddy's side, looks at the machine spin.

It's thump, thump, thump and more coins fall into the coin tray. The sound of metal against metal, coins dancing around.

"You're on a roll," B.J. says.

"Looks that way," Daddy says.

"We should go," I say.

B.J. shoves on my shoulder with his whole hand.

"Go?" B.J. says. "He's winning."

Daddy looks across the casino and he squints like it's bright in here even though it's dark.

"She's right," Daddy says. "You two get us a table and I'll try one more time."

"But Dad," B.J. says.

Daddy takes a quarter out of the tray, holds it up between him and B.J.

"If you take your sister and get us a table," Daddy says, "I'll put this one in for you."

B.J. looks at me, looks at the quarter.

"Okay," B.J. says.

B.J. presses his hand on my back and I walk faster so he can't touch me.

There is the sound of the money in the slot, the handle pulled, and when I look back Daddy's face is lit up from the light on the slot machine.

We get a booth and B.J. pulls out a Keno card, fills in numbers with a black crayon. I sit on the edge of the booth, smooth out my dress, look back at the slot machines, except I can't see Daddy anymore. Auntie Carol's ponytail makes my head hurt and I shake my head a little.

A waitress comes over and she has bright orange hair piled up on top of her head. She smiles red lipstick at B.J. and me.

"All alone?" the waitress says.

B.J. tilts his chin low to his chest and looks mad at the waitress.

"My father is coming," B.J. says.

The waitress looks over at the casino, looks at me, at B.J. She puts three menus on the table and smiles again.

"Okay," she says. "Be back in a sec."

B.J. takes a menu, holds it over his face, and all I can see are his fingers over the plastic.

I slide all the way into the booth, take the menu, and open it flat.

"What a streak of luck," Daddy says.

Daddy's hands are full of quarters and he sits down, spills money over the middle of the table. Coins roll around on the table and then they spin until they fall flat. B.J. puts his menu down and his eyes are wide open.

"How much?" B.J. says.

B.J. stacks quarters.

"At least enough for breakfast," Daddy says, "plus some extra for you, buddy."

Daddy settles into the booth and picks up his menu. The waitress comes back with a pot of black coffee.

"Hey, Bud," the waitress says. "Are these your kids?"

"They are," Daddy says.

She fills his coffee cup, her hand over her heart.

"Well, I had no idea," the waitress says. "What good-looking children."

Daddy smiles and looks at me, at B.J.

"Say thank you," Daddy says.

"Thank you," I say.

B.J. takes his hands off the money, puts them in his lap, eyes down. He looks at the waitress and looks down again. The waitress laughs.

"Your boy is a real heartbreaker," she says.

B.J.'s face and neck are a bright red stain and the waitress laughs some more.

"Be back in a minute," the waitress says.

Daddy opens his menu again. B.J. opens his menu. I close my menu.

"I know what I'm having," I say.

"French toast?" Daddy says.

Nodding my head, I push my menu across the table.

"Can I have hot chocolate?" B.J. says.

"Sure," Daddy says, closing his menu and putting both hands around his coffee cup.

I reach behind my head and work my finger into the rubber band around my ponytail, but it's too tight for my finger.

The waitress comes back and she pulls the pencil out of her hair.

"Ready?" the waitress says.

Daddy says it's just coffee today, I order French toast, and B.J. gets scrambled eggs with bacon. Both of us get hot chocolate.

B.J. stacks quarters again, eight little piles, a bunch of quarters still lying loose.

Daddy sips his coffee and clears his throat.

"Well," Daddy says.

He clears his throat again and his eyes are on the coffee in his cup.

"Well," Daddy says. "There's something I need to tell you guys."

The casino is the sound of change into metal slot machine trays. B.J. takes his hands off the quarters, looks at me, looks at Daddy.

"Your mother had to go to a special hospital," Daddy says.

Daddy looks up at B.J., at me, and then he looks down again.

"At least I thought she should be there," Daddy says.

"Dad?" B.J. says.

Daddy's eyes blink like he's surprised we are here and he clears his throat.

"Anyway," Daddy says, "we need to find a different place for your Mom. I think the best place for her is in California and that's where she is right now."

"California?" B.J. says.

"Right," Daddy says.

"When will she come back?" I say.

It's quiet at the table again, Daddy looks around the restaurant like he wants something.

"Well, that's the thing," Daddy says. "She's not coming back."

"She's not?" B.J. says.

"No," Daddy says. "We are going to her."

"To California?" I say.

"Right," Daddy says.

"We're going to California?" B.J. says.

"Right," Daddy says.

"Forever?" I say.

"For now," Daddy says.

"But, Dad," B.J. says, "what about school?"

"What about Moshe and Diana?" I say.

"What about all my friends?" B.J. says.

"What about our house?" I say.

Daddy puts his fingers up to the top of his nose and squeezes tight. When he lets go there are two little white spots where his fingers were.

"Look," Daddy says, "we'll come back and visit. We'll find a new house, a better house, and Moshe, well, we'll find a place for him too."

"What about Diana?" I say.

Daddy puts his hand on my shoulder, warm fingers pressed down.

"Juniper," Daddy says, "everything will be fine. Business opportunities, good schools, the ocean, sunshine year around, you guys will love California."

B.J. presses all the way back in his side of the booth, his eyes on the quarters, his mouth wide open.

My head aches behind my eyes and around my ears. I push my finger into the rubber band again and my finger finally fits. I pull hard and the whole thing falls off, my hair around my face again. I look at the ribbon and the rubber band like I don't know what they are.

Daddy reaches over, takes the rubber band and the ribbon.

"Oh, Jenny," Daddy says, "why did you do that?"

"It was too tight," I say.

The waitress comes with two mugs of hot chocolate, whipped cream sprayed in a circle. She sets both mugs down on the end of the table and Daddy makes himself smile. He holds the ribbon and rubber band up like he's showing the waitress.

"Looks like you've got your hands full," the waitress says.

Daddy laughs, but the sound isn't right and he shakes his head.

"I guess we'll manage," Daddy says.

The waitress laughs and nods her head the way grown-ups do when they don't know what to say. She tears our check out of her book, lays it facedown on the table, and walks away.

part two

Hermosa Beach, California

1970–1971

four

Every morning I wish I was waking up in my pink bedroom in the house on Mary Street. When I open my eyes, B.J.'s bunk bed bottom is the first thing I see and I know we're not in the house on Mary Street, nowhere near Carson City.

We live in Hermosa Beach. Daddy says Hermosa means beautiful in Spanish.

Beautiful Beach. Hermosa Beach.

If you like the beach, if you like the ocean, I guess it's true, Hermosa Beach is nice. The thing is, I don't really like the ocean, too loud, too scary, and you can't see the bottom like you can at Lake Tahoe.

You can see the ocean and the beach from our place. We live up the hill, just a couple blocks away, except our street doesn't have a name like Mary Street or Minnesota Street. Here the street is a number, twenty-eight.

Our place isn't our place either, it's a triplex, which means apartment, except Daddy says he likes the sound of triplex better. B.J. says it doesn't matter what you call it, we rent an apartment and that means it's not really our place. A triplex is three apartments built together and we live in the apartment called Number One.

Number One on 28th Street.

Number One is small. Come in the front door and you're in the living room. Five steps and you're in the kitchen. Ten steps and Momma and Daddy's bedroom door is just past the refrigerator. Half a turn, four steps, and there's a bathroom across from the washer and dryer. Four more steps and you're in the bedroom B.J. and me have to share.

Our room faces the sunrise and it's bright sun first thing. B.J. sleeps through anything, but when the sun shines that way, I can't sleep at all. I slide out of the bottom bunk bed and go eight steps up the hall to my parents' room. I know Momma isn't in there, but it feels good to lean my face against the door and listen. If I close my eyes, I can see Moshe and Diana the way they were, sand-colored cat bodies, deep blue cat eyes. When I open my eyes there's no Moshe, no Diana. I don't know where they are now.

When Momma's not home, there's no rule. I put my hand on the doorknob and turn extra slow, extra quiet so I don't wake Daddy. Momma and Daddy's room faces the sunrise too, but heavy drapes block it out. The only sign of light is the thin white line where the drapes pull together.

There is the sound of breathing through his nose and I know Daddy is in the deep part of sleep.

Extra slow, extra quiet, I go in, close the door so California sunshine won't come in and wake him up.

My eyes separate the light-dark from the dark-dark and my hands reach ahead until I feel the edge of the California King.

Even though she's gone, Daddy always sleeps on his part of the bed and I can see how he lies on his back, see the outline of his straight nose, his long jaw, and his squared-up chin.

Momma's in the hospital again, seems like she's been in the hospital ever since we moved to Number One. After we moved in, she was here for a couple days and then she left. She came back for a couple more days and then she left again. Daddy says she's in the hospital for an operation and after the operation, things are going to get better again. Daddy says that's a promise. No kids are allowed at the hospital, that's the rule, and since I can't go see Momma for myself, I do the best I can to believe.

Extra slow, extra quiet, I climb on Momma's side of the California King, lie down where she belongs. There's always a blanket folded up on the end of the bed, Momma calls it a throw, and I pull the throw blanket up until it's under my chin. Curled on my side, I listen to Daddy breathe and when the dark isn't so dark, I see how he has his hands together over his chest, over his heart.

This close to Daddy and it's nice, probably the best thing about Hermosa Beach. I look at him for a long time, I don't know how long, and then I close my eyes and fall back to sleep.

Warm under the throw blanket, I open my eyes and Daddy sits on the edge of the bed. He has on a short sleeved T-shirt and boxer shorts the lightest color of green, mint green. The nightstand lamp is turned on and warm yellow light circles on his half of the California King. Daddy yawns and shakes his head. He looks at his watch and his eyes are serious the way they get about time.

"When did you sneak in here?" Daddy says.

"I don't know," I say.

"Well, we overslept," Daddy says, "it's almost eight."

Daddy pats his hand on the California King, pat, pat, get up.

"Better get a move on," Daddy says, "we're burning daylight."

He walks around the California King, opens the door, and goes down the hall to the room B.J. and me share.

"Hey, sleepyhead," Daddy says, "rise and shine."

On Momma's side of the California King, I lean over and turn on her lamp. In Hermosa Beach, there are way more pill bottles on her nightstand, I count twenty bottles, almost every color of pill inside. There's Darvon, Valium, Nembutal, Seconal, Thorazine, every letter in the alphabet, A to Z. I like to arrange the bottles, smallest to tallest, or sometimes in a circle around the base of the lamp, or in a triangle. Daddy says the pill bottles aren't for my hands, says I should leave them alone, so now they're just pushed together in a bunch with no shape at all. Even though it's against the rule, I almost touch the bottles, but Daddy comes back up the hall, stops for a second to look in the room.

"Don't mess with those," Daddy says, "get up now."

Daddy moves around in the kitchen and I know he makes a pot of coffee.

I smooth my hands over Momma's side of the bed, the wrinkles from my body all gone. Daddy sleeps so still, his side of the bed is hardly messy at all and I pull the sheet up, then the blanket, then the bedspread. If you punch the pillow, it goes from flat to fluffy and I punch the pillow three times. It's nice when the bed is made up, looks neat and tidy.

Daddy opens and closes the refrigerator, runs water in the sink, and puts dishes and silverware on the kitchen table.

"BeeJer," Daddy yells, "come on now, let's get up."

The throw blanket is on the floor and I pick it up, shake it long. Daddy comes in, his hair messed up the way it is in the morning, rough whiskers on his squared-up jaw.

"Thanks, Juniper, I'll finish up," Daddy says. "Make sure your brother gets up and has breakfast, I'm going to take a shower."

B.J. only has on the bottom half of his pajamas, says California is too hot for pajama tops. B.J. rubs his face with his hand and then falls back into his pillow and rolls on his side.

"Daddy says you better get up," I say, "it's past eight."

"Go away," B.J. says.

"We're going to be late," I say.

B.J. lies still, asleep still, knees curled up to his chest, and I give up.

I go to the hall bathroom and shut the door. I get dressed, brush my teeth, rub a hot washcloth over my face and into the corners of my eyes. Daddy says you should always get the sleepy gunk out of there and I lean my face close to the mirror to see if all the sleepy gunk is gone.

My hair is long dark brown around my shoulders and I brush from the top down. Daddy says I should use a comb and start from the bottom since my hair tangles easy, but I don't like the comb, it takes too long and hurts when there's a tangle.

"Bryan Joseph," Daddy yells. "Get up."

I open the bathroom door and look down the hall. Daddy has on a clean undershirt, nice work pants with the little pleats, and shiny black shoes he calls wingtips. Daddy looks down at me and puts both his hands up, drops them against his legs.

"At least you're ready," Daddy says.

I have on a green corduroy jumper dress and a T-shirt with little purple and green flowers all over. I press my hands down over the front of the jumper.

"One print, one solid," I say.

"I see," Daddy says, "you look very pretty."

B.J. walks to the bathroom and drags his feet on the floor. His crew-cut hair isn't so crew-cut anymore and it sticks up around his head.

"I'm tired," B.J. says.

"Well then, you should go to bed earlier," Daddy says, "we're burning daylight."

B.J. goes around Daddy and into the kitchen, his feet still dragging on the floor.

"You always say that," B.J. says.

Daddy takes a deep breath in and makes his face smile.

"Teeth?" Daddy says and looks at me.

"All done," I say.

"Face?"

"Done."

"Ready for hair?"

I hold out one rubber band and a purple ribbon.

"One ponytail, please," I say.

Daddy looks at his watch. "How about barrettes?" he says.

"You can't have long hair with a jumper," I say, "the hair covers the little snaps at the shoulders. It's a ponytail day."

"All right, fine," Daddy says.

Daddy takes a deep slow breath and reaches for the brush. He brushes one, two, three long strokes and the brush gets caught.

"Damn," Daddy says.

"I hate tangles," I say.

"No comb, no ponytail," he says.

I put the rubber band and the ribbon on the bathroom counter and take the comb from Daddy. He looks at me in the mirror and I nod my head.

"Good girl," Daddy says, "comb from the bottom up, then bring me the rubber band and I'll do your ponytail."

Every school morning is the same. B.J. won't get out of bed, my hair is tangled, B.J. can't find his homework, I burn my toast and have to make it again since there's no way I'm going to eat burnt toast, and Daddy calls his office and tells someone he's a little late.

Daddy hates being late, says time is money and when you're late you're losing cash. After he hangs up the telephone, he gets that look, mad pretending he isn't mad, lips tight in the corners.

"Come on," Daddy says, "let's get going."

Out the door, Daddy locks up Number One with a key on a heart-shaped key chain that says *I Love California*.

Red is parked at the curb, low to the street, slanty front end. My spot in Red is behind the front seats in a place called the cargo hold. I climb in the back, sit on the middle hump, were I can see out the front window and the side windows.

Daddy gets in Red, shuts his door, and B.J. gets in on the passenger side, slams the door hard. Daddy leans his head back in his seat, looks tired even though it's still early in the morning.

"Okay now," Daddy says, "here's the deal."

Daddy says he has a meeting in the city, says he has another meeting in the valley, says he's coming home by four-thirty, maybe five.

"That means you need to go to Jenny's school and walk her home," Daddy says.

"Dad," B.J. says.

"Don't Dad me," Daddy says. "Just get your sister home safe."

B.J. moves his hand over so his bangs swoop over his forehead and his cheeks get that red stain deep under his tan skin.

Daddy looks at me in the rearview mirror.

"Wait at the front door of your school for B.J.," Daddy says, "okay?"

I sit up tall, shoulders back, chin tucked.

"I can walk alone," I say.

"Absolutely not," Daddy says, "there are all sorts of weirdos out there. You wait at the front door and your brother will come get you."

B.J. tucks his chin and his eyes are on the glove box. I don't know how Daddy can't see all the mad in B.J. I can see it and when B.J. is mad like that, it's not a good thing. I look at B.J., look at Daddy, look at B.J. again.

"Do not walk home alone," Daddy says, "am I clear?"

"Yes, Daddy," I say.

Daddy shifts around in his seat, starts Red, the engine loud inside the car, and the radio is on, plays "Good Day Sunshine." I love the Beatles, B.J. hates the Beatles. B.J. turns the radio down, the music almost gone, and Daddy drives up the hill.

❧

In kindergarten you draw, you paint, you sing songs. Kid stuff. The best part about kindergarten is when the bell rings and it's time to leave.

My teacher says my box is too full, says all the other kids

take their paintings home once a week and she gives me a pile of my paintings.

"Take these to your mother," the teacher tells me, "and she'll hang them on the refrigerator."

My paintings are mostly handprints, all different colors, and I wish I could throw them in the trash since there's no way Momma is going to see them, let alone hang them up on the stupid refrigerator. Handprint paintings don't matter when you're sick and you can't get out of bed and you have to go to the hospital to see stupid doctors and have stupid operations.

Stupid teacher, stupid kindergarten.

In front of the school, I wait at the front door and hold the handprint paintings against my chest. None of the other kids wait by the door, they all run out to meet the moms who wait out on the sidewalk. There are all kinds of ladies out there: tall, short, fat, skinny, yellow hair, brown hair. One kid, one mom, and they hug each other, kiss too.

I look at my handprint paintings and they're not so bad since there are lots of great colors and my hands are all over the place. Maybe I'll just hang them myself and Momma will see them when she gets home. When she's better.

I smooth my jumper under my butt and sit down on the step by the front door. I hold my handprint paintings in my lap and press my knees together.

The steps are concrete and they are all warmed up by California sunshine. The front of my school is sidewalk, steps, grass, and there's a flagpole with two flags, one for California, the other for America. It's windy and the flags flap-snap on the poles.

Between the street and the school are a row of trees and way down the sidewalk, B.J. walks with his head down. He kicks a rock on the sidewalk, follows the rock, and kicks it again.

Off the steps, I go down to the sidewalk, handprint paintings against my chest.

"You're late," I say.

B.J. looks at me through his eyebrow shadows and then he walks to the crosswalk with the stoplight. B.J. presses the button to change the light and he looks down at me like I smell bad.

"What's that supposed to be?" B.J. says.

I hug the handprint paintings to my chest.

"Paintings," I say, "handprint paintings for Momma."

"That's stupid," B.J. says.

"No, it's not," I say.

The light changes from DON'T WALK to WALK, red to green, and B.J. steps off the curb. I stay at the curb, look at his back.

"It's not stupid," I yell.

B.J. walks across the street and the light blinks DON'T WALK. I run across the street, so I cross before the solid DON'T WALK.

B.J. and me walk apart, him on one side of the sidewalk, me on the other, like we're together and not together at the same time. Up ahead is the park and a pond and people throw bits of bread into the water. Ducks and geese swim close and fight each other to eat soggy bread.

All the way on the other side of the pond are two white swans who float around in lazy circles. They don't try to eat the bread, they just hold their heads up on their long necks like the only thing that matters is how beautiful they are. I like that about the swans.

After the pond, the rest of the park is a long stretch of grass and so many trees it's like a forest. On the other side is another crosswalk, no stoplight.

B.J. steps off the curb, steps into the street.

I put my hand on B.J.'s arm and hold his windbreaker between my fingers.

"Hey," I say. "You can't cross here."

B.J. stops, looks at my hand and looks at me. I let go of B.J.'s windbreaker.

"Dare you to cross," B.J. says.

I look both ways, four lanes across, cars everywhere.

"No way," I say.

"Go on," B.J. says, "double dare."

B.J. watches me and there's a bad feeling up and down my back. I look at the street again, and it's just the sound of traffic and wind and not that many cars. I look at B.J. again.

"If I do it," I say, "no more dares."

"Deal," B.J. says. B.J. makes a big smile with lots of teeth, but it's not the real thing. There's no smile in his eyes.

I take a deep breath, look both ways, and step off the curb. I run as fast as I can and all my eyes see is the curb on the other side of the street, just the curb. Halfway across the street, there is a loud honk sound, too loud. My feet, my legs, my eyes, all of me stops and I am in the middle of the busy street, a car right at me. I turn around to run back. Another car honks and where there were no cars before, now they are everywhere, cars all around and horns loud in my ears.

Back on the sidewalk, B.J. stands stiff and still like he's a statue. I squeeze my eyes shut, put my hands over my face, and my handprint paintings fly up, fly away.

Brakes squeal, horns honk, white papers fly, and just like that it's a clear path between me and B.J. I run back to the curb, back to B.J.

B.J. stays completely still, eyes wide open, and then he looks down at me, at the street, at me again. My handprint paintings are everywhere and cars drive over the papers. I push both my hands against B.J.'s chest and shove all my weight into him. B.J.'s body is strong and solid and he barely moves.

"Look what you did," I yell, "you made me lose my paintings."

B.J. pushes my hands off his body and shoves me back like I'm nothing.

"Knock it off," B.J. yells.

I point at the road, my arm out from my body.

"Get them," I yell, my voice loud in my head.

"Shut up," B.J. yells.

"You shut up," I yell. "You have to get them, get them now."

B.J. moves his jaw, the bones back and forth under his skin, and he squints his eyes and looks across the street. My handprint paintings are white squares on the black road.

B.J. looks side to side and runs into the road. It looks easy the way B.J. does it, stop, start, dodge side to side. Cars honk and he doesn't get scared, just moves like he knows. B.J. stops, swerves, dodges, and pretty soon he has a whole pile of papers in his hands. He runs back to where I stand and his face is red and sweaty.

B.J. bends over, hands on his knees, and breathes hard. He holds the papers up, tire prints, handprints.

I pull the papers from his hand and smooth them out, my fingers over the tire prints and wrinkled paper.

I step back from B.J and put a safe distance between us.

"What?" B.J. says.

B.J. steps close to me and reaches out like he's going to punch my arm. I back up another step and his hand misses my shoulder.

"I was just kidding around," B.J. says.

"No, you weren't," I say.

"I didn't think you'd do it," B.J. says.

I look at B.J. and B.J. looks at me, and who knows if he was kidding or not. B.J. pushes his hands into his pockets and tucks his chin. His dark eyes look down, look at the sidewalk, and his face is a low red stain to his ears.

The wind smells like salt and seaweed, and it blows my hair into my eyes. I stand up tall, shoulders straight, chin tucked, and I walk to the crosswalk where you can get across the street without getting hit by a car. I can feel B.J. behind me, can feel him watch and I don't care, just pretend there is no B.J.

When you come into Number One, the living room is the first thing and it's all packed with our stuff. The long green sofa is under the window, the TV is against the wall, the big purple grape is in the corner. Daddy's lounger chair, the dining room furniture, and my bedroom stuff is in the garage since Number One is so small.

When we get to Number One, B.J. unlocks the door with the *I Love California* key chain and puts the key back under the doormat. In the living room, I drop my paintings on the big purple grape, hold my breath like I do when I'm mad but I don't want to show it. B.J. goes into the kitchen.

I let my breath out slow, slow and bite my bottom lip between my teeth. The only good handprint paintings are the ones without tire tracks. The best one is of three red handprints in a circle. I pull that painting out and go into the kitchen, open the everything drawer where there are odds and ends, see-through tape, and a pair of scissors.

"What are you doing?" B.J. says, mouth full.

There's a jar of peanut butter open on the counter and B.J. eats bread with peanut butter smeared on. I look past him and pull a piece of tape.

B.J. wipes his hand over his mouth.

I put the tape on the top of the painting and stick it to the refrigerator.

"It's crooked," B.J. says.

When you're mad at someone, really mad, you wish they would just go away, except in Number One, there's no place to go. I don't look at B.J., just act like he's not even here, and I make the handprint painting straight.

B.J. leans against the counter, chews with his mouth open, and I can feel his eyes on my back.

Arms crossed, I look at the refrigerator door. It's too much white door and not enough painting. I go back to the big purple grape, pick two more paintings, and stick them on each side of the red handprint painting.

B.J. stands right next to me.

"How many are you going to put up?" B.J. says.

B.J.'s voice is the only sound in Number One and I step away from him like he isn't here at all.

B.J. reaches out and I jump back from his hand.

"You can't stay mad forever," B.J. says.

I sidestep out of the kitchen and into the living room. For every step I take, B.J. closes the distance.

"I was just kidding," B.J. says.

"Go away," I say.

B.J. reaches out like he is going to grab my arm and I run to the big purple grape. B.J. gets me in the middle of the living room, his arm around my neck, his hand on my arm, and pulls me against his chest.

"Just listen to me," B.J. says.

"Let go," I yell.

B.J. moves his leg around my leg, trips me down, and I'm under, him over. His body is heavy against my side and he breathes peanut butter in my face.

"You stink," I say. "Get off."

I pull my arm free and slap at the air, slap at his head, his face, his arms. My heart beats hard in my chest like it wants to jump out.

B.J. laughs and his face is red angry and excited and something else. He puts his hands around my wrists, his fingers into my skin, and he turns me on my back.

"That hurts," I yell, "you're hurting me."

"Just listen," B.J. says.

B.J. sits on my stomach and pins my wrists under his knees.

"I can't breathe," I say.

B.J. puts his hand over my mouth, over my nose.

"Just shut up," B.J. yells.

His hand is hot on my face, smells like peanut butter, and he presses his fingers into my skin.

"It's not my fault," he says.

I turn my head side to side and he pushes his hand harder. There is no air between his fingers and my chest burns.

That's the way it is with B.J. now, he grabs like there is no me, pins me under his weight, makes me stop, and then he says how he didn't mean it, and it doesn't matter what happened, it's never B.J.'s fault.

There's not enough air for me anymore and I feel smaller and smaller until I can't feel, can't think, and it's just black and warm all over.

Number One is quiet the way it gets when no one is here and I know B.J. is long gone. My wrists hurt, my chest burns, and my face is tight from dried-up tears. I roll over on my stomach and rub my face with my hands.

Off the floor, I walk slow steps to the long green sofa and look out the big window. The sun is a circle of gold on the edge of the ocean and the gold shines so bright that the ocean is all blue-white shine. B.J. is in the driveway doing skateboard pops and hops and I look pure hate at him, like it is going to make any difference.

Down on the sofa, I cross my arms over my middle and I can still feel B.J. on my stomach, his hands on my wrists. I could tell Daddy when he gets home and get B.J in trouble, but that's no good since B.J. and me will be alone again and then I'll just get it worse.

The best time in Number One is when Daddy gets home from work and we all have dinner. Sometimes it's pot pies, sometimes it's TV dinners, sometimes Daddy brings home pizza.

After dinner, Daddy drinks one beer and watches the news. I sit as close to him as possible, my body into that warm place under his arm against his side, and I look at the TV too. Most nights it's Walter Cronkite and he talks about business and natural disasters and the war in Vietnam. Daddy doesn't say anything about the news, just sips his beer and watches, and I wonder what he's thinking.

One time Momma told me that Daddy is a genius, which I guess means he's smarter than everyone else. Momma says he has a special kind of brain that thinks faster and deeper and when he was in college, he never had to study since he could just take the tests and get straight A's.

Me and Daddy on the sofa, B.J. on the floor with his homework, Walter Cronkite on the news, and I wonder if Daddy's genius is a good thing or a bad thing. I bite my fingernail and wonder if B.J. is a genius too, or maybe if I am going to be extra smart, even though I don't think so since I can't even read yet.

The last thing Walter Cronkite says is how many American boys were killed in Vietnam and then he says good night.

After dinner, I take a bath in one bathroom and B.J. takes a shower in the other bathroom and we put on our pajamas.

Daddy tucks B.J. in first, pulls the covers up under B.J.'s chin.

"Good night, son," Daddy says.

"Good night, Dad," B.J. says.

I go into the sliding door closet, get *Snow White and the Seven Dwarfs* off the shelf. There are two kinds of *Snow White and the Seven Dwarfs* stories. There's the Disney story, where the princess is cute and the dwarfs are cute and everything is happily ever after. Then there's the Grimms' story, where the princess is beautiful, the dwarfs are kind of scary, and in the end, the evil stepmother dances herself to death in a pair of hot steel shoes.

Daddy says I have a dark side since I like the Grimm story better.

I get in bed and Daddy tucks the daisy sheet and fuzzy pink blanket around my body. He sits right next to me and puts his arm around my shoulders. This close he smells like cigarettes and chicken pot pie.

"Ready?" Daddy says.

"Ready," I say.

On the top bunk, B.J. rolls on his side and then it's quiet up there.

Daddy reads in his story voice, deep and clear, words through his body and into the place where I lean against him.

The best part of *Snow White* is how much her mother loved her, even before Snow White was born. The worst part of *Snow White* is how the mother dies when she is born. It doesn't seem fair for the queen to get her wish and then not be a part of the life she wished for.

"It's a lesson about life," Daddy says, "when we wish for something, we think it's what we really want. Just shows you have to be careful what you wish for."

"But why?" I say.

"I don't know," Daddy says. "Maybe the queen wasn't specific enough."

I don't know what Daddy means by specific and I guess that must be genius. I look at the drawing of the queen, how she looks like she would have been a good mother, and I still think it's not fair that she didn't live to see her wish come true.

After the queen dies, there's an evil stepmother who's really a witch and the evil stepmother talks to a mirror. The mirror always tells the evil stepmother that she's the most beautiful woman in the land, but one day the mirror says it's Snow White.

The evil stepmother tries to have Snow White killed by a huntsman, but the huntsman can't do it and he lets her go in the forest. Snow White runs and runs until she finds a little house with seven little men. She stays in their house, takes care of them, cooks and cleans, and she is finally happy, until the evil stepmother talks to her mirror and finds out Snow White is still alive.

I hate how the stepmother makes a poison apple and then disguises herself as a nice old lady giving away regular apples. I want to warn Snow White to run, get away, throw the apple in the trash. It doesn't matter. Turn the page and Snow White eats the apple. All it takes is one bite and she falls down like she's dead.

I wipe my hands over my eyes, tears on my nightgown, on the daisy sheets.

"You are so silly," Daddy says, "you know how it ends."

"I know," I say, "it's still so sad."

The whole thing gets turned around when the prince comes and sees Snow White in death as beautiful as she was in life. The prince asks the dwarfs if he can have Snow White's body so he can take her to his castle where he can look at her forever. The dwarfs say yes, and when he's moving Snow White, the tiny piece of apple falls out of her mouth and she was never dead to begin with.

The scariest part of the story is how the evil stepmother finds out Snow White is alive and happy and about to marry a prince. The stepmother goes to the wedding, puts on a pair of steel shoes, and dances until she is dead.

It's scary and crazy and it doesn't make any sense.

"Some people just can't be happy," Daddy says.

"Why?" I say.

"When the other guy has more than you," Daddy says, "it can make you miserable, even crazy. Understand?"

"Sure," I say, "I guess."

Daddy smiles and closes the *Snow White*. My head is tangled with Snow White and evil stepmother and how the happy ending is really a sad ending and Daddy tucks me in tight and pulls the blankets under my chin.

"Sleep tight," Daddy says.

He kisses me then, just on the forehead, and I look right into his brown eyes.

"I miss Momma," I say.

It's quiet in our room, but I know B.J. is still awake. Daddy looks at me for a long time and his face is close to my face.

"She misses you too," Daddy says, "but she'll be home soon."

"When?" I say.

Daddy fusses with the sheets and covers even though I'm already tucked in.

"Soon," Daddy says.

Daddy kisses my forehead again and stands up straight.

"Sleep tight," Daddy says, "don't let the bedbugs bite."

❧

Two days into February, Daddy brings Momma home while B.J. and me are in school. No warning and she's back, just like that. On top of no warning, Momma's asleep and sick and I can't go in to see her even though Daddy promised she was going to be better this time.

"She just needs rest," Daddy says.

"But I want to see her," I say.

"Not now," Daddy says.

I sit on the long green sofa, cross my arms over myself, and look at her closed door. Daddy stands between me and Momma's door, says he's going to the grocery store for bread and milk.

"Come on, Juniper," Daddy says, "come with us."

"She's pouting," B.J. says.

"No, I'm not," I say.

Daddy kneels down in front of me so my eyes have to look at his face.

"I know you're mad," Daddy says, "but I'm telling you she needs her rest and that's that."

There are tired lines around his mouth and his brown eyes are tired too.

"I don't want to go to the grocery store," I say.

Daddy lets out a deep breath between his lips and the air pushes his lips and cheeks out.

"Have it your way," Daddy says, "but you can't stay mad forever."

All of his genius and Daddy is way wrong, I can stay mad forever.

They leave and it's quiet in Number One. I stay mad and still, but then the mad slips away and the only thing there is is Momma, just on the other side of that door.

I look out the window, down the hill, and 28th Street is empty. No Red, no Daddy, no B.J.

If I just open her door a little and look fast, there's no way Daddy will know.

I look out the window again.

Careful, quiet steps, ten steps through the kitchen, and I reach for the doorknob. The Frigidaire kicks on and I pull my hand back, tingles up my neck and around my face.

I breathe in and breathe out. The front door is still closed and the apartment is still quiet.

Breathing in, I turn the doorknob.

The light is on in the bathroom and a rectangle of yellow light reaches to the end of the California King. Momma lies on her back, face up, curls of brown-black hair all over her pillow.

B.J. says Momma has been gone for two months and two months is so long I almost forgot how she's Snow White beautiful, white skin, dark hair, black eyebrows and eyelashes too.

I stand on tiptoe and go slow steps to the side of the bed, no sound at all in the room except my heart in my ears.

Momma's face is a line of smooth bones just under her white skin and I trace my finger from her jaw to her chin like drawing her face in my memory.

Momma moves her head up and down like dreaming and I pull my hand back.

The room is the same except it's different with her in here.

A small travel suitcase sits on the floor by the closet and the top is open, her lemon meringue nightgown and robe are folded on top, and there's a blue sweater I never saw before.

On the night table, pill bottles are pushed together, new bottles with the old ones.

The smell is different too, a bad smell, bitter. I follow the smell to the floor and down there is a plastic something. I squat down, touch the plastic with the tips of my fingers, and it's full of cold yellow water. I lift the bedspread up and the plastic is a plastic bag hooked to a plastic tube and the tube goes up and up until I can't see anymore.

When something's wrong, my skin knows first.

I drop the bedspread fast and stand up.

My ears listen for Red, for Daddy, for B.J., but Momma's breath in and out is the only sound. I look at the floor again, at the plastic bag, and I know it's pee, her pee.

I take a deep breath and move her hand into my hand. I squeeze my fingers into her fingers, just me squeezing, her hand soft and loose.

Momma says when you can't make sense of things, you have to look inside and find what you can believe. Momma says the thing you believe has to come through your experiences, through your heart.

My eyes look at the bag again, at the pee, and I try not to look, just look at her face, her perfect Snow White face.

Just like that, I know.

Momma believes in me and I believe in her and if I just stand here and hold her hand, she will wake up, she will have that special look, she will be better. She will.

I squeeze my eyes shut and push what I believe through my fingers into her fingers. I open my eyes, but her eyes are still closed and her fingers are loose.

When you believe in something, when that something picks you, you can never, never give up. Momma didn't say that, but now I know it's true.

I let go of her hand and sit on the floor. I lean my shoulder against the California King and take her hand again.

On the fifth day of being home, Momma squeezes my hand back and her eyes are wide open with the special look for special people.

"I dreamed you," Momma whispers.

Momma squeezes my hand, her bones, my fingers.

"I dreamed you came to save me," Momma says.

"I did," I say.

Momma smiles.

"You've been asleep for a long time," I say.

"How long?" she says.

"Five days," I say.

"Where is everyone?" Momma says.

"Daddy's at work," I say. "B.J.'s out on his skateboard somewhere."

Momma clears her throat, the sound deep in her chest.

"I missed you," Momma whispers.

"I missed you too," I say.

"I missed you more," Momma says.

"Bet you didn't," I say.

Momma smiles and her dark eyes have that special look that's just for me.

Momma wants her robe and it's the peach silk over her arms and around her hips.

She wants a cigarette and I go into the everything drawer, dig out a white pack of Parliaments and a pack of matches.

Momma wants a glass of water and I let the water run fresh and cold and just right.

Momma up in bed with her back resting against her pillows, the peach silk robe and a white Parliament cigarette between her fingers, and it's just like it was before except it's different too.

Momma's so skinny you can see her bones through her skin. Momma used to say you can't be too thin, but now she says she's wasting away.

All around her head, her hair is long and wild and I brush all the curls smooth the ways she likes.

Momma closes her eyes when I brush and she smiles a slow sad smile.

"You're my girl," Momma says.

"Special gift," I say.

Momma nods, dark eyes closed.

"Why do you say that?" I say. "Special gift?"

Momma is quiet for a long time, dark eyelashes against the blue hollows under her eyes.

"It's a good story," Momma says.

Momma opens her eyes then, moves her head back to look at me.

"I never got to travel," Momma says, "I always wanted to travel."

Momma's eyes stop-start and the room is quiet and dark.

"I thought I was going to die," Momma whispers. "But then you came and I knew."

"What?" I say.

Momma licks her lips, the tip of her tongue on the middle of her top lip. She puts her hand on her cheek, thin fingers on her thin face.

"What?" Momma says.

"What did you know?" I say.

Momma looks at the drapes pulled tight, her lips together in a tremble.

"Can you keep a secret?" Momma says.

"What?" I say.

"Can you promise?" Momma says.

"I can keep a secret," I say. "I promise."

Momma blinks and she pushes the covers back, pulls up her peach silk nightgown.

Momma's stomach is white skin, a belly button, and a bunch of lines, red and purple, and they look like a knife cut her. I bite my lip so hard it hurts and I look at Momma's face, at the line on her stomach again.

"It's terrible, isn't it?" Momma says.

Momma moves her hand over the lines and stops at the big purple line, as big as a big fat earthworm, and the line is stitched together with black thread.

"No way I'm going to be a swimsuit model now," she says.

"Did you want to be a swimsuit model?" I say. Momma shakes her head and laughs into a cough. The lines shake and her stomach shakes and she stops laughing.

"You can touch it," she says, "it's nothing but an ugly scar now."

The purple line is angry and sore and the more I look at it in the light, the less scary it is. I set the brush on the California

King and trace my finger on an old line, my finger from one end to the other.

"Why are there so many?" I say.

Momma sucks in air and her stomach is flat and tight.

"Stupid doctors," Momma says, "they just can't get it right."

My finger doesn't have to lift up to trace another line going up the other way and then another line.

"Daddy says this time you're going to get better," I say.

Momma shakes her head and looks down at her stomach. She puts her hand on my hand and lifts so I am not touching her anymore. She lets the peach silk fall over her stomach and her eyes are wet with tears. She tilts her head to the side.

"Who's going to love me all cut up like this?" Momma says.

The tears in her eyes, the sound of her voice, the way she looks, and it's the saddest thing ever.

"I love you," I say.

Momma's face smiles and she puts her arm around my shoulders. I lay my head down on her stomach, close my eyes, and cry and cry, just the two of us crying, where I begin and she ends, the same place.

Every day, Momma sleeps less and less, but she's still not right. She can't remember little things like what day it is or big things like what pills she is supposed to take. The worst thing, though, is how Momma doesn't remember how she is supposed to get out of bed and go to the bathroom.

Momma cries when she goes to the bathroom in bed, not loud crying, little whimper cries and hiccups. Momma just sits there on the California King, tears down her Snow White beautiful face, and she points at the bed, whimper cries and hiccups.

B.J. says Number Two.

Daddy says crap.

I say poop.

When she messes the California King, poop smell is everywhere and Momma cries and hiccups until Daddy changes the sheets and she is cleaned up again. After that Daddy burns matches and it's poop smell and burned match smell.

Then there's how she pees in a bag.

The bag hooks to a plastic tube and the tube runs up there, into the place where Momma has black hairs that look just like the legs of daddy long-legged spiders. I hate spiders.

If Momma forgets, someone has to change the bag or it overflows on the carpet and makes the whole room smell like pee. Most times Momma remembers, but sometimes Daddy has to do it, sometimes me. B.J. never changes the bag. Never.

If I have to change the bag, I keep my eyes on the place where the tube hooks to the bag, never look up where the tube hooks into her. You have to empty the bag, clean it, and put the bag on again, and you have to do it quick so she doesn't accidentally pee through the tube and onto the carpet.

Holding my breath, I unhook the tube where it connects to the bag, and go straight to the bathroom, empty the bag into the toilet, bitter pee smell in my face.

Flushing the toilet, I rinse the bag in hot, hot water. Daddy says the water should almost burn your hands so it kills any Germans in the bag. I like the way he says that, Germans instead of germs. Daddy says it's an old war joke even though it's not really that funny since we're mostly German.

I stand in the bathroom, let the hot, hot water fill up the bag, and look at me in the mirror. I don't really like how I look. There are too many freckles, my lips make a crooked smile and my nose is way too big. I smile, stop smiling and squint like I'm mad.

Daddy says you have to rinse the bag out three times. I turn the bag over, empty it out, fill it up again. Steam lifts between the me who waits and the me in the mirror.

One more time over, hot water out, more hot water in, and my hands are red and tingly. By the third rinse, it's steam all around, no more me in the mirror and the pee smell is finally gone.

❧

It's a dream with voices and no pictures, a dream where Momma yells and Daddy yells and when I open my eyes, the yelling doesn't stop.

A white fingernail moon is out the window, dark blue sky all around, stars too. B.J.'s head blocks out the fingernail moon, just his head over the bunk bed, voice a whisper.

"They're fighting," B.J. whispers.

Down the hall, it's the refrigerator, the front of the washing machine, the dryer, the bathroom, a thin line of light under their closed door.

"Who is it?" Momma yells.

Daddy's voice is low and I can't hear his words.

"You're lying," Momma yells.

B.J.'s head is gone, just the fingernail moon in the window, lines of clouds here and there.

"You didn't even sleep here last night," Momma yells.

"I told you," Daddy yells, "I stayed at the office."

"You didn't call," Momma says.

"He did call," B.J. says.

"I did call, Janet," Daddy says.

Something falls, the sound of glass breaking.

Daisy sheet, fuzzy pink blanket, and I push the covers back, put my feet on the floor, eight steps up the hall.

"Hey," B.J. whispers.

On this side of their door, I press against the wall. There is moving around and the door opens, Daddy out, Momma's whimper cry and a hiccup, and then Daddy shuts the door with a click, walks into the dark kitchen.

Daddy still has his work shoes on, white shirt with the sleeves rolled up, and he bends over, opens the cupboard door under the sink, and drops something in the trash.

"Daddy?" I say.

Daddy jumps a little and stands up tall again, so big in the little kitchen. Three steps and Daddy flips on the kitchen light, bright light, and I cover my eyes.

"Jesus," Daddy says, "you scared me. What are you doing there?"

"Did she mess her bed?" I say. "Do you want some help?"

Daddy bends over and puts his hands on my arms. His fingers are cold through my nightgown and the look on his face is someone who is in real trouble except they are trying to hide it, wide-open eyes, eyebrows half circles, lips tight, tired lines all over the place.

"No, Juniper," Daddy says, "everything's fine."

"Did she break her glass?" I say.

"Yes," Daddy says, "but it was an accident, she's fine, I'm fine. Go back to bed now."

Daddy moves his hands up and down on my arms to make me warm, except I'm not cold. He stands up there and puts his big hand on my head and walks me back to the bedroom. B.J. shifts around on his bunk, moves the covers around. Daddy whispers to B.J. to go back to sleep, everything's fine, and then Daddy tucks me into the bottom bunk, daisy sheets, fuzzy blanket, all the way up to my chin.

"All right now?" Daddy whispers, "Comfy?"

Daddy in the dark, face all angles and shadows, and the trouble is still in his eyes. I put my hand on top of his hand, his skin cold.

"You shouldn't be fighting," I say.

Daddy stops fussing with my covers and looks at me for a long time.

"We're not fighting," Daddy says.

"Sounds like a fight," B.J. says.

B.J.'s voice is clear in the dark and Daddy shifts on the bunk bed, looks up in the dark, looks at me again. Daddy takes a deep breath in and shakes his head.

"I'm sorry, you guys," Daddy says, "everything is fine, I promise. Mom just got a little upset, but it's all right now."

Daddy stands up then, fusses around with B.J. up there.

"Go to sleep," Daddy says, "everything's fine."

Saturday mornings are sleep-in mornings. No sleepyheads, no burning daylight, no school. The sun shines bright in our room and B.J. snores up there, deep snore in his nose. B.J. can sleep through anything.

There is the sound of Daddy's shoes in the kitchen, That Man cologne up the hall, and then the front door closes.

B.J.'s bunk bed bottom is wood slats and the brown cover on his mattress pressing through.

Red starts up, spit and sputter, and Daddy revs the engine.

I get out of bed and go down the hall.

Momma and Daddy's door is open and it's all dark in there except for an orange glow and I know she's smoking a cigarette.

"Momma?" I say. "Can I come in?"

"Sure," Momma says.

"Can I turn on a light?" I say.

"Sure," she says. "Not the overhead though."

I feel up the nightstand lamp and turn the switch. Lamplight falls over her pills, the lift of her legs under the covers, and the ashtray she holds on her lap. Momma's eyes are shadows and her curly hair is tucked behind her ears. She taps her cigarette on the ashtray and her hand shakes.

"Are you okay?" I say.

Momma's dark eyes stop-start and she puts her cigarette between her lips, the tip glows bright, and she puts her cigarette into the notch on the ashtray that holds the cigarette in place. She clears her throat, sniffs in one quick sniff.

"Quite frankly," Momma says, "we're all a bit tired of the whole thing."

"Momma?" I say.

Momma blinks a couple times and looks at me, dark eyes squinting, and she reaches out and moves my hair behind my ear.

"When did your hair get so long?" Momma says.

I sit on the edge of the California King, mattress dent under my behind.

"It's always been long," I say.

"That can't be right," Momma says.

Her fingers tuck more hair behind my ears, both her hands on the side of my face, her fingers so cold.

B.J. walks barefoot from our room to the bathroom, shuts the door. Momma jumps at the sound, looks at the door, her eyes wide open stop-start.

"What was that?" she says.

"B.J.," I say.

"B.J.?" she says.

Momma looks at me, eyes wide like she can't remember. I touch her hand with my fingers.

"You know," I say, "Bryan."

The toilet flushes and B.J. comes to the door, looks in. He has on pajama bottoms and he stands there, pushes his hair over his forehead.

"Good morning, Bryan," Momma says.

Momma never calls B.J. Bryan. He looks at me with his eyes wide open and I shake my head back and forth.

"Come here, son," Momma says.

B.J. lets his hands off the door, one step into their room, and then he stops.

"Where's Dad?" B.J. says.

"Come, come," Momma says.

B.J. walks slow steps, looks at me, looks at Momma, that mixed-up look in his eyes, like he isn't going to get too close but he wants to be close all at the same time.

Momma makes a sound in her throat, arms up and down, the ashtray on her lap bouncing, and I put my hand out to steady it.

"I thought so," Momma says, "look at you. Look at your hair."

B.J. moves his hand over his face, pushes his bangs out of his eyes.

"What?" B.J. says.

"What?" Momma says, "your hair is in your eyes, this one's hair is way down her back."

Momma is all business, serious too, and B.J. laughs, stops laughing, pushes his hair out of his eyes. B.J. looks at me and I bite the side of my thumb.

Momma puts one hand on my shoulder, the other hand on B.J.'s shoulder and she looks right at us, eyes steady.

"Haircuts, that's what we're going to do," Momma says. "I need scissors."

It takes a while for Momma to get all set up, slow walk to the bathroom, slow walk back, and then she puts on a peach robe over her white silk nightgown.

B.J. has the scissors and I have a towel and we both stand there while she moves slow, slow getting her robe on and then walking to the bed.

"Momma?" I say. "Do you want the white robe?"

Momma has one hand on her robe, the other hand holding the plastic pee bag. She sways a little and moves her peach robe so it's closed over her white nightgown.

"Why?" Momma says.

Biting my lip, I look at B.J. and B.J. just shrugs.

Slow and careful, Momma sits down on the edge of the California King, circle of lamplight over her knees, her feet, the bones in her feet. She leans over slow, sets the pee bag on the floor by her foot, and then she looks at us, back and forth, hands on her knees.

"You first, son," Momma says.

B.J. looks at the pee bag, makes a nasty face, and he turns around, sits down slow. B.J. sits on the floor between Momma's legs and he looks down at the pee bag, scoots away from it, and looks at it again. Momma takes the towel and puts it over B.J.'s shoulders, dips the black comb into her glass of water and combs B.J.'s dark hair.

On the floor, I sit cross-legged.

"Quit squirming now," Momma says.

"I'm not," B.J. says.

"Yes, you are," Momma says. "Don't worry about that bag, it's not going to bite you."

"I'm not," B.J. says.

Momma holds B.J.'s head between her hands and makes him look down.

"It's been a long time since I cut your hair," Momma says.

"Carson," B.J. says.

"That's right," Momma says. "I used to cut your hair once a month, remember?"

B.J. tries to nod, but Momma has her hands on his head, turning him so she can look at both sides of his face, look at the back of his neck.

Just like that, she starts to cut and it's quiet, quiet, the whisper of scissors blades. B.J. stays extra still, looks down at the floor, and Momma cuts a straight line across the back of his neck, straight line sideburns and a straight line of bangs right over his eyebrows. She cuts steady and sure, like she knows exactly how, all the lines just right. I don't remember haircuts, not here, not in Carson, but the way she cuts and the way B.J. lets her, I know it must have happened.

Momma stops cutting, shakes her arms a little, and takes a deep breath in.

"I forgot how tiring this is," Momma says.

B.J. looks up, looks at the wall past me, dark eyes moving around.

"Do you want to stop?" B.J. says. "Do you want to rest?"

Momma shakes her head and takes another deep breath, little bits of sweat over her lip.

"No, no," Momma says, "what good am I if I can't do a haircut in one sitting?"

B.J. rolls his lips together, eyes on the floor, fingers on the little cuts of hair in the carpet. B.J.'s haircut is over his ears,

higher on his neck, and his bangs are in the middle of his forehead, neat and tidy, clean.

Momma stops combing B.J.'s hair, puts her hands on his
shoulders, and bends forward, the side of her Snow White
face to B.J.'s tanned face. Momma does something I don't
remember her doing in such a long time, she kisses B.J. on the
neck, holds her lips against his skin and closes her eyes.

B.J.'s face goes red and his eyes are all over the place, not
sure, and then he tucks his chin close to his chest. Momma lets
him go then and she sits up tall, shoulders straight, chin
tucked, posture of a lady. She wipes hair off his shoulders,
his neck.

"All done, my handsome man," Momma says.

B.J. gets up quick, pulls the towel off his shoulders, eyes on
Momma like he is seeing her for the first time, like he doesn't
know. He hands her the towel and touches his hands around
his head, feels the lines and edges of trimmed hair, stops his
hand where Momma kissed him.

"Thanks," B.J. says.

Momma smiles and moves his bangs around over his forehead.

"Remember to keep your hair neat," Momma says.

"Okay," B.J. says.

"Why don't you get dressed now," Momma says, "and
have your breakfast."

B.J. has a look on his face like he doesn't know what to do
and he goes out of her room, looks back one time, and then
he's gone.

Momma wipes hair off her nightgown, little cuts of B.J.'s
hair on the carpet.

"You're next, Jenny," Momma says.

"But I like my hair," I say.

"No, no," Momma says, "it's out of control. Now sit."

Holding my breath, I sit on B.J.'s old hair and she puts the towel around my shoulders. Momma's knees are on each side of my back, bones on the other side of the white silk nightgown, and I sit stiff, hold the towel together with my fingers in a fist.

The way I'm sitting, I can't see anything, just the shadow of her on the green carpet. Momma turns my head this way and that way and then she starts to comb through with the black comb dipped into her glass.

My hair is dark brown, long past my shoulders, and it's mostly straight except for a little curl at the ends. You can do anything with long hair, ponytails, braids, barrettes. I love my hair.

Momma picks up my hair, all of it in her hand, and I can see the shadow of her arm, the other hand with the scissors. My breath in, and one, two, three, my hair on the floor.

My breath out, and I can't help tears in my eyes, my long hair like something dead on the green carpet. I touch the hair and it's cool and soft.

B.J. comes up the hall and grins a big stupid grin, all the way into his dark eyes.

"Wow," B.J. says, "you're practically bald."

"Don't exaggerate," Momma says.

"Well, short anyway," B.J. says.

Momma cuts and cuts, shorter pieces of hair around my legs, cool on the back of my neck. I look down at the carpet, the shadow of her arms, the shadow of the scissors.

"You look like a guy," B.J. says.

"This isn't a place for young men who are going to be critical," Momma says, "scoot out and let the ladies finish."

B.J. laughs a snort laugh and he's gone into the kitchen,

the sound of cereal in a bowl and then the refrigerator opening.

Momma combs and cuts, turns my head this way, that way.

It's not the end of the world, feels like it though, my stomach a wide-open hole with the end of the world falling
through it.

Momma leans her face over my ear, voice warm, cigarette
smell.

"Short hair is neat and tidy," Momma says. "Very
European."

"European?" I say.

"You need to look just right if we are going to see the
queen," Momma says.

"The queen?" I say.

"Sh," Momma says.

Her voice isn't her voice and I bite my lip hard.

B.J. yells how he's going out to skateboard and Momma
says he should be careful and then Momma finally puts the
mirror over my shoulder. The front door closes with a slam
and I hold the mirror with both hands, not me in the mirror
now, someone else. Momma fusses around my shoulders,
dusts the hair off, and little wet pieces fall on the floor.

"Pixie," Momma says, "that's your style."

"It's all gone," I say.

"Pixie," Momma says, "don't you remember?"

There are little slices of hair all over the carpet, like blades
of grass, and they're stuck on my nightgown, on the towel, on
the California King, down the front of her nightgown.
Momma's curly hair sticks up all over the place, sweat over
her lips, dark eyes wide open. Momma puts her hand over her
mouth, air in fast.

"Don't you remember?" Momma says.

Momma moves her foot over my hair on the towel, my hair on the floor, and her dark eyebrows are bunched together over her eyes. Momma reaches out to touch my hair, stops, and lets her hand fall palm up on her white nightgown, peach robe open.

"I remember," Momma whispers, "don't you remember?"

"It's okay," I say, "I remember too. Let me clean up now."

Momma shifts back slow and careful, stop-start eyes blinking and blinking.

"I'm so tired," Momma whispers, "I have to get some sleep now."

I move the pee bag so it's not tangled, wipe hair off Momma's nightgown, off her feet, off the California King.

On the floor, I rake the carpet with my fingers, pull B.J.'s hair and my hair into a ball, pile it up on the white towel, a brown nest of hair, long and short, hair everywhere.

In the bathroom, I shake all the hair into the trash and the me in the mirror isn't me now. Pixie. European.

"Can you get me some fresh water?" Momma says.

Momma messes around with her pill bottles and I take the glass of water off her nightstand, carry it back to the bathroom, pour the water and pieces of hair float into the sink. I lay the comb on the counter, and I rinse out her glass three times, fill it with fresh water.

In her room, Momma pours a whole bottle of green pills on her lap, must be thirty pills. Momma drops the empty bottle on the bed, takes another bottle, looks close at the label. She shakes her head, puts the bottle down, picks up another one. She reads the label, opens the brown pill bottle, and turns it upside down. Red pills fall on the pile of green pills, the sound like water, like candy, like beads you can string for a necklace.

"What are you doing?" I say.

Momma looks up, dark eyes steady, Snow White beautiful face. I set the glass down on her nightstand. Momma looks at the pills again, runs her fingers through the pile on her lap, and lets them fall down between.

"Momma?" I say.

"Like Christmas," Momma says.

She picks up a green pill and a red pill, puts them side by side on her open palm.

"What's the green for, Momma?" I say.

"For sleep," Momma says.

"What's the red for?" I say.

"What?" Momma says.

"The red pill," I say.

She tilts her head to the side like listening and her voice is so low I have to lean in.

"Be a good girl," Momma says, "and go play now."

Momma puts the two pills in her mouth, sips water, and puts her head back.

My heart beats in my ears, my skin prickles over my head, my stomach moves like throwing up. It's more wrong than ever and I should do something, except I don't know what.

Momma takes two more pills, one red, one green, and she looks at me, eyes stop-start. The back of my neck is smooth and I move my hand over all the prickles under my skin.

"Why don't you go play now," Momma says, "let me rest for a bit."

Swallowing, I wipe my hand over my nose, my eyes. I look at her, at the pills in her lap.

"Are you sure?" I say.

"I'm sure," Momma says.

Momma's room is quiet, the sound of her pills tapping

against each other and my nose is prickles, like a nosebleed without the blood. Momma takes two more pills, sip, head back, swallow.

Slow steps, backward steps, I go to the door and pull it open. The sunshine comes through the front room, falls on the kitchen floor, and slices into the shadows of her dark room.

"Be sure and close the door, honey," Momma says.

The clock over the stove is little hand on the ten, big hand on the twelve. Ten o'clock. My hand over the back of my neck, short hairs on my fingers, and I look in our room.

No B.J.

Past her door, I stop and hold my breath. It's quiet on the other side of the door, quiet in there.

Ten steps through the kitchen.

Five to the front door.

Hand on the cool metal doorknob, turn, pull.

On the front stoop, I squint against the sun, pull the door closed.

Outside wind blows, always blowing, sun shines, always shining.

I hate it here.

I walk to the curb, look up the hill, down the hill, nothing.

No B.J.

Sitting on the curb, knees up, arms around, hand up to push hair out of my eyes, but there isn't any hair and my neck is cold. Standing up, the bottom of the hill is nothing but cars back and forth on Highway 101. Beach and ocean past the highway.

No B.J.

Up the hill, houses are lined side by side, cars parked on the street.

No B.J.

He probably took his skateboard to the park and is wheeling around up there, hops and pops. Up the hill, my arms swing back and forth, I breathe hard, but I can't get enough air. At the top of the hill, I look down just in case.

No B.J.

The park is trees and grass, little kids, grown-ups.

No B.J.

At the pond, it's ducks and geese, white swans apart from all the other birds.

No B.J.

Back through the park, I run to the crosswalk, push the button until DON'T WALK is WALK, and I run all the way back to Number One.

Inside, the clock says ten-thirty and I turn the knob on Momma's door, push it open just a crack. Momma is leaned against her pillows, face to the side, eyes closed. She breathes deep and loud, mouth open a little. She's fine, everything's fine, and I close the door.

Maybe it's all right about the pills since she has to take so many pills anyway.

Number One is quiet, just the tap of the Frigidaire motor before it clicks on.

Our telephone is on the wall next to the kitchen table and the cord is twisted around itself. I pull out the kitchen chair, climb up, and take the talk part off the telephone. Daddy's work number is on a piece of paper taped to the telephone and I dial that number, my finger in the hole, the dial turning a big circle after each number.

With both hands, I hold the receiver and listen to the ring and ring and ring.

No Daddy.

In her room, Momma sleeps exactly the same way, mouth open, eyes closed, loud breathing.

Eleven o'clock.

Out on the curb, I sit and look at the bottom of the hill.

No B.J.

Daddy's office number rings and rings and I count one hundred rings before I hang up the telephone.

Momma stays asleep, looks the same, her breathing is like deep sleep, except maybe not. I lean my face close to her mouth, the air out on my cheek.

She's fine, everything is fine.

Noon.

On the curb, I watch down the hill. From up the hill is the sound of skateboard wheels and B.J. rides down the middle of 28th Street, wide *S* turns. B.J. bends his knees, arms out to his sides, and he has a brown bag in one hand.

The back of my throat hurts, scared stiff in my legs and arms, and I've never been so glad to see B.J.

B.J. takes one foot off the board, stops at the curb.

"Where have you been?" I say.

B.J. pops his skateboard over the curb, everything normal, just like always, and maybe it's just me, maybe I'm worried for nothing.

"Around," he says.

B.J. pushes his skateboard so it rolls up to the front door and he sits down on the curb, opens his paper sack, and looks inside. He pulls out a pack of Twinkies, rips the package open with his teeth.

"Something's wrong," I say. "Something's wrong with Momma."

B.J. spits out the corner of the Twinkie wrapper, two fingers fishing a Twinkie out of the package.

"I mean it," I say. "Something is wrong. I mean, I think something is wrong."

B.J. shoves the Twinkie into his mouth and white filling pushes between his fingers. B.J. rolls his eyes and he says something I can't understand.

The smell of Twinkie, the wind, the sunshine, the idea of a Twinkie, Momma not right, and my stomach rolls and my mouth waters. Daddy says mouth watering is a warning and when you get a warning, always run to the bathroom.

Up the sidewalk, I run into the house, to the bathroom, push up the toilet seat, and wait. Spitting into the water, clean toilet water, a gray stain line around the bowl.

Daddy calls it vomit.

B.J. calls it puke.

I call it throw-up.

I hate to throw up more than anything, hate the taste in my mouth, the burn up my throat, the way I shake after. Throwing up into the toilet water, nothing inside me but yellow water, and I cry and cough and cry some more until there isn't anything left to throw up.

I wipe the back of my hand over my nose, push the tears off my face and on my shirt. Up off the floor, I flush the toilet and shut the lid.

Turning on the water, I cup my hand under, sip, spit, sip, spit. I look at me in the mirror and now I'm short hair, white face, and wide open dark eyes.

One o'clock.

In her room, I walk quiet, quiet, and Momma is the same except there isn't the sound of breathing, seems like no air out of her at all. Momma's hand is too cold and her face is cold too.

You are never, never supposed to wake her up, that's the

rule, but I put my hands on her shoulders, peach silk robe soft under my fingers.

"Momma?" I whisper, "Momma, are you okay?"

Her head tips like it's not hooked up to her neck and I put my hands on her face, cheekbones, dark under her eyes, try to get her head back.

"Momma?" I yell.

B.J. blocks out the sunshine in the doorway, white frosting on the side of his mouth.

"Something's wrong," I yell.

I let go of her face, Momma's head to the side again. My fingers into her fingers, I squeeze hard and it's nothing, just bones and cold.

"Come on," I yell, "you have to wake up."

B.J. puts his hand against my shoulder and pushes me away. B.J. stands close to Momma, not close enough to touch and he turns his head to listen to her not breathing. B.J. touches her face with the back of his hand, almost not touching, he's that slow and careful.

"She's cold," B.J. says.

B.J. lifts Momma's hands and puts them under the covers, touching like he doesn't want to touch, like she's made of glass.

"What are you doing?" I yell. "What's the matter with you?"

B.J. pulls the bedspread and blanket up and they slide down off her peach silk robe.

"She's cold," B.J. says.

"Who cares if she's cold," I yell, "she's not waking up. She took too many."

"Too many WHAT?" B.J. yells.

"PILLS," I yell.

"Stop yelling," B.J. yells.

"You stop yelling," I yell. "I looked everywhere for you, I called Daddy, it rang one hundred times, it's been since ten o'clock, and now she won't wake up."

Up on the California King, I hold the empty pill bottles, turn them over and back up again.

"She took them all," I say.

B.J. looks at me for a long time, I don't know how long, his eyes blink, blink, and then he looks at Momma, at me again.

B.J.'s face is red from his neck to his cheeks and he runs to the kitchen.

Momma doesn't move at all and I run into the kitchen.

B.J. holds the telephone and looks at Daddy's telephone number.

"The operator," I yell, "dial zero."

B.J. pushes his finger into the hole, spins the dial, and he looks at me, dark eyes, bottom lip between his teeth.

Scared is in my arms, my legs, up the back of my neck, my heart beats in my head. B.J.'s arms shake and he looks at the floor, starts to talk and cry at the same time.

"Help," B.J. says, "help, my mother is sick, we need help."

One time, a hundred times, everything in between. It doesn't matter how many times Daddy asks me what happened, I can't remember anything else about that day.

There was a haircut, there were a lot of pills, I threw up, and I yelled at B.J. After that I don't know. When I close my eyes tight and make myself remember, the only things are bright lights and voices yelling and then I feel like I took all her pills and I am the one floating away.

B.J. says it was a mistake.

Daddy says it was an overdose.

I don't say anything since I don't know.

Daddy says Momma tried to hurt herself and that's why she has to go to a special hospital with special doctors who take care of people who try to hurt themselves.

After that day, Momma is gone in the special hospital and Daddy calls Carson City, talks with his head in his hand. Daddy talks to Grandpa Ed like nothing ever happened, says business is good and B.J. and me are growing like weeds. After Grandpa Ed, Daddy talks to Grandma Maggie, says he doesn't know what to do, says he's running on empty with the bills and the kids and nothing is the way it's supposed to be. After Grandma Maggie, Daddy calls Auntie Carol and they talk for a long time too. When Daddy hangs up the telephone, he says help is on the way.

five

Steve is long dark hair and whiskers on his face. B.J. says Steve is Steven, our cousin from Carson City, but there's no way. The Steven I remember was part of my wild pack of cousins, part of Steven, Andy, Mark, Bobbie Lou, Tracy, and Faith Ann. Steven was short hair, clean face, and a white button-up shirt.

"Steven is going to stay with you guys until Mom gets better," Daddy says.

"Steven's so square, man," Steve says. "Just Steve."

Steve's beard is patches of dark hair here and there, looks like a cat after a bad fight. Steve's dark hair is in a ponytail and he has on torn jeans and a tie-dyed shirt.

"What happened to you?" Daddy says. "You don't look like the same kid."

Steve looks down at himself and laughs. Steve's laugh is high with a cough at the end, sounds like a cat coughing up a hairball.

"That's true, Uncle Bud," Steve says. "I'm on a personal quest for transformation."

"Transformation?" Daddy says. "Looks more like degeneration."

Steve nods his head, cat laugh, cat cough.

"That's what my old man said," Steve says. "He's such a square."

"What's a square?" I say.

B.J.'s eyes are all over Steve and he smiles a slow grin, black mole over his top lip.

"A square is an uptight person," B.J. says.

"Very uptight," Steve says.

B.J. laughs and pushes his hands up and down on his legs like his hands are dirty. Steve laughs with his head back, cat laugh, cat cough. Daddy watches B.J and Steve, clears his throat, and offers his hand out for shaking.

"Well, it's good to have you here anyway, son," Daddy says.

Steve laughs some more and then he gives Daddy a weird handshake, all twisted up, palms and fingers flipping around. Daddy's eyebrows go high and he looks at his hand getting flipped around.

B.J. laughs so hard he falls off the sofa.

Steve sits on the long green sofa with his arms wide on the back of the sofa and his knees spread out. Daddy sits on the big purple grape with his elbows on his knees and he talks with his hands clapped together, apart, and then together again. I sit close to Daddy, close enough to feel the heat off his body. I pull my legs up to my chest, arms around, make a little ball.

Daddy tells Steve how things are. How B.J. and me go to school, what time we get home, what we eat, what we can do, what we can't do. No television until homework is done, stuff like that.

Steve mostly listens, dark almost black eyes, shadows all over him.

B.J. watches Steve and nods when Steve nods, crosses his arms when Steve crosses his arms, laughs when Steve laughs, even when nothing's funny.

Daddy says it's tax time and he has lots of work to do, says that means late nights, maybe all night, and then he points his hand to a bunch of telephone numbers written on a piece of paper by the telephone.

Steve nods, blinks, nods some more.

The feeling of Momma is all gone now, like she was never here at all. I move my hand over the back of my neck, no hair where there was hair, and I know she was here, no hair the only proof.

Daddy talks, Steve nods, and then Steve puts his dark eyes on me. He just looks at me and I look down.

In Carson City, there was the pink girls' room and the blue boys' room, girls always separate from the boys. I never even saw Steve unless it was mealtime and even then I never talked to him.

I bounce my feet around a little, but I can feel Steve's eyes. I look his way, just to make sure. Steve smiles a little bit of a smile and I look away again, prickles up the back of my neck, over the top of my head, down into my nose.

Here's how it is with Steve.

In the morning, there's no more sleepyheads, no more burning daylight, no more running late. Daddy bought us a radio alarm clock and shows us how to set the wake-up time for seven o'clock so we have one hour to get ready and walk to school.

When the alarm clock goes off, I get out of bed and look up at where B.J. is a lump of sleep under the covers. If he moves or says something, anything, I know he's awake. If B.J. is quiet, I know he's asleep. This morning, B.J. is quiet.

"You better get up," I say.

"Go away," B.J. says.

I go eight steps up the hall to Momma and Daddy's room and look in. The California King is all made up, neat and tidy, and it's cold air in there, air like no one slept there last night.

B.J. says Daddy has to work a lot so he can make his million dollars.

Steve says Daddy is on his own journey of personal transformation.

I don't say anything, but I wish Daddy would come home, at least for the nighttime.

Across the kitchen and in the living room, Steve is on the long green sofa, blue blanket over him, blue pillow under his head, still asleep.

I go into the bathroom, turn on the light and the fan, lock the door behind me. The sound of the fan is the only sound and it's nice the way it hums and moves the air around. Under the lights and the fan, I get myself put together, brush my hair neat and tidy, and then I look close in the mirror to make sure there's no gunk in my eyes.

When I'm done, I turn off the light and the fan, open the door.

Number One is quiet the way it is when everyone is asleep and I walk through the kitchen to the living room, the sound of my shoes on the linoleum the only sound.

Steve sleeps on his back, hands over his chest, mouth wide open. This close is morning breath and tobacco and I can see whisker hairs up his nose. If you stand there long enough and just look, Steve wakes up fast and jumpy.

"Hey," Steve says. "What the . . . ?"

"Time for school," I say.

Steve backs away on his elbows, sits up on the sofa, knees

wide. The blue blanket falls between his legs, black hairs, knobby knees, boxer shorts.

"Shit," Steve says, "you scare the shit out of me when you do that."

Steve rubs his face, his eyes, and I just stand there, just look at him. Steve pulls the blanket around his legs and leans all the way back against the cushions again. He looks at me looking at him.

"You're a spooky little chick," Steve says.

"B.J. is still asleep," I say. "We're going to be late."

"All right," Steve says, "all right."

Steve clears his throat and yells at B.J. to get up. Then Steve gets off the sofa, turns on the TV, and changes the channels around.

In the kitchen, I make one slice of toast and eat it standing up.

Steve stops on the channel with the Dick Tracy cartoons and that's when B.J. gets up too. B.J. walks with his arms out in front of his body, eyes half open, heavy footsteps. B.J. looks like Frankenstein in cowboy and Indian p.j. bottoms. When B.J. does that, Steve laughs and then B.J. laughs too, just like Steve.

First grade is like kindergarten except it's all day.

In my classroom, four desks are pushed together to make one big table. My desk is next to a chubby kid named Charlie, across is Emily, and Bobby sits on the corner from me. Bobby wears eyeglasses.

My teacher is Mrs. Cabbage and some kids laugh when she says it. Mrs. Cabbage doesn't care about being named after a vegetable, so she laughs too.

In first grade, we make name tags and draw pictures around our name. Mrs. Cabbage says our pictures should be something we can look at and enjoy every day, like our favorite things around our names.

I move my hand slow, spell my name in all capitals. Off the side, I draw an oval face, dark eyes, dark curly hair, bright red lips, and just a whisper of color high on the cheeks. There is only enough room for a neck and I draw it long and thin.

"Is that you?" Mrs. Cabbage says.

Mrs. Cabbage wears a flowered skirt and a flowered blouse and Momma is right, the only thing I see is flowers.

"It's my mother," I say.

"Oh," Mrs. Cabbage says.

Charlie draws a baseball bat and a baseball, Emily draws daisy flowers, and Bobby draws four ice cream cones. I push my hands down between my knees, shoulders in, and I try to touch the brown crayon down to the floor.

"It's not very good," I say, "my mother is lots prettier than that."

Mrs. Cabbage looks at the drawing and she shakes her head.

"No, no," Mrs. Cabbage says, "your drawing is very pretty, it's just I've never seen a child draw their mother on their name tag."

I sit up tall, shoulders back, chin tucked, posture of a lady. Charlie, Emily, and Bobby try to see Momma too and Mrs. Cabbage puts her hand over her heart.

"It's just wonderful," Mrs. Cabbage says, "your mother is very lucky."

Mrs. Cabbage pats her hand on my shoulder and then she walks around the other tables. Momma looks at me from the drawing and I wish I could draw better.

The girl who lives upstairs is Malibu Suntan Barbie pretty, blond hair, blue eyes, long tan legs. She comes home from work about the same time we come home from school.

On the long green sofa by the window, I look up the stairs until I can't see her tanned legs anymore.

"She is hot," Steve says. "And she's single."

B.J. looks at Steve and Steve looks at B.J. and they both laugh like it's some kind of joke.

Steve, B.J., and me sit in the living room and watch TV. TV before homework is against the rules, but Steve says it's cool to hang out with the tube as long as no one narcs.

Steve sits on the floor and leans against the side of the big purple grape, a tiny cigarette pinched between his thumb and finger. He makes his own cigarettes with a pack of small white papers and a baggie of loose tobacco. Steve smokes by sucking in with a loud air sound and then he talks with the smoke still inside.

"What's single, B.J.?" I say.

"Not married, twerp," B.J. says.

"Man, you gotta get your name back," Steve says.

B.J. laughs when Steve talks that way, laughs so hard he hiccups, and Steve laughs too and then he puts his hand on B.J.'s shoulder.

"I'm serious," Steve says. "B.J. That's fucked up."

B.J. presses his lips together like he wants to be serious and then they push out, his laugh out like he can't help it. Steve closes his eyes and moves until he's laid out long on the floor, face to the ceiling.

"B.J." Steve says, "that's just cruel."

B.J. stops laughing for real this time, looks at me. I don't know what Steve is talking about, don't know what he means most of the time, and I shrug my shoulders.

There's something about Steve, I'm not sure what, but he

makes me feel shaky from the inside out, like when you see a black hairy spider run across the kitchen linoleum and you didn't think there were any spiders. I like Steve, I guess, since he's my cousin, but I don't trust him very much, and the way he looks at me, I know he knows I don't trust him.

"Hey, Jenny," Steve says, "why don't you go hang out, you know, outside somewhere?"

"Why?" I say.

"B.J. and me," Steve says, "we need to discuss this B.J. business."

"No," I say. "I don't have to leave."

B.J.'s mouth hangs open and his head moves around slow and strange.

Steve sits up and looks at me, a smile on his face.

"You're a spunky little chick," Steve says.

B.J. laughs a high laugh and slaps his hand on his leg.

I cross my arms over my chest and tuck my chin.

Steve's cigarette is just a nub between his fingers. He presses the burned end and puts the nub into his plastic bag. Steve talks with his face down, his voice far off and dreamy.

"Spooky," Steve says, "one spunky, spooky chick."

Steve stands up, thin legs in his bell-bottom pants, and he puts his hand on the big purple grape.

"If that spooky little chick isn't going to leave," Steve says, "we'll hang in your room."

B.J. stands up then, his hand on the big purple grape too, and they stand close together like they can't stand up at all. Steve puts his arm around B.J. and they lean together, walk that way through the kitchen, around the corner, until I can't see them anymore.

There is the sound of the door closing, that little click

sound, and then it's quiet. On the television is a Dinah Shore interview and she has a smooth sleepy voice and just like that, I'm tired all over. Lying on the long green sofa, I put my hands between my knees, curl up, and close my eyes, Dinah Shore smooth sleepy voice inside my eyes and my head.

The rule is bedtime at eight o'clock, but I'm the only one who follows rules around here.

B.J. and Steve stay up and watch television. They laugh all the time and Steve rolls and smokes his little cigarettes.

When it's eight o'clock, I brush my teeth, put on my nightgown, and get into the bottom bunk with *Snow White*.

Since there's no one to read to me, it's a story of drawings and no words, but that's okay since Daddy says drawings in a book mean something important about the story.

The first drawing is the queen sewing stitches into a little white hat. The next drawing is Snow White barefooted in the forest, wild animals all around. Snow White has on a blue dress and she looks scared, eyes wide open at the forest behind her. Animals are drawn into the leaves of the trees and bushes, nineteen when you add them up.

The drawing is complicated and I look at it for a long time. Here's Snow White, thrown out of her home, almost killed, and now she's alone without anyone to take care of her. But maybe she's not really alone after all, and if she's extra careful, the animals will show her how to be in the wild world. Maybe, if Snow White isn't careful, the animals will hurt her, except it doesn't look that way. All the animals on the page have wide open scared eyes, Snow White eyes, and maybe they really came from inside Snow White, like a dream of all the good and not so good things in her life.

I like the idea of all the animals being a part of Snow White and I close my book, the hard cover against my arms, against my chest.

I can hear the television from the living room, hear B.J. and Steve cat laugh, Steve cat cough.

I wonder where Momma is tonight, if she's being extra careful.

I lay my book under the bed, roll over so my back is to the wall, hold my pillow against my chest, and close my eyes.

The next day it's after school and I'm supposed to wait for B.J. at the pond, but there's no B.J. The ducks and geese squawk for dried-up hunks of bread, the swans float around being beautiful. I wait and wait, but there's still no B.J.

I don't know how, but I know B.J. isn't going to meet me today. I look around just one more time and then I walk home alone.

B.J. sits on the little cement step in front of Number One, the door closed behind his back, and I don't know why I'm glad to see him.

"Hey," I say. "What happened to you?"

B.J. scrapes the *J* off his skateboard with a rock, part of his tongue out of his mouth while he works.

"Where were you?" I say. "You're supposed to walk me home."

B.J. keeps his chin tucked and his dark eyes look up at me, shadows all around.

"You're here, aren't you," B.J. says, "you're fine, aren't you?"

B.J. scrapes and scrapes on his skateboard, the *J* almost gone.

"What are you doing?" I say.

B.J. throws the rock on the sidewalk, picks up a thick black Magic Marker and pulls on the top.

"No more B.J.," B.J. says.

"What's wrong with B.J.?" I say.

There's a deep red on B.J.'s face, not mad but something else. B.J. writes the letters *R Y A N*.

"It's a guy thing," B.J. says. "Steve says it's a guy thing."

B.J. pushes the cap on top of the Magic Marker, holds the pen in his fist.

"No one calls me B.J.," B.J. says, "not anymore."

"What about Daddy?" I say.

"No one," B.J. says, "not ever."

When B.J. is mad, it's trouble, and I get up off the step, go to the front door.

"You can't go in," B.J. says.

"Why not?" I say.

"You just can't," B.J. says.

Up on the step, I turn the doorknob, except it won't turn. Under the doormat, the *I Love California* key chain is gone, just dirt where the key should be.

"Steve," I yell, "open up."

"You better cool it," B.J. says.

"Stop talking like him," I say.

B.J. shrugs. I hit my fist on the door.

Inside is the sound of people, voices high and low, and then something thunks like it fell. B.J. dusts off the butt of his jeans, puts one foot on his skateboard over the new *Bryan* written on.

The door opens, Steve in the crack, and he has on a pair of jeans, no shirt.

"Let me in," I say.

"Hey," Steve says, "home so soon?"

"Soon?" I say. "It's late."

I push the door and it hits against Steve's body. He holds the door closed, the smell of sticky sweet smoke all around.

"Hey," Steve says, "cool it. Tell this spooky little chick to cool it."

B.J. puts his hands out to his sides and shrugs.

"I tried, man," B.J. says, "but you know."

I look at B.J., look at Steve in the door crack.

Steve is face whiskers, pointy nose, pointy eyes, pointy chin. He looks back into our apartment and looks down at me again.

"I've got a little company here," Steve says, "so I need you to lay low and kill an hour. Can you do that?"

"What?" I say.

Steve digs his hand into his back pocket and pulls out his billfold, takes out some money. He pushes a rolled-up dollar bill through the crack in the door.

"Give this to Bryan there," Steve says, "and you guys can go to the store, get me a pack of Marlboros, and then keep the change."

B.J. reaches over, his arm heavy on my shoulder, and he takes the dollar bill between his fingers.

"No problem," B.J. says.

"What store?" I say, "there's no store close by. Plus we can't buy cigarettes anyway, you have to be a grown-up."

Steve looks at me for a long time, quiet in his eyes.

"You're a real pain in the butt," Steve says.

"Go on now, Bryan," Steve says, "and take this one with you. Got it?"

"Got it," B.J. says.

Just like that, Steve shuts the door in my face. The lock turns and it's us outside, him inside.

I hit the door, open hand, the sting up my arm to my elbow.
"Hey," I yell.

B.J. puts his hand on my shoulder and I shrug my arm so he can't touch.

"What's going on?" I say. "Why can't we go in?"

"Be cool," B.J. says.

"Quit talking like him," I say.

Wind blows up the hill, lifts his hair up around his head, and it blows in his eyes. B.J. puts his hand on his forehead, squints, and holds his hair out of his eyes.

"Steve's in there with the chick from upstairs," B.J. says, "they're making out."

"Making out?" I say.

"Fooling around," B.J. says.

"Fooling around?" I say.

B.J. looks down, foot on his skateboard, and all I see is the top of his head, dark straight hair. He looks at me again, storm cloud eyes.

"You better get lost," B.J. says, "just kill an hour, just hang loose."

"Stop talking like him," I say.

"Fine," B.J. says, "do what you want. I'm going."

B.J. pushes his skateboard off the sidewalk, all the wheels on the street, and he takes off down the hill, wheel roll sound on asphalt. B.J. rides all the way to the bottom without falling, makes a tight left turn, and I can't see him anymore.

I look up the hill, down the hill, turn around, and look at the door for Number One. I walk to the curb and next door to Number One is a green house and then a blue house and then a gray house. Ingleside Drive is at the top of 28th Street and I look both ways and cross over.

I go up two more streets, turn the corner, and touch my hand on a white fence in front of a gray house. Inside the fence is a little black dog with a tiny bark. It's funny how that dog barks, yapping serious, and I laugh at how serious and loud it tries to be. The dog jumps and barks more and I squat down.

"It's okay," I say, my hand to the little dog through the slats in the fence, "see, it's okay."

The dog weaves around, sniffs my fingers, backs up, and starts to bark again.

"You can pet her," a voice says. I pull my hand back, stand up.

The voice is a lady with white blond hair in a ponytail that's tied with a scarf. On her lips she wears shiny pink lipstick, the nicest shade of pink I've ever seen. The lady opens the gate and it swings into her yard. The little dog runs over and jumps up, its paws just to my knees.

"That's Chloe," the lady says.

I kneel down to Chloe, let her lick my face, dog breath. I lean my head back and rub both hands behind her ears. The lady watches, her eyes behind sunglasses.

"That's a funny name," I say, "Chloe."

"It is a funny name," the lady says.

The lady's voice is high and sweet, like flowers if flowers could talk.

"We used to have cats," I say, "one named Moshe, one named Diana."

The lady takes off her sunglasses and kneels down on one knee, her hand petting Chloe.

"Moshe Dayan," the lady says, "is an Israeli who led a war against Egypt."

"Really?" I say.

"Really," she says.

Her eyes are green and blue and gray, like ocean water when the sun sets.

"I like your lipstick," I say.

The lady presses her lips together.

"Really?" she says, "it's a frosted, it's new."

"It's great," I say, "matches the colors in your scarf too, just perfect."

The lady touches the scarf in her hair, eyes on my face.

"Do you live around here?" she says.

"Just on the next street," I say, "Number One on 28th Street, it's a triplex."

She stands up, looks around, looks at me.

"Are you all alone?" she says.

"Just out for a walk," I say, "I have to kill an hour."

The lady laughs and the wind chimes on her porch ding together at the same time.

"Kill an hour, huh?" she says.

"I have to be cool and lay low," I say.

The lady laughs, puts her hand up to her mouth to stop laughing.

"How old are you?" she says.

"Six," I say, "almost seven, I'm in first grade, my teacher is Mrs. Cabbage, I'm not kidding, that's really her name."

The lady laughs so hard she has to bend over, hand on her side, and it's nice to make someone laugh like that.

Chloe sniffs along the fence, working her way down the sidewalk.

"Hey, Chloe," the lady says, "get back here."

The little dog walks up the sidewalk, tail wagging behind her little dog body.

"I'm Gayle," she says.

She shakes my hand all formal, her hand soft and her fingernails done in the same soft pink as her lips.

Sometimes you meet someone and it's like you knew them forever. That's how it is with Gayle.

Gayle has some lemonade and asks me to have a glass since she was about to take a break from her garden. Since I have an hour to kill, I say why not and sit with Gayle on her front steps. The two of us drink lemonade and talk and talk.

I tell her how we are from Carson City and Gayle says her husband has family in Reno. I say Daddy works in money, except I don't know what that means, and Gayle says her husband works at a bank, that maybe Daddy works at a bank. I say I don't think so. I say my favorite television show is *Bewitched* and Gayle says that's her favorite too. Gayle says we have a lot in common and it's nice having things in common with someone.

Gayle looks at the watch on her wrist, a slim silver watch with the face so small I didn't even know it was a watch.

"It's four," Gayle says, "your hour is up."

"We killed it," I say.

Gayle laughs at that and I look in my glass, just ice.

"I better get going," I say.

"Is someone waiting for you?" Gayle says, "your mom?"

Clearing my throat, I look at the ice cubes, think, think. I don't want to tell about Momma.

"Oh sure," I say, "she's just resting."

"Is that why you have to lay low?" Gayle says.

"Something like that," I say.

I set my glass down on the porch. Chloe puts her head up, sniffs.

"Thanks for the lemonade," I say.

Gayle crosses her arms over her knees, sits pretty, and looks at me with her head tilted to the side.

"You're welcome," Gayle says, "and you can come up and visit anytime."

"Okay," I say.

"Maybe we can watch *Bewitched* together some afternoon," Gayle says, "if you tell your mom."

"Sure," I say.

I let myself out the white gate, shut the gate so Chloe won't get out. I wave at Gayle and she waves back, Miss America wave, elbow, wrist, elbow, wrist.

Every day it's hanky-panky.

Every day it's B.J. and me locked out.

Every day I go to Gayle's house. We sit on her porch and she always asks about Momma, if it's okay that I'm out alone, stuff like that. I tell Gayle that Momma needs lots of rest and it's okay, and after that Gayle lets me stay and sometimes help with her garden. Gayle shows me how to pop the heads off the dead flowers, shows me how to pull weeds at the root so they don't grow back, shows me how to find snails hidden in the shade and put them in a little can.

When we work in the garden Gayle tells me she wants a baby of her own, says it's taking a long time. Gayle's eyes are sad when she talks about a baby and I wish I could think of something to make her laugh. Deep inside, in the place that has secrets, I wish Gayle wouldn't make a baby since she wouldn't have time to talk with me anymore, but right away I feel terrible for thinking that way. I tell Gayle all about Mrs. Cabbage and how she dresses in all flowers, how Mrs.

Cabbage is a clasher, not a matcher, and that makes Gayle laugh and laugh, the sad baby look gone.

Gayle makes the best ham on toast sandwiches in the world, says the secret is to keep it simple and use the right mayonnaise.

"You must use Best Foods," Gayle says, "they call it Hellman's in the East."

Gayle and me sit in her kitchen with white cabinets and white appliances. Even the floor is white. Gayle says white is a clean restful color. She stands at the counter, spreads Best Foods on toast, lays thin slices of pink ham on, puts the whole thing together, and cuts diagonal. I love how she does that.

After slicing, Gayle puts the best ham sandwich in the world on a nice plate, red rose painted in the center, a green line of trim around the outside. Then Gayle puts two slices of orange off to the side of the best ham sandwich in the world, sets the whole thing down on the white kitchen table.

Gayle sits down across from me, puts her chin in her hand.

"It looks so nice on the plate," I say. "Momma says presentation is everything."

"Your mother sounds like she has wonderful taste," Gayle says.

"She does," I say, "she's bursting with style."

Gayle smiles at "bursting with style."

"Aren't you having one?" I say.

"No," Gayle says, "I already ate."

It's bad manners to eat in front of someone who isn't eating, and I don't know what to do. I look at the best ham sandwich in the world, look at Gayle.

"Go ahead," Gayle says.

"Momma says it's rude," I say.

"It's okay," Gayle says.

Careful, careful, I pick up one diagonal of sandwich, toast crumbs on my fingers, and I bite off the pointy end, ham and mayonnaise and toast in my mouth.

Gayle bites her lips like she is thinking about something.

"We're getting to be pretty good friends, aren't we?" Gayle says.

It's rude to talk with your mouth full and I just nod.

"Well, I was thinking that maybe," Gayle says, "maybe I could come to your house and meet your mother."

I breathe toast crumbs down my throat and cough hard. Gayle gets up quick, fills up a glass with water, and sets the glass on the table.

"Are you okay?" Gayle says.

I drink the water, that scratchy feeling down my throat, my eyes watered up.

"You can't," I say.

"What?" Gayle says.

I wipe my hand over my mouth and press my lips together.

"You can't come over," I say. "My mother, she's sleeping."

"Is she sick?" Gayle says.

I like Gayle, I like her a lot, and now I'm lying to my friend and I know she knows. Up the back of my neck, over my head, it's prickles and tears too. I pinch the top of my nose, but the tears are already out.

Gayle gets out of her white chair, kneels down, and puts her hands on my knees. Her fingers are soft and she smells like flowers and earth and mayonnaise. Gayle hands me a napkin and I press it over my eyes.

"It's okay," Gayle says, "you can tell me the truth."

The wet napkin between my hands, Gayle with her warm

soft hands on my knees, her face so serious and worried, and I don't know what to do.

"I'm sorry I lied," I say.

Gayle pats my knee, puts her hand on my arm.

"It's okay," Gayle says.

Gayle's eyes are full of everything that is good and they just wait for me to tell the truth. Before I can stop, I tell her everything about Steve, the hanky-panky, about Momma in a special hospital for I don't know how long. I tell about Daddy and how he's boy-next-door drop-dead handsome except I don't see him anymore and I don't know why. I tell everything I know, all the way back to Mary Street, and it's like the whole ocean out of my mouth and into the all-white kitchen. Gayle holds my hand in her hand and listens and finally, I'm all out of words.

Gayle looks at me for a long time and then she lets go of my hand, sits down in her chair again, and puts both her hands over her heart.

"My goodness," Gayle says.

It's quiet in the kitchen, the kind of quiet that says everything.

The best thing about Gayle is how she is so normal and happy. My story is sad and it's not normal and I wish I didn't say any of it now. I wish I could say I was just kidding and Gayle and me could be like we were before. Normal.

Sitting up straight, I roll my shoulders back and tuck my chin. Inside my stomach is restless and I know I should go. I get up then, take my plate to Gayle's sink, and rinse it off. Gayle clears her throat and stands up too, says I shouldn't worry about the plate.

I wipe my hands off on my jeans, look around at everything, at Gayle. I'm never coming back here, not ever, and I know it the way you know things you can't explain.

Gayle and me walk to the door and I go out on her porch, pink and blue in the sunset sky.

"If you need anything, anytime," Gayle says.

Gayle's voice is different, sad and quiet and wrong. I nod my head and look at my feet going down the steps, down the sidewalk, out the gate. I close the gate carefully, feel Gayle's eyes, and I look at her one more time, smile like everything is just fine, and wave my hand.

Gayle lifts her arm up too, waves Miss America, and then she drops her arm against her leg.

When I get home, Red is parked at the curb and the front door is open partway. Voices yell inside, Daddy, Steve, B.J., but it's mostly Daddy who yells.

Trouble is all around and I stand outside the door, hold extra still, not even breathing in. Daddy says Steve has to leave and B.J. says it's not Steve's fault and Daddy says he doesn't give a damn about fault, he isn't going to tolerate sex and drugs and god knows what else has been going on in his house.

I lean my whole body against the side of the door, try to see in, but it's just shadows.

"Just be cool," Steve's voice says, "Uncle Bud's right, I gotta move on anyway."

"But you're hanging here," B.J.'s voice says, "we haven't even gone surfing yet."

"For crying out loud," Daddy yells, "be a man."

Daddy's voice is out the door, into the wind. B.J.'s voice is a low throat sound in his chest and he says something, I can't believe what he says.

"I wish you weren't my father," B.J. says.

Inside Number One, it's quiet, quiet, a terrible quiet.

Tears are in my eyes, sting and hot down my face, and I wipe them away. I walk down the sidewalk, out to the curb, and sit down. My face into wind, into the sunset, and I close my eyes.

Steve leaves on a Wednesday and B.J. is on extended, indefinite restriction. B.J. can go to school and come home, but that's it, no beach, no skateboard, no television. Daddy says I have to watch B.J. and tell if he breaks his restriction.

I don't like being the one who has to narc on B.J.

B.J. says if I narc, I suck.

Now that Steve's gone, B.J. says everything sucks, restriction sucks, I suck, Daddy sucks. B.J. says that when you suck, it's really bad.

"So when you say 'suck,'" I say, "it's like a swear?"

"No," B.J. says, "it's like slang."

B.J. and me are in the living room and the television is on, the sound off. Daddy didn't say no TV without sound, so B.J. says it's cool.

"A swear is like 'shit' or 'fuck,'" B.J. says.

"You shouldn't swear," I say. "You get your mouth washed with soap for swearing."

"That's your problem," B.J. says. "Too many rules. Too uptight."

B.J. puts his hand in a fist, his middle finger up and the two fingers on each side curled up next to the middle finger.

"Try this," B.J. says.

My hand in a fist and I hold my middle finger up like B.J.

"You're doing it wrong," B.J. says.

B.J. crosses the living room on his knees and grabs my hand. He moves my fingers so they are all bent except the middle one.

"There," B.J. says. "Now hold it up high. With authority."

I lift my hand in the air and B.J. does it too, our middle fingers to the ceiling.

"Fuck you," B.J. says.

I drop my hand, my fingers unrolled.

"You shouldn't say that," I say.

"Why not?" B.J. says.

B.J. keeps his middle finger up, points it to the ceiling.

"Fuck you, upstairs chick," B.J. says.

B.J. rotates his hand, points his finger at the television.

"Fuck you, TV," B.J. says.

The telephone rings and B.J. turns his hand around, points his finger at the kitchen.

"Fuck you, telephone," B.J. says.

B.J.'s middle finger looks like a cannon about to shoot.

The telephone rings again and B.J. drops his hand and walks to the kitchen, picks up the telephone.

"Hello," B.J. says.

Daddy calls every day, tells us when he's coming home. B.J. says yeah and uh-huh and okay and then he rolls his eyes, looks at the ceiling. B.J. holds the telephone out to me and nods his head up.

"He wants to talk to you," B.J. says.

Off the big purple grape, I walk to the kitchen. B.J. holds the phone against his chest.

"Don't narc," B.J. whispers.

I hold the telephone in both hands. B.J. holds up his middle finger and points it at everything, the refrigerator, the sink, the open jar of peanut butter on the counter.

"Hey, Juniper," Daddy says, "is everything okay?"

"Yeah," I say. "Everything is okay."

"Is B.J. behaving?" Daddy says.

B.J. turns his hand, pushes his middle finger into the peanut butter.

"Yeah," I say. "He's fine."

B.J. pushes his middle finger into his mouth, sucks the peanut butter off, and holds his finger up again, says "Fuck you," without the words, and I don't know if B.J. means it to be for Daddy or for me or just everything and everyone.

B.J. says Momma has been gone for a whole year. Daddy says more like ten months. Momma won't say anything.

She comes home on a Saturday and everything about her is like it was, like she's better. I'm so happy she's home, I sit as close to Momma as I can, so close it's like I could just climb inside of her body.

Momma is on the big purple grape and she smokes Parliament after Parliament, taps the ash off in one of Daddy's beanbag ashtrays. She has on a pair of orange slacks, a brown sweater with orange and red leaves in the design, and a funny pair of white plastic tennis shoes like a nurse would wear.

Daddy sits on the long green sofa, smokes Marlboro after Marlboro.

Momma looks at the carpet, at her hand on the big purple grape, at the end of her cigarette. Daddy looks out the big window.

B.J. sits in the middle of the living room, lips rolled together, his dark eyes on Daddy, on Momma, on Daddy again.

Momma has been gone for so long, it should be like a

celebration, but something is wrong. Shoulder to shoulder, arm to arm, I scoot in closer and Momma laughs at how I sit so close, and puts her arm around me.

"Don't worry," Momma says. "I'm not going anywhere."

Daddy laughs too, the two of them laughing, and they look at each other and then, just like that, they stop laughing, stop smiling.

Momma lifts her chin, smokes her Parliament, and squints her eyes. Daddy looks at his hands, at the Marlboro between his fingers, and he snuffs his cigarette out in his beanbag ashtray.

I bite my thumbnail. Momma puts her hand on my hand.

"Don't bite," Momma says, "that's a nasty habit."

B.J. bites his fingernail too, his middle finger, and he holds it up like "Fuck you," takes it down again fast, and tries not to laugh.

"Well," Daddy says, "I have a couple things to do at the office so . . ."

"You're leaving?" B.J. says.

Daddy rubs his hands together, dry skin sound of his fingers.

"Gotta pay the bills, son," Daddy says.

Sun shines in the big window and the room is full of light. Momma smokes her Parliament and all of her face squints against the sunlight.

"Do you need help getting settled?" Daddy says.

Momma blows smoke out in a thin line.

"No, thank you," Momma says. "My children can help me."

Daddy stands up and puts his hands into his pockets.

"Well, all right then," Daddy says.

Momma nods, eyes on me, like Daddy is already gone.

B.J. looks at Daddy, at Momma, at Daddy again, like he

doesn't know what to do. The red under B.J.'s skin is up from his neck to his cheeks and he gets off the floor and follows Daddy to the door.

"When are you coming back?" B.J. says.

Daddy takes his keys out of his pocket and opens the door.

"Later," Daddy says.

B.J. stands between the big purple grape and the front door, fingers into fists by his legs.

"But," B.J. says, "what about us? What about Mom?"

Momma reaches her hand out, fingers on B.J.'s sleeve.

"Let him go," Momma says. "It's fine."

Daddy stands in the doorway, sunlight and wind into Number One, and he looks at us, all three of us, looks at Momma and shakes his head.

Daddy shuts the door and that's when Momma lets out a deep breath. She lets go of B.J.'s arm and leans her weight on me.

"Well," Momma says, "that is that."

When the lights are out for movies in my classroom, I put my arms on my desk and lay my head on my arms.

The lights are off for a movie called *Compounds, Atoms, and Molecules* because that's what we do in second grade, we watch lots of movies. On the screen, tiny round things float around and they look like colored bubbles or marbles. The man in the movie says the whole world is made of atoms and atoms paired up are molecules. The round things float together and make different shapes. The man says atoms and molecules are so small, you can only see them through a microscope. Then the round things split apart and float on the screen and the movie is over.

When the lights are on, I sit up straight, blink my eyes used to the light.

"Now it's time for you to make a molecule," Miss Evans says.

Miss Evans has a box of colored toothpicks and a bag of sugar-covered gumdrops. She goes around the room and puts some on each desk. I get fifteen gumdrops and ten toothpicks.

"Don't eat the gumdrops," Miss Evans says, "make your molecule first, make sure I see it."

Miss Evans is tall and skinny and she talks in a high voice. I don't like her half as much as Mrs. Cabbage. I pick up a gumdrop, red candy under white sugar, and I try to see the million molecules that are impossible to see. Squeezing the candy until it's flat, I open my fingers and it springs into a circle again. I drop it on the desk, watch it roll in a circle. Gumdrop, grains of sugar, gazillions of molecules.

Miss Evans stops at my desk.

"You have to build a molecule," Miss Evans says, "or you can't eat the candy."

"It doesn't make sense," I say.

Miss Evans kneels by my chair.

The clock on the wall is big hand on the eleven, the little hand on the three, and school is almost done.

"What doesn't make any sense?" Miss Evans says.

"Well," I say. "It's just how millions and millions of molecules make up everything and they're so small you can only see them through a microscope and if that's true, then these toothpicks and these candies are made up of molecules too and you can't make them into molecules since they are molecules and it's just impossible."

Miss Evans looks at me for a long time and her eyes just blink and blink. Finally, she looks at the clock.

"All right, Jenny," Miss Evans says. "Why don't you stay after for a minute."

Miss Evans claps her hands and that means school is all done. All the kids push chairs under their desks, get their lunch boxes and coats, and then they leave.

I want to leave too except I know I can't.

Miss Evans is at her desk and she writes on a piece of paper, folds the paper, and pushes a safety pin through the note. She looks at me and does that thing with her finger like she wants me to come to her desk.

I push my chair under, walk ten steps to her desk.

"Take this home," Miss Evans says.

Miss Evans pins the note to my daisy T-shirt, pins it right on the stem.

"I can carry it," I say.

"No," Miss Evans says, "this way I know your mother will see it."

You don't talk about Momma's being sick, not ever. Daddy says it's our business and other people won't understand. Ever since Gayle, I know that's true and I know I can't tell Miss Evans about Momma.

Miss Evans fusses with the note and stops, drops her hands on her knees.

"Have your mother call me," Miss Evans says, "tell her it's important."

That wrong feeling is up the back of my neck.

"Am I in trouble?" I say.

"No," she says. "I just want to talk to your mother."

"Why?" I say.

Miss Evans takes a deep breath and lets the air out through her nose.

"I always talk to parents," Miss Evans says, "it's normal. I just haven't had a chance to talk with your parents this year and it's time, so be sure to give that note to your mother."

Miss Evans stands up then and smiles her nice teacher smile. I don't care what Miss Evans says, I know I'm in trouble.

Halfway through the park, I stop at the pond, sit down on an empty bench. Ducks and geese swim my way, a V behind them in the muddy pond water. On the other end of the pond the swans swim alone.

Even though I'm not supposed to, I undo the safety pin and the note falls off the daisy stem and lands in my lap. Miss Evans's note is thick paper folded three times, Momma's name on the front. I hold the note in my hand, press it flat against my palm.

Momma's only been home for a month, maybe less, and some days she's good enough to get out of bed, get dressed, even cook. Other days, Momma takes pills and sleeps, takes more pills and sleeps some more. Sometimes she messes her bed too and I hate that most of all, especially if I'm the only one home to clean her up.

B.J. says there's no way Momma is ever going to get better, Daddy never says anything about it, doesn't even make promises. I know she's going to get better, I can make her get better, but a note from Miss Evans could mess up the whole thing. Maybe make Momma worse.

Miss Evans's note is all in cursive writing and I can't read the words, not even the little ones. Maybe the words say I'm too stupid to make a molecule.

A duck reaches my end of the pond and jumps out, waddle-walks in my direction. I rip a corner of the paper and roll it into a little wad, toss it up in the air. The duck lifts his head and eats the paper, looks at me again.

"It's paper, you stupid duck," I say.

The duck flaps his wings and quacks.

I rip another corner, then another, then the whole sheet of paper, and I feed it all to the stupid ducks. On the other side of the pond, the white beautiful swans never look my way. Swans are too smart to eat paper. I like that about the swans.

When I get home, it's all wrong. Momma is on the long green sofa and she is dressed in a pair of slacks and a light yellow V-neck sweater. Her hair is combed smooth and she has makeup on too. It's been such a long time since she's put on makeup, I just stand there and look at her, at the color over her skin.

"Here she is now," Momma says.

Momma waves both hands, her fingers dancing in the air. Her smile is like a big crack on her face.

"Shut the door, sweetie," Momma says, "we've got company."

A stranger lady sits on the other side of the long green sofa, knees together, blue suit with a skirt. I touch the daisy on my shirt, daisy stem, no note.

"Come on, silly," Momma says.

Momma smiles and looks at the stranger lady.

"She's shy," Momma says.

It's four steps from the door to the sofa and I sit next to Momma, my yellow tights along her navy pants. Momma puts her arm over my shoulders and smiles down at me.

The stranger lady has brown hair up in a bun and she would be pretty except for those glasses, black frames and thick lenses that make her eyeballs look huge, frog eyes under water.

"Hi, Jenny," the stranger lady says. "I bet you are wondering who I am?"

Momma sits up tall and takes her arm off my shoulders.

"This nice lady is Mrs. Axton. She's from the County," Momma says.

The stranger lady has a clipboard on her knees, a white sheet of paper clipped on, and she puts both hands over the paper.

Momma crosses her legs at the knee and her pee bag isn't on the floor, isn't anywhere. Momma taps me on the shoulder and shakes her head like I should stop looking for her pee bag and she reaches for her pack of Parliaments.

"Would you care for a cigarette?" Momma says.

Mrs. Axton shakes her head no and writes on her sheet of white paper. Momma drops the pack of cigarettes like she changed her mind.

Mrs. Axton stops writing, clears her throat, makes her face into a grown-up smile.

"Jenny," Mrs. Axton says, "I'm here because there was a call to our office from one of your neighbors."

"A call?" I say.

"I was just explaining," Momma says, voice high, too high.

Momma clears her throat, a deep cough in her chest.

"I was just explaining how I was in the hospital," Momma says, "and you were taken care of by your cousin Steven."

The wrong feeling is up the back of my neck and Mrs. Axton writes something on her sheet of white paper.

Momma puts her hand on my knee and squeezes. Her face is a long line from cheekbone to chin. This close, I can see how she's got on too much powder and how the lipstick is crooked too.

"I'd like to ask you a few questions, Jenny," Mrs. Axton says.

Momma looks at me and smiles a tight smile. Momma's

eyes are fast, too fast, and they go back and forth, on me, on Mrs. Axton. Stop-start eyes.

"It's okay, honey, " Momma says.

Mrs. Axton holds her pen tip on the paper, big eyes on me, on Momma, on me.

"How old are you?" Mrs. Axton says.

"Seven," I say.

"Really?" Mrs. Axton says.

"She's a tall seven," Momma says.

"Very grown-up," Mrs. Axton says.

I try to smile, but my face isn't right, my smile more like a wiggle on my face, like an itch on my lip. Mrs. Axton stops her smile and I stop my smile.

"I want to ask you about the time your mother was in the hospital," Mrs. Axton says. "Were you ever left alone?"

"Alone?" I say.

"Yes," Mrs. Axton says, "were you ever alone in the apartment?"

"No," I say.

"Never?" Mrs. Axton says.

"Never," I say.

Mrs. Axton writes on her paper.

"Your cousin was always here?" Mrs. Axton says.

"No," I say.

"No?" Mrs. Axton says.

"After Steve left," I say, "he wasn't here then."

Mrs. Axton crosses her arms over her paper, leans forward again, stupid smile on her face.

"So you were alone then?" Mrs. Axton says.

"No," I say.

"Who was watching you then?" Mrs. Axton says.

Momma nods at me like it's okay.

"B.J.," I say.

"Your brother?" Mrs. Axton says. "Who is nine?"

"Right," I say.

"Almost ten," Momma says, "a very grown-up ten."

Mrs. Axton writes and it's the sound of pen on paper.

Momma reaches for her cigarettes and sits back like she changed her mind again. She bites her bottom lip, lipstick off on her tooth.

I lean against Momma and she looks down at me.

I move my finger over my tooth so she knows and Momma moves her finger over her tooth, rubs the red off. Momma leans back, looks at her finger, at the red lipstick she rubbed off, and she smiles at me. Her dark eyes are steady again and she puts her arm around my shoulder and holds me against her side.

Mrs. Axton clears her throat.

"I just have a couple more questions," Mrs. Axton says, "okay?"

"When you were here with your cousin Steve and your brother, B.J.," Mrs. Axton says, "did you stay inside or did you go outside?"

Mrs. Axton talks slow and careful the way grow-ups do when they think you're stupid. I slow talk back.

"I-play-inside," I say. "And-sometimes, I-play-outside."

Momma starts to laugh, a little laugh, and she covers her mouth with her hand.

Mrs. Axton looks down at her paper without writing, takes a deep breath in. Mrs. Axton clicks the top of her pen, holds it between her fingers, rolls it around and around.

"Okay," Mrs. Axton says, "let me ask you one more question and I want you to think really hard and just tell me the truth."

Momma's body is stiff next to me, her breath in, and I sit up straight.

"If there was a plate of cookies on the table," Mrs. Axton says, "would you ask for one or would you wait until it was offered to you?"

It's a stupid question since there aren't any cookies on the table. I want to tell Mrs. Axton it's a stupid question. I want to say how all her questions are stupid and she should leave since Momma is sick.

"Jenny?" Mrs. Axton says.

"I don't understand," I say.

"It's simple," Mrs. Axton says, "pretend there are cookies on the table, chocolate chip, whatever kind you like. Would you ask for one or would you wait until your host offered it to you?"

It isn't really a question, feels more like a test. I don't know what to say since I love chocolate chip cookies and would probably ask for one. The way the question just sits there, the way Momma and Mrs. Axton look at me, I know what I would do might be wrong.

"I would wait?" I say.

Momma lets out a loud breath, her body leaned against my body.

"Of course you would wait," Momma says. "Jenny is a good girl."

Mrs. Axton watches Momma, watches me.

I hate Mrs. Axton. I hate her thick glasses and her frog eyes. I hate how she sits so still with her navy blue suit and her matching pantyhose and her stupid pen.

Just like that, Mrs. Axton stands up and she says stuff like, "Sorry to bother you," and "Thank you for your time."

Momma stands up too, moves slow, her hand on my shoulder. Mrs. Axton says she can show herself to the door and thank you again and Momma smiles her hostess smile, dark eyes stop-start.

When there is no more Mrs. Axton, Momma sits down on the sofa and her body shakes.

"Momma," I say.

Momma puts her hands around my arms, her fingernails into the soft part of my skin.

"Do you know who that woman was?" Momma says. "She came to take you away."

She shakes me one, two, three times, the back of my head to my neck, and her face is like a scream, lines of tears in the powder.

"Never," Momma yells. "Never ask anyone for anything, especially a stranger."

Her voice is in my ears, all around Number One.

"You can't trust anyone," Momma yells, "you can't trust them."

"Momma," I whisper. "You're hurting me."

Momma's eyes stop-start on my face, on my arms, on her hands on my arms. She opens her fingers and puts her hands over her face. My arms are hot where she pressed and it's like she still holds on even though I'm free.

White sunshine comes through the window and falls over the living room carpet. Momma takes her hands off her face and looks at her feet.

"Oh no," she says.

"Where is your bag?" I say.

"In the bathroom," Momma says.

She tilts her head to the side and she has a sad deep in her eyes.

"I didn't want it out here with that woman," Momma says. "I thought I could hold it."

"It's okay," I say.

In the hall, I get a towel from the closet.

Momma hugs her arms around her middle, looks at the pee puddle on the green carpet.

I push the towel around her feet and it's warm and wet through to my fingers.

I look at the front door. No B.J. No Daddy.

I roll the towel up and help her stand. Momma and me walk slow steps through the kitchen to her bedroom and the smell is more than pee. The smell is bitter and strong and I know she pooped too.

We don't talk, just do like we always do. You take off the dirty clothes, run them in clean water, put them into the washing machine. You clean up the mess on her too, wipe until her skin is white and clean and the way it was. You always hold your breath to keep the smell away from your nose, but it doesn't work.

After she is into her nightgown and under the covers, you need to hook the bag to the plastic tube.

The pee bag is in the bathroom and you rinse it with hot water, rinse again, and then rinse one more time. Three times kills the Germans.

Momma lies with her head deep into her pillows, dark curls around her face, curls on the white pillowcase.

I don't look at her face, look at the floor, the plastic tube.

"I'm so sorry about this," Momma says.

"It's an accident," I say.

I hook the bag to the tube and balance it upright so it doesn't spill.

"Everyone has accidents," I say.

"No," Momma says, "that's not what I mean."

Her dark eyes are steady on my face.

"I'm so scared," Momma whispers.

My throat hurts and I swallow.

"It's okay," I say. "You're going to be okay."

Momma puts her fist up to her mouth, coughs. Her shoulders lift off the pillows when she coughs and the sound is deep in her chest. I put my hands on her shoulders, silk and bones into my fingers. Momma wipes her hand over her mouth, all the lipstick off now, and she leans back into her pillows again.

"I don't want you to remember me like this," Momma says, "weak and sick."

"You're not weak," I say.

I stand away from her, look at her nightstand, at the pill bottles. I open the bottle with the Darvons, take out two, just two. I open the Thorazine, take out two, just two.

"Jenny?" Momma says.

"You just need to rest," I say.

I hold my hand to her and she looks at me, her dark eyes back and forth on my face. She looks at me like she wants to say more and then she looks at my hand. Momma opens her hand, palm up.

I open my fingers and drop the pills into her palm.

"You are such a good girl," Momma says. "What would I have done without you?"

I put the lids on the pill bottles, move all the bottles to the far edge of her nightstand.

"Do," I say.

"What?" she says.

"You mean 'do' without me," I say. "What would you do without me?"

Momma looks at me then, nothing in her eyes, and then she nods her head like she knows.

"Right," she says. "What would I *do* without you."

Momma lets out a deep breath, her eyes on the pills in her hand. She pops them into her mouth and takes the water glass, drinks, closes her eyes, and swallows.

I take the glass out of her hand and set it on the nightstand.

Momma and me, pills and water, every day, forever. I don't know any other way and I don't care because she's here and she's my mother and without my mother, there's nothing else. I want to tell her that she's going to get better, that today was just a bad day, that it's my fault and I'll just try harder tomorrow.

Momma's eyes stay closed and her face is quiet and still, powder around the edges. I look at her for a long time, just look, and then I pull the covers over her shoulders, tuck her in, and Momma smiles then, sleepy smile, and rolls on her side.

Across the street from Number One, I sit on the curb, my chin on my knees. The sun makes a shadow of me on the black asphalt.

It's hot but I'm cold.

B.J.'s shadow is in my shadow and I look up at him, my hand against my forehead to shade my eyes.

"Where have you been?" I say.

B.J. sits down and he smells like the beach.

"She was sick again," I say.

My shadow and B.J.'s shadow are on the street and his shadow is wide.

"Poop and pee," I say.

I rub my face on my shoulder.

"Are you crying?" B.J. says.

"No," I say.

Wind blows up the hill, my hair whipped into my eyes and my mouth. I pull a long piece of hair out of my mouth.

"You're too uptight," B.J. says.

"Uptight?" I say.

"Uptight." B.J. says. "And high-strung. Steve told me that, he said you're different, high-strung."

"Steve is an idiot," I say. "Daddy called Steve an idiot too."

B.J. moves his head back like I hit him.

"Dad didn't say that," B.J. says.

"Yes, he did," I say. "He told me after Steve left, he said, 'That Steve is just an idiot kid.'"

B.J. moves his lips together, rolls them in, and clears his throat.

"Dad's wrong," B.J. says. "Steve was cool, very cool."

"Yeah," I say. "Steve, Steve, Steve. Big deal."

B.J. is quiet again and he bites the inside of his cheek the way he does when he thinks. B.J. leans closer, his face in my face.

"Steve knows about you," B.J. says.

"What?" I say. "What about me?"

B.J. looks up the hill, down the hill, and then he stops his dark eyes on my face.

"You're adopted," B.J. whispers.

"I'm what?" I say.

"Adopted," B.J. says, "not real. Not one of us."

Wind blows up from the ocean and the air is hot. I breathe in and the air is hot into my throat, into my body.

B.J. talks and his words move around in my head. He says Steve told him how these gypsies in a circus are my real parents, except they didn't want me so they put me into a Dumpster or a trash can or something like that and then they left, my real parents, the gypsies, they left, and no one ever saw them, not ever again.

On the street, my shadow is the dark part of me that lies

flat on the street and I move my head side to side. My shadow head moves side to side too.

B.J. talks and talks, his voice just sound in my ears, over my head.

I move my fingers so the middle finger sticks straight and the rest of the fingers are bent. My shadow hand is "Fuck you" too.

B.J.'s voice stops and it's just the sound of wind on 28th Street.

"You suck," I whisper.

I open my hand and push myself off the curb.

"What are you going to do?" B.J. says.

It's twelve steps and I'm across the street, eight steps to the front door, and I bend over, take the *I Love California* key chain from under the mat, and open the front door.

"You can't tell," B.J. yells.

Inside Number One, I slam the door as hard as I can and lock the door.

Momma is asleep in her room and I stand in the doorway and look at her body under the covers. I want to wake her up and ask if it's true, but I just stand there, the sound of my own breath the only sound.

There is a bang on the door, B.J.'s fist, and he yells to let him in.

The telephone is on the wall over the kitchen table and the cord is all tangled up. I climb up on the chair, take the receiver, hold it to my ear.

B.J. is in the big window, his fists on the glass.

"No," B.J. yells. "Stop."

I dial Daddy's number, listen to the ring, my finger into the tangled cord.

B.J.'s fists shake the window glass, and I look at Momma's room, the door closed.

A woman's voice says hello and I ask for Bud Lauck. The woman says to hold on and there's music in the telephone, quiet piano music.

"Hello?" Daddy says.

"Daddy?" I say.

"Juniper?" Daddy says, "What's wrong? Are you okay, is your mother okay?"

B.J. yells, "Fuck you," and his face is red.

"Daddy," I say, "come home. Please, can you come home now?"

"I can't come home," Daddy says, "I have to work. What's wrong?"

"Please," I say.

"Is your brother there?" Daddy says. "Let me talk to B.J."

B.J.'s hands are open on the glass, his forehead pressed on the glass too, and his eyes are round wide open.

"Jennifer," Daddy says. "What's going on?"

"B.J. says I'm adopted," I say. "B.J. says Steve told him."

It's quiet again and it shouldn't be quiet. Daddy should say it's not true, should say it's a lie, should tell me to hang up the telephone and forget the whole thing.

"Daddy?" I say.

"I'll be right there," Daddy says.

Daddy hangs up the telephone and it's that sound, dead-end sound, a buzz in my ear. I stand there, look at the telephone like something's going to happen, and then the buzz stops, no sound at all.

The story goes like this. There wasn't any circus, there wasn't any gypsy, there wasn't a trash can or a Dumpster. Daddy says the true story was two young people who made a mistake and had to give their baby up for adoption. Daddy says their mistake was a good thing since Momma and Daddy got to bring me home.

Daddy and me at Dairy Queen, two hot fudge sundaes on the plastic table, and it's the first time I can't eat ice cream. I sit on my side of the table and look at Daddy talk, not my Daddy, not really.

Daddy holds my hand, his fingers into my fingers, and he says how lucky they were to get me and how happy they were when I came. Daddy says it was Momma who wanted another baby, but she couldn't have one, not after Bryan was born and the doctors found the tumor in Momma's spine. Daddy says I was born to be Momma's daughter, says that when I came, Momma got better for five whole years and everyone knows it was because of me, because I was like a lucky charm. At least until the luck ran out.

Daddy says adopted doesn't change how much he loves me, doesn't change how much Momma loves me.

It's a lie, I know it's a lie. All this time, them and me, a lie. Them and me.

There are no shadows in Dairy Queen. The lights are those bright white tube lights that make everything bright white too. On the table, the hot fudge sundaes melt in the white and red dishes, red plastic spoons stuck in the ice cream.

Daddy says he was going to tell me about being adopted when I was older, says it's not right how Bryan told me, says he's glad the truth is out though.

The truth.

I can't look at Daddy, my face away from his face, my eyes on the trash can, the window.

My real parents are out there, somewhere. Maybe they are over by the soda machine, maybe they're ordering a hamburger basket, maybe they're in that car that's driving away.

"Juniper?" Daddy says. "Are you listening?"

Daddy's not the same, never will be the same again. Daddy, not my Daddy.

The space between us is a red Dairy Queen table, but it's like a mile, like forever.

"What happens now?" I say.

Daddy rubs his chin with his hand.

"What do you mean?" Daddy says.

Looking down at my hands in my lap, my hands, my lap, just me on my side of the table. Maybe my real parents are old enough now, maybe they want me back, maybe I should go and find them.

"Where do I belong?" I say.

Daddy tilts his head and moves his body off his side of the table, sits with me on my side of the table. Daddy puts his arm around my shoulders, That Man cologne, the smell of cigarettes.

"You belong right here," Daddy says, "with us."

All this time, all the special looks for special people, and she never told me, not once, and now I don't know who I am or where I belong and it's all mixed up in my head.

Even when you don't want to cry, you cry and that's the worst thing. Right there in Dairy Queen, people all around, white light over, melted ice cream, and I can't stop. Daddy takes his handkerchief out of his pocket, pushes it into my hands, and rocks me side to side.

That night, I want to see Momma and I don't want to see her. Daddy says Momma is not feeling well and we can all talk about it in the morning.

I don't want to talk about it, not in the morning, not ever.

I lie in my bunk bed, the wood slats of B.J.'s bunk bed overhead, just like always. B.J. is quiet up there, too quiet, and I know he's in some kind of trouble, big trouble.

Out the window is a full moon with rips of white clouds. The white moonlight shines through the clouds, makes them look like tissue paper.

Daddy asks if I want to read *Snow White and the Seven Dwarfs*.

I don't want to read anything, not ever again.

Daddy says everything will look better in the morning.

B.J. stays quiet. I stay quiet.

Daddy turns off our light and says good night.

It's quiet in our room, quiet in Number One, and I hear the television turn on in the living room.

B.J. moves around up there, rolls around.

I hate B.J., hate how he knows everything, how he's always right. I look hate up through the bunk bed bottom, hate right into B.J.'s body in his bed.

I roll on my side, the pillow in my arms, against my chest.

I'm always going to be adopted, I'm always going to be different, and a good night of sleep isn't going to change that.

❧

It's the darkest part of night, deep sleep all around, and Daddy shakes me awake.

"Get up," Daddy says, "you have to get up now."

Daddy says the same thing to B.J.

"Mom?" B.J. says.

"No," Daddy says, "it's me, son. Mom's sick, we have to get her to the hospital. Get up. Get up now."

Nothing's right in the middle of the night. Your head is

dizzy and you can't think and nothing makes any sense. B.J. puts a big T-shirt on and then a sweatshirt with a hood. I pull my jeans on, tuck my nightgown in, and run down the hall.

Daddy yells at B.J. to open the front door.

Daddy carries Momma out of their room and Momma is half wrapped in a blue blanket, her head against his wide chest, and Daddy carries her like she's nothing.

Momma has on her lemon meringue silk nightgown, just the nightgown. In their room is that terrible smell, poop and pee and maybe throw-up. I push my hand over my nose, my mouth. The lemon meringue robe is on the floor like a yellow puddle and I take the robe in my hands, hold the softness against my chest.

Daddy yells for me to come on and I run out the front door, lemon meringue silk in my arms.

"We're not all going to fit," B.J. says.

Daddy puts Momma into the low front seat.

"Yes, we are," Daddy says, "go around and get in on my side."

B.J. goes around the back of Red, gets in the cargo space behind Daddy's seat.

"What about her robe?" I say.

Daddy squats down, wraps Momma's legs in the blue blanket, snaps the seat belt around her middle.

"I can barely fit," B.J. says.

"There is enough room," Daddy says.

"What about her robe?" I say.

Daddy closes the door carefully.

"Later," Daddy says, "get in the car now, I'll shut the front door."

B.J. is right, there isn't any space, just a sliver of space half my size. I don't want to be close to B.J., don't want my body close to his body.

Momma moves her head side to side, curly hair all over the place.

"No," Momma says, "I don't want to go."

Daddy jogs up the sidewalk, keys in his hand.

"Get in, Jenny," Daddy says.

"We can't fit," B.J. says.

"Get in now," Daddy says.

I shove into the back, my shoulder on B.J.'s side, and he shoves himself against me.

Daddy pushes his seat back, my knees into the leather, and he adjusts the seat forward.

"We're fine," Daddy says, reaching out and pulling his door closed, "we're in."

"Bud," Momma says, "I don't want to go. Please, Bud."

Daddy puts his hand on her hand, tucks it back into the blue blanket, moves the blanket around her shoulders.

"I know," Daddy says, "but you are sick, you have to see a doctor."

Daddy drives with his face close to the windshield, both hands on the wheel. He goes through all the red lights, turns without his blinker on, makes the tires squeal.

B.J. breathes in my hair, my ear, around the side of my face, nasty nighttime breath smell. B.J. keeps himself stiff, like we don't touch at all, and I hold the back of Daddy's seat, press my head into the leather, and close my eyes tight.

Daddy makes a hard turn and stops fast. Ambulances are parked under white lights and it's quiet here, too quiet.

Daddy pushes his whole hand over the steering wheel, honks the horn loud and long, and it's the only sound in the black night. Daddy gets out of Red, jogs around, opens Momma's door. He pushes his arms under her body, looks at us through the open door.

"You guys stay here," Daddy says, "don't move a muscle."

Two men in white coats run out, move around Daddy, all of them talking over each other, deep voices, words mixed, Daddy in the middle, and he carries Momma. Her feet are bare and her nightgown floats around Daddy's arms like it's trying to float away.

The sliding glass doors slide open and they all go inside. The sliding glass doors slide shut and they are all gone.

Inside Red, it's quiet and B.J. climbs into the front seat.

I can still feel B.J. on my body, my shoulder, can still smell him too and I wipe all over myself like wiping him away.

"Knock it off," B.J. says.

"Screw you," I say.

I wipe my shoulder off again.

"Screw you," B.J. says.

B.J. sits deep in the front seat and slams the door.

Momma's robe is in my lap and I press my fingers into the lemon meringue silk, the softness like water in my hands.

Daddy jogs out of the sliding glass doors, arms bent at the elbows.

"Everything's okay," Daddy says, gets in Red, "everything is going to be fine."

Daddy drives Red to a parking lot, stops under a white circle of light coming from a tall street lamp.

"What's wrong with her?" I say.

"I don't know," Daddy says.

Daddy closes his eyes, pinches the top of his nose.

"Dad?" B.J. says.

Daddy opens his eyes, blinks like he forgot.

"You have to stay in the car," Daddy says, "no children are allowed in the hospital."

"Dad?" B.J. says.

"It's fine," Daddy says, "everything is fine."

Daddy opens his door and swings out of the car.

"Daddy," I yell.

I hold the lemon meringue silk robe to him and he takes it out of my hands.

"Thanks, Juniper," Daddy says.

Daddy shuts the door and it's just B.J. and me.

Outside, it's sidewalk and a line of street lamps, circles of white light on the sidewalk and into the parking lot. In between the circles of light, it's nighttime shadows and dark.

It's quiet inside Red, quiet outside too, and I lean my head against the little side window, cool glass against my forehead.

seven

Birthdays are the most special days of the whole year, even more than Christmas. You get to do anything you want on your birthday. "Within reason," Daddy says. When it's my day, I always go to Disneyland.

B.J. sleeps in past eleven o'clock and then he says he wants breakfast for lunch and Daddy says that's reasonable.

Daddy, B.J., and me go to the International House of Pancakes and B.J. says we have to sit in a booth since it's his birthday and he likes booths best.

We get a booth next to a window and Daddy sits next to B.J. I sit by myself in the middle of the other side. B.J. sits slouchy and looks at the menu. Daddy looks at B.J., smiles, and looks at his menu.

The House of Pancakes is waitresses with pots of coffee, the sound of plates and forks and voices talking and all around is the smell of breakfast.

Momma came home and then she left again, came home, and then had to go back to the hospital. B.J. says she has been in the hospital six times altogether since we moved to Number One, but I lost count. The last time she left was August and now it's the new school year.

Daddy puts his menu down and puts his hand on B.J.'s head.

"Ten years old," Daddy says.

B.J. pulls his head away, that mad look in his dark eyes, and he looks around the House of Pancakes like everyone is looking at us.

"Sorry, buddy," Daddy says. "I guess you're too big for all that now."

The waitresses at the House of Pancakes wear dresses that go past their knees, blue aprons over with white lace around the edges. Our waitress pours Daddy coffee, smiles at him, moves her hair around her ear.

"Today is my son's tenth birthday," Daddy says.

"Dad!" B.J. says.

The waitress smiles a bigger smile with her bright red lips.

"Ten years old," the waitress says, "you're too young to have a ten-year-old son."

Daddy laughs and shakes his head.

"Not that young," Daddy says.

The waitress laughs and Daddy laughs.

"Well, it's breakfast on the house on your birthday," the waitress says.

Daddy puts his hand on B.J. again, touches his shoulder like a punch, and B.J. leans away from Daddy's hand.

"There you go, buddy," Daddy says.

The waitress sets her pot of coffee on the table, takes out a pad of paper. I order strawberry waffles with a pile of whipping cream, B.J. and Daddy order eggs over easy with bacon and hash browns.

When he's all done eating, Daddy pushes his plate away and stirs his coffee.

"What's it going to be, big guy?" Daddy says, "Knott's Berry Farm? Disneyland? Maybe take a sailing trip? You name it."

B.J. holds his fork in his fist, bends over his plate when he eats. He looks up at Daddy, shakes his head side to side.

"No good?" Daddy says.

B.J. looks at me and then he looks at the table, his eyes on his food.

"I was thinking," B.J. says, "how old do you have to be to go into the hospital?"

Daddy rolls his lips in.

"Fourteen," Daddy says.

"Really?" I say.

B.J. pushes hash browns around in his egg.

"Maybe we could just go by," B.J says, "you know, maybe she can come to her window."

Daddy looks at B.J., just looks at him. It's quiet at the table, restaurant sounds all around, and I don't know why B.J. wants to see Momma since he never wanted to see her before. Daddy looks at me and I look at Daddy and then Daddy looks at his watch.

"Okay," Daddy says, "why not."

Daddy lifts his hand in the air and nods. The waitress with the bright red lips rushes over, mouth in a little frown.

"Done already?" the waitress says.

"Looks that way," Daddy says.

She stacks plates on her arm and dips into her pocket with her other hand. She pulls out a slip of paper and lays it upside down on the table.

"Well, happy birthday, little boy," the waitress says, "you're just as handsome as your daddy there."

B.J. rolls his eyes and his face is all red.

Daddy takes out a ten-dollar bill and puts it on top of the paper.

"Keep the change," Daddy says.

Daddy parks Red under a tree spread out over the parking space, cuts of white light through leaves. We all sit there in Red, quiet all around. Daddy bounces his keys a little like he doesn't want to go into the hospital.

"Is there any special reason you wanted to come here?" Daddy says.

B.J. looks back at me, looks away.

"I don't know," B.J. says, "I guess I just wanted to tell her it's my birthday."

Daddy presses his lips together, his mouth in a frown.

"She knows it's your birthday, buddy," Daddy says.

Daddy puts his hand on B.J.'s shoulder, keeps it there.

"Well, just tell her I'm in the car," B.J. says.

"Anything else?" Daddy says.

B.J. shakes his head side to side, bites his top teeth on his bottom lip, looks out the windshield.

I want Daddy to tell Momma that I know about my other mother, but that I don't care since Momma is my mother. I want him to tell her to get better and when she gets better everything will be good again.

Daddy looks at me over his seat and I know he waits for me to say something. All the things I want to say are around and around in my head and my mouth is all dry.

"Just tell her hi," I say.

"Okay," Daddy says, "I'll be back soon."

Daddy gets out of the car, shuts the door, just B.J. and me inside. Daddy walks up the sidewalk to a set of sliding glass doors and they open for him and then close after he walks through.

B.J. takes a deep breath in, crosses his arms.

"Tell her hi," B.J. says. "God, you're stupid."

"Shut up," I say.

"Hi," B.J. says.

"Shut up," I say.

B.J. shifts around in his seat, his arm between the seats. I press myself all the way back in the cargo hold, kick at his arm. B.J. turns all the way around in the seat, makes his hand into a fist, and tries to punch. I kick his arm again.

The car door opens.

"Hey," Daddy says, "what's going on?"

B.J. pulls his arm back, moves around in his seat.

"Nothing," B.J. says. "What happened? How is she? Why are you back so soon?"

"Fine. Everything is fine," Daddy says, "I have good news."

Daddy moves fast, keys in, car started, gears shifting around. He looks out the back window and backs up Red.

Daddy smiles right at me and the way his face looks so happy, I get bumps on my arms like a cool wind is all around.

"Is she coming home?" I say.

"Not today, Juniper," Daddy says.

"What did she say?" B.J. says. "Did she remember my birthday?"

"Of course she did," I say.

"Dad?" B.J. says.

Daddy drives through the parking lot and stops, looks both ways.

"Dad?" B.J. says.

"I'll tell you everything when we get home," Daddy says.

Daddy's voice is quiet and I turn around so I can see the hospital one more time. I wonder which one is her window, if she sees us, if she is waving.

I wave my hand just in case.

Daddy makes a right turn, drives to the freeway, the hospital farther and farther away. I wave until I can't see the hospital anymore, just in case.

It's the middle part of the day, the sunlight on the ocean, whitecaps on the water. If you squint your eyes, you can see the white sails of boats out there too.

Daddy, B.J., and me go into Number One and Daddy sits us down on the big purple grape, B.J. on one side, me on the other. Daddy puts his arm around me, around B.J., and it's quiet all around. Daddy never sits this way, never, and I get a bad feeling up the back of my neck.

"Mom died," Daddy says.

Daddy's voice is so quiet it's like a whisper in the wind. I look at his face, at his mouth, at his chin.

"What?" B.J. says.

"Your mother is dead," Daddy says.

The words aren't right at all, and it's like I can't understand even though I do understand.

Daddy talks and his words are full of quiet deep sounds. He says Momma is in heaven now where she belongs. He says she lived her whole life in terrible pain and now she's out of pain.

"It was just time, it was her time," Daddy says.

Daddy's arm is heavy around my shoulders and I can't breathe.

"You're both lucky, you're young, you can put this behind you, you can move on," Daddy says. "In a few years, you'll forget."

"Forget?" B.J. says. "I'll never forget."

My head is heavy on my neck and I look up slow. B.J. stands away from Daddy and his face is bright red stain all the way to his ears.

"B.J.," Daddy says, "come on now, buddy. I didn't mean it that way."

"No," B.J. yells, "it's my birthday, it's my birthday."

B.J. hits his chest with his fist, hits hard, a thump against his heart.

"Come on, B.J.," Daddy says.

Daddy reaches out again and B.J. looks at Daddy's hand and then he slaps it away.

"No," B.J. yells.

Just like that, B.J. runs to the front door, pulls it open, and runs out. Daddy runs out the door too, yells "B.J." over and over, except B.J. doesn't come back.

It's one hour, two hours, three hours, and Daddy says he might have to call the police. Outside Number One, he looks down the hill, up the hill, hands on his hips.

Wind blows hair back from his forehead, shows his whole face, the bones of his cheeks, squared-up jaw. I watch him from the window and he's the same except he's not the same. He's like someone I know but I never really knew, not really.

Daddy comes into Number One, his hair all messed up by the wind.

"I can't just stand here," Daddy says, "I'll look at the beach, you go up to the park."

"He never goes to the park," I say.

"Check anyway," Daddy says.

Daddy walks down the hill and I go up.

At the top of the hill, I look down and Daddy's just a speck down at the light. I put my hands around my mouth, yell. Daddy doesn't turn around, just stands at the crosswalk and waits for the light to change.

I drop my hands, let the wind blow against me, and I close my eyes for a second. It's nothing but wind and I open my eyes again.

The park is trees and grass.

I walk where sidewalk and grass meet and the grass looks like all the ducks and geese were here and pooped all over the place. Bending down, I look closer and it could be dirt, it could be poop, I don't know.

"That's not what you think," B.J. says.

B.J. has one foot on his skateboard and his shadow is long on the sidewalk. I put my hand up to shade my eyes.

B.J. is all calm and quiet, the red gone from his face and his voice low.

"It looks like goose shit," B.J. says, "but it's dirt and grass."

"Daddy's looking for you," I say.

"It's just dirt," B.J. says.

"He's at the beach right now," I say.

B.J. pushes his foot on the end of his skateboard and it tips up on one end. He swings the skateboard under his arm and walks toward the pond.

"He's going to call the police," I say.

B.J. stops.

"Just go away," B.J. says.

"Daddy wants you home," I say.

B.J. drops his head, chin to his chest, and his eyes are darker with the shadows of his eyebrows. I don't know if he's mad or sad or what, but I walk so B.J. and me are toe to toe. I don't know what to do, what to say, and I reach out to touch his arm.

B.J. holds his head up and back, eyes down on me.

"She's not your mother," B.J. whispers.

I drop my arm, hand on my leg, and his words sting down my neck.

"She is too," I say.

"Just go away," B.J. says.

B.J. drops his skateboard on the sidewalk and rides away. I stand there, my arms at my sides, and my head hurts between my eyes.

I walk to the middle of the park and stand at the edge of the pond. The water is all gone and it's an empty circle of cement with a slime of green stuff around the edge, no ducks, no geese, no swans.

The wind blows around my legs, around my head, and pieces of hair get into my mouth and my eyes.

Without Momma there is no purpose and it's like being lost, like being on the edge of the world and you don't have anywhere else to go.

❧

My temperature is one hundred and two on the thermometer and Malibu Suntan Barbie is lost. I look everywhere, but she's just gone.

Daddy says there isn't time to look for her anymore. He says he and B.J. have to drive to Carson City by tonight for the funeral tomorrow. Says I have to go to Chuck and Suzy's house, even though I don't know Chuck and Suzy.

It doesn't matter what he says, I sit down on the floor, all of me covered with sweat, and I cry.

"Look, Jenny," Daddy says, "your Barbie will turn up, I promise, but right now we have to get going."

Daddy squats down too, his hand on my back, his other one on my head.

"You're burning up," Daddy says, "come on now, Juniper, let's get you out of these clothes and over to Chuck's so you can rest."

"No," I yell, "I'm not going. Not until we find her."

"I'll get you another one," Daddy says.

"I don't want another doll," I yell.

Daddy just looks at me, his eyes wide open, and I cry so hard I can't talk anymore. Daddy hates it when you throw a fit, but I can't help it.

"Dad, I've looked everywhere," B.J. says, "I don't know where she put it."

Daddy touches me again, his hand light on my shoulder.

"All right," Daddy says, "that's enough now. You need to settle down right now, am I clear?"

My eyes are puffy and heavy and I wipe my face on my nightgown. Daddy presses his handkerchief into my hands, but I let it fall on the carpet by my foot. He picks it up again and presses the white material over my whole face and wipes off tears.

"I know you're upset, but let's stay focused," Daddy says.

Scratching my cheek, I look at Daddy, just a quick look, and I sniff hard. Daddy presses his handkerchief into my hand and stands up straight.

"Come on now," Daddy says, "Chuck and Suzy are waiting."

Chuck and Suzy are supposed to be my godparents, but I didn't know anything about them until now. Daddy says it's the only place I can go since I'm sick, says that's what god-parents are for.

B.J. waits in Red and Daddy walks me to the door. He carries a bag with my clothes and my toothbrush.

Suzy has on white shorts and a pink fuzzy sweater that looks like bird feathers.

"Well, here you are," she says, "I was getting worried."

Daddy shakes my hand to my arm.

"Say hi," Daddy says.

I let go of Daddy's hand and look down.

"You have gotten so big," Suzy says, "she has gotten so big, Bud."

Daddy takes a deep breath.

"Sorry about the late notice and everything," Daddy says, "but Jenny came down with a fever and I can't drag her to Carson with the flu."

"Of course you can't," Suzy says.

"No, I mean it," Daddy says, "I really appreciate it, especially after all this time."

Suzy laughs and laughs and she puts her hand on Daddy's arm, her other hand on my shoulder.

"Get in here, you goose," Suzy says, "let's get this one off to a comfy bed so she can rest."

Suzy shuts the door and her house is all modern with lots of windows and high ceilings. It's the nicest house I've ever seen. The way Daddy looks, I know it's the nicest house he's seen too.

My head hurts and all of me is hot. I lean against Daddy's leg, my head against his side, and he puts his hand on my shoulder.

"Jenny lost her Barbie today," Daddy says.

"She did?" Suzy says. "Well, that's no good."

Suzy bends at the waist, her face into my face.

"She'll be back before you know it," Suzy says.

"She didn't run away," I say, "she's a doll."

Daddy laughs a little and then it's quiet in the big house.

"Jenny's pretty run down," Daddy says.

"Well, of course she is," Suzy says, standing up again. She puts her arm out to me, pulls me her way, and I look at Daddy.

"Daddy?" I say.

He sets my bag down and puts his hand on my arms.

"You're going to be okay, Juniper," Daddy says, "just let Suzy here take care of you and I'll be back in two days."

He holds up two fingers like I'm stupid.

"I know two, Daddy," I say.

Daddy drops the fingers and nods at me, eyes serious.

"Get some rest," Daddy says, "get better."

"Come on now, honey," Suzy says.

Suzy flaps her hand at Daddy.

"Go on now," Suzy says, "us girls will be just fine."

Me and Suzy walk up a step and down a hall and I look back, but I can't see Daddy, just hear the door open and close again.

Suzy chatters like a bird, turns down one hall, goes up two steps, turns down another hall. She says she has a great dinner going, how it's going to be just fine here, how she's sorry the house is such a mess. Looking around, the house is so clean it looks like no one lives here. Suzy stops and opens a door.

Inside is a double bed with a white bedspread, frills and lace everywhere, looks more like a cloud. She puts my bag at the end of the bed and moves her arm wide.

"Here we go," she says, "home sweet home. At least for a couple days."

Suzy drops her arm and holds her hands together.

"I am so sorry about your mom," Suzy says, "she was just lovely."

I don't know what to say and I just stand there in the big room, my arms at my sides.

"Well," Suzy says, "you need some help getting out of those clothes and into bed?"

"No," I say.

"Well, let me get out of here then, and you just climb into bed and sleep a little."

Suzy backs out of the guest room, closes the door.

There is a big window on the other side of the bed and I could just open that window and crawl out. Going over, I look out the window and it's a long drop down a hill to the driveway. Maybe not.

Kicking off my shoes, I climb on the white cloud of lace and cotton, lie on my side, my hands tucked between my knees.

There's a knock at the door, three knocks, and I can barely open my eyes, they're that heavy. The door opens and Daddy is there, head in the door a little.

"Are you still awake?" Daddy says.

"Daddy?" I say.

Daddy comes in and closes the door. He has a big box behind his back. Daddy swings the box around and lays it on the bed.

"Surprise," Daddy says.

The box is pink with red writing all over and inside is a big baby doll.

"Her hair grows," Daddy says, "see."

Daddy sits on the edge of the bed, points to the picture at the bottom of the box where a girl pulls the doll's hair and pushes in her belly button.

"And then it gets short again," Daddy says, "when you twist the arm."

The doll has on a jumper kind of dress and her hair is dark brown. I pick up the box and she has eyes that look like marbles and close when you tip her backward.

"I know she's not a Barbie," Daddy says, "but I wanted to get you something."

I put the doll on the bed between us and her marble eyes close.

"She's really nice," I say, "thanks, Daddy."

He presses his lips together and he knows I don't like the doll. I put my hands on the box and pull it on my lap.

"No, I mean it," I say, "she's great, I never had a doll like this before."

Daddy smiles, tired lines around his eyes, his mouth.

"Well," Daddy says, "let's get you in bed now."

He moves the covers on the bed and I crawl in between the sheets. I wish I had my *Snow White* book here so he could read it to me. He pulls the covers up around my shoulders and kisses my forehead, his lips dry, That Man cologne and cigarettes.

"Sleep tight and get well," Daddy says.

Daddy puts the big doll in the corner of the room and I close my eyes.

When Daddy comes back, he picks me up at Suzy and Chuck's house. Daddy says B.J. is at the apartment with Auntie Carol, says Auntie Carol came down from Carson to help us get straightened out.

Daddy and me sit in Red, me up front where B.J. always sits, and that's when I open the glove compartment door. Inside the dark space is a pair of suntan doll legs, Malibu Suntan Barbie, my Barbie. Not lost. Here the whole time.

You don't always know you're happy unless you have been so low and sad that you forgot what it was to feel happy.

My hand around Malibu Suntan Barbie's legs, her in a green and white checkered sundress, and I hold her up for Daddy to see. I'm so happy I cry, tears down my face and into my mouth.

Daddy starts up Red and says he knew she would turn up, says I got all upset about nothing.

Number One is full of wind and light, curtains tied in knots and all the windows are wide open. There are dark brown stains on the green carpet, little black cigarette burns on the white kitchen linoleum, curled-up bits of dried cheese from tacos, hard cereal flakes spilled off a spoon who knows when.

Auntie Carol says the place is a pigsty, says she can't believe we lived like this.

B.J. stays quiet and I stay quiet.

Daddy takes off for some U-Haul boxes.

Auntie Carol is big and heavy like I remember her, and she's all dressed in black. What's different about Auntie Carol is her hair. Brown hair before, white hair now, gray-white like she saw a ghost.

Auntie Carol scrubs the floor on her hands and knees, vacuums the carpet, washes dishes, even the ones that are already clean in the cupboard.

B.J. and me sort out all our stuff, toys and clothes. Auntie Carol says we have to throw away toys that are broken and clothes that don't fit.

Number One smells clean and feels clean, like we were never here. Auntie Carol says the last thing is Momma's room and she goes in there and shuts the door.

Outside the door, I lean my ear and listen and it's the sound of water in the bathroom. I turn the knob, go in, close the door, and lean against the wall.

The curtains are pulled and the windows are open and there's sunlight all over the place. Auntie Carol has the sheets off the bed, the pillows out of the pillowcases, and all the bedding is a pile in the middle of the California King.

Auntie Carol turns off the water and she has a pile of towels in her arms.

"Go on out of here," Auntie Carol says. "Go play with B.J."

I cross my arms and set my feet wide.

"Not B.J.," I say.

Auntie Carol stands at the end of the California King and the sunlight makes an outline around her wide body. She opens her arms and the towels drop into the pile of dirty bedding.

"That boy may want to be Bryan," Auntie Carol says. "But he's always going to be B.J. to me."

Auntie Carol wipes nothing off her hands and looks at me with one eye closed like she's thinking, and that's when I remember how she has special powers, how she can read your future by looking at your hands.

"You shouldn't be in here," Auntie Carol says.

"Why not?" I say.

She puts her hands on her hips, her fingers rolled into fists.

"Because," Auntie Carol says, "I'm going to sort through your mother's things and you don't need to see this."

I press myself all the way against the wall, my leg against the cool wood of the nightstand.

"I've been here all the other times," I say.

Auntie Carol looks at me for a long time and I know she

knows what I've seen here and I know I don't have to say anything more. She opens Momma's closet and takes a box off the top shelf.

"Well, don't just stand there," Auntie Carol says. "Come give me a hand."

Auntie Carol and me sort through everything, my hands and her hands, Momma's things all around. There are hats and gloves and all the pretty clothes she never wore since we moved here. Auntie Carol says to take all the clothes off the hangers, fold them careful and make piles for pants, tops, sweaters.

I touch Momma's stuff extra careful, my hands on the silk of her nightgowns and her robes. I want to ask if I can keep something, but Auntie Carol is so quiet and so serious, I'm scared to say anything.

When we are done, it's piles of clothes and shoes and hats and scarves and purses. The sun is over Number One and the light through the windows is bright white and shadows at the same time.

Auntie Carol moves her hand through her white hair and then she reaches into a pile next to the closet door. She holds up a small white book and a little black velvet bag, and all around her hands, small pieces of dust float in the light.

"Here," Auntie Carol says.

She sets the book and bag between us and shifts her legs around to sit cross-legged.

I shift around too, my legs crossed and my hands in my lap.

Auntie Carol picks up the white book and holds it careful in her hands like a baby bird. She traces her finger over the swirly gold letters on the cover.

"It says 'Our Wedding,'" Auntie Carol says.

She touches the bottom right corner and lifts the cover open with one finger. Inside is a black and white picture of Momma in a beautiful white wedding dress. She smiles and stands on her own and she has the prettiest round cheeks and darkest sharpest eyes. Momma is so perfect, it hurts to look at her.

Auntie Carol moves her whole hand over the photograph, closes her eyes, and smiles a sad smile.

"She looked like a princess," Auntie Carol whispers.

Auntie Carol opens her eyes and looks at me.

I bite my lip and look away from her face, my eyes on the black and white photo.

Auntie Carol moves her finger to the bottom right-hand corner and turns the page.

The picture is Momma with Grandma Rowena and Grandpa Ivan in front of some house, and a cat is asleep in the shadow of Momma's dress.

"The wedding was in Reno," Auntie Carol says.

Auntie Carol looks at me and I look at her and it's quiet in the room, so quiet it's like time has stopped. She takes a deep breath, moves her whole hand over the photograph, touches the bottom right-hand corner, and turns again.

Momma stands next to a car and some man holds the door. The wind blows Momma's veil the wrong way and she smiles and has her arm up to keep it from blowing away.

"It was a sunny day," Auntie Carol says. "Windy too."

Auntie Carol moves her whole hand over the photograph and turns the page again.

The photo is Daddy in a white tuxedo with three other men in white tuxedos too. Momma is in her beautiful white wedding dress with three women in short light-colored dresses. Everyone smiles.

"There's Uncle Charles as an usher," Auntie Carol says, "and Aunt Ruth was a bridesmaid."

Auntie Carol points at the faces and I nod my head like I know the people, even though I barely remember.

Auntie Carol moves her whole hand over the photograph, touches the bottom right-hand corner, and turns again.

The photo is of Momma and Daddy up the aisle. Daddy's eyes are happy, his nose wrinkled, and his squared-up jaw has a little dent right in the middle.

Auntie Carol closes her eyes and puts her face to the ceiling.

"Bud used to say how lucky he was to marry Janet," Auntie Carol says.

She drops her head and opens her eyes wide.

"Lucky," Auntie Carol says, "can you imagine?"

Auntie Carol shakes her head, puts her hand over the page, her finger on the bottom right corner, and she turns again.

Momma and Daddy stand behind a three-tier wedding cake and Momma has a piece of cake in her hand. Daddy has his mouth wide open, his hand on her arm, a smile in his eyes and around his lips.

I look at Auntie Carol, but she just shakes her head again. She puts her whole hand over the picture and turns the book closed.

"It's not good to look at too many at one time," Auntie Carol says. "So many memories can hurt."

Sunlight reflects off the window frame and a bright beam of light comes in low through the window. Auntie Carol pushes the book to me and she lifts up the black velvet bag.

"Hold your hands open," she says.

Auntie Carol unties the strings on the bag and tips it over into my cup hands.

Like water out of a faucet, a line of pearls slides out and then a round circle of metal. Auntie Carol puts her finger into my hand and lifts the string of pearls out so they are in the shine of the sunlight.

"They are the real thing too," Auntie Carol says. She takes the pearls and moves them over her front teeth. The sound is like a rock against a rock and she smiles and rolls her lips together.

"Fake pearls don't feel like that," she says.

Auntie Carol circles the pearls around and puts them in my hand again. The pearls are warm against my skin.

She picks up the ring then, holds it on the tip of her finger, and the line of diamonds shines in the sunlight.

"This is her wedding band," Auntie Carol says. "And inside it's engraved with the date they were married."

"Really?" I say.

Auntie Carol holds the ring away from her face and squints her eyes like she's reading. She nods and lets the ring drop into my hand again.

I look at Auntie Carol, look at the ring, look at the pearls.

I open my hands and let the ring and the pearls down on the green carpet, rub the feel of them off my hands.

"Maybe I shouldn't," I say.

"Of course you should," Auntie Carol says.

"Maybe you should give them to Bryan," I say.

Auntie Carol looks at me, eyes so brown and hair so white, Auntie Carol who knows what you think and what you feel. I look down, my face away from her eyes.

Auntie Carol takes the ring and pearls, puts them back into the black velvet bag, and ties the string so the bag is closed. She holds my hands in her hand, puts the black bag into my hand, and closes my hand over the bag.

"Listen to me," Auntie Carol says, "listen very close."

I look at her face, at her eyes, and she clears her throat.

"You are Janet's daughter," Auntie Carol says, "it's your job to hold her treasures. It's your job to remember her life."

The room feels heavy and my face stings with tears that I won't cry, not now, not here.

"Do you understand me?" Auntie Carol says.

I look at the floor, the bed, at my hands in her hands.

"But I'm not," I whisper, "not really."

Auntie Carol clears her throat and looks at my eyes, her voice low.

"You are," Auntie Carol says, "you really are."

Auntie Carol and me and Momma's stuff all around, and that's when I know it's true. I am Momma's daughter, her special gift, the baby she waited for, the baby she wanted, her reason for living.

Tears come out of my eyes and roll down my face.

Broken heart tears.

Not knowing where you belong anymore tears.

Truth tears.

part three
Los Angeles, Fountain Valley,
and Huntington Beach
1971–1973

It's dark and even in the dark, LA looks dirty. On the concrete walls under bridges and on the sides of buildings, there is spray paint writing everywhere. Bryan says it's graffiti, says gangs spray on graffiti to mark their territory.

Daddy stops at a light, his blinker on for a right turn.

"Don't scare her," Daddy says.

"It's true," Bryan says.

"What's a gang?" I say.

"A bunch of guys looking for trouble," Daddy says.

"A bunch of guys looking for little girls," Bryan says.

"Enough," Daddy says.

Daddy turns right into a neighborhood with lots of big old houses built close together. He pulls Red to the curb, turns off the engine, and it's quiet in the car. Daddy shifts around in his seat, looks at Bryan, looks at me.

"Okay now," Daddy says, "I want you on best behavior, am I clear?"

Bryan looks at me and I look at Bryan.

"I mean it," Daddy says. "This is a friend of mine, a very good friend, and I brought you here to meet her and to meet her kids."

Bryan moves his hand around like the "Fuck you" finger is just about to come out and he rolls his lips together to keep from laughing.

"Why?" I say.

Daddy looks at me for a long time, quiet all around, and then he smiles.

"Because," Daddy says, "I think it's time we made a few friends."

Best behavior is shoulders straight, arms against your sides, being seen and not heard. Out of Red, Bryan and me stand shoulder to shoulder, best behavior stiff. Daddy is down on one knee and he reties Bryan's shoes, tucks my hair behind my ears. Daddy stands up, hand flat over his slacks.

"Tuck in your shirt, buddy," Daddy says.

"Dad," Bryan says.

"Jenny, pull up your socks," Daddy says.

"They aren't supposed to be pulled," I say, "they're fold-downs."

Daddy's boy-next-door drop-dead handsome face is every kind of nervous and when he acts this way, I'm nervous too. Daddy lifts his arms up, lets them fall against his legs, and he shakes his head.

"Let's just go," Daddy says.

Daddy holds our hands, walks up the sidewalk, and then up steep steps. It's twenty steps altogether and at the top is a brown house with a long porch across the front. If there were really haunted houses with witches inside, this could be one, it's that dark and big and scary.

Before Daddy even knocks, the big door opens and a lady stands there, a smile wide on her face. This lady is just like any other lady except she wears the special look for special people.

"Finally," the lady says, "I was getting worried."

I look at Bryan and he looks at me.

Daddy smiles and the lady smiles and Daddy pushes his hands on our backs so we have to walk into the house.

The lady steps back to make room and she has deep red hair that falls straight and long around her narrow face. She has green eyes that are so light they can almost be blue, except they aren't blue, they're green. The only time I've seen eyes like that is on a cat.

The lady shuts the door on the afternoon sunlight. The sound of the door is deep and hard like there's no way to get out again.

The lady looks at Bryan, looks at me, looks at Daddy with her special look.

Daddy clears his throat and the lady laughs, ha ha ha, like she's nervous.

"Well, kids," Daddy says, "this is my, ah, friend."

The lady shakes her head and her hair moves all around her face like a curtain.

"Oh, Bud, you fool," the lady says. She slaps her hand out at Daddy, a playful kind of hit. Daddy's face is embarrassed red on his cheeks.

"Men," she says to Bryan and me. "My name is Deborah, but you kids just call me Deb."

Deb and Daddy and the way they are together, there's something I don't know, don't understand.

It's being on the outside looking in.

It's knowing something's up even though you don't know what.

It's a bad feeling up the back of my neck, over my head and into my nose.

Deb and Daddy laugh about something and Deb says we

should all go into the living room. She walks through an open doorway and Daddy presses his hands on our backs again, pushes us into the big room.

On the sofa are three kids and they all wave at Daddy. Daddy and these kids, they're like a whole other family that he's a part of and we're not.

Deb says her kids are Christopher and the twins, Kendall and Veronica, except Kendall goes by Kenny and Veronica goes by Ronny. Kenny and Ronny look like boys anyway, so it makes sense they would go by boys' names.

Deb's living room is crammed with big old furniture, musty smell all around. Bryan sits on the edge of one of the big chairs and I sit with Daddy in another big chair. Deb perches on the edge of the sofa, talks grown-up talk with Daddy. Deb says introductions are always awkward and Daddy says the worst is past us and then they start to talk about some client of Daddy's named Smith.

Kenny and Ronny both have light-colored eyes just like Deb's except Kenny's eyes are more green and Ronny's eyes are more blue. Both of them have red hair too and freckles all over their faces. When girls look like boys, Momma says they are tomboys and I can tell Kenny and Ronny are tomboy girls.

Christopher is nothing like Deb or Kenny or Ronny. Christopher is blond curly hair, the deepest brown eyes, and a round face that's almost pretty the way a girl's face is pretty. Christopher has a quiet all around him and he sits so still, it's like best behavior stiff is normal for him.

Daddy says Kenny and Ronny and me are the same age.

Deb says the twins turn eight on November fifteenth.

Daddy says I turn eight on December fifteenth.

Deb claps her hands at that and says we can celebrate our birthdays together.

The twins both look at Deb like she's gone crazy, their mouths wide open and their faces messed up like they ate sour lemon candy.

"We already do something special for Jenny's birthday," Daddy says, "it's a little tradition we do every year."

Deb's round face has thin eyebrows that look like painted-on half-loops in the middle of her forehead and she lifts them even higher.

"Oh, really?" Deb says.

Daddy looks at me and smiles a nice smile.

"Right," Daddy says.

"Disneyland," I say, "just me and Daddy."

My voice is too loud in the big house and I press my mouth shut. Everyone looks at me. Bryan, Christopher, Deb, even Daddy. Kenny and Ronny look too and then Ronny sticks her finger in her mouth, and makes a choking sound.

"Disneyland?" Ronny says. "Disneyland sucks."

"Totally sucks," Kenny says. Kenny laughs at Ronny and Ronny laughs at Kenny.

Bryan laughs too and it's a snort sound in his nose.

Christopher doesn't laugh at all, just looks around like he wishes he was somewhere else. I wish I was somewhere else too.

"Well," Deb says, "there will be lots of other chances for us to be together."

Deb looks at Daddy with the special look and something else, an edge in her eyes. Daddy looks at Bryan and smiles and then he looks at me and smiles again.

It's a perfect round moon in a black sky. Daddy sends Bryan and me to the car and he stays at the front door with Deb.

Bryan leans his butt on Red and crosses his arms high over

his chest. I lean on Red, cross my arms the way he does, but it feels too weird. I uncross my arms, cross them the other way.

Bryan kicks his foot at a patch of grass.

I kick my foot at a patch of grass.

Streetlights shine circles of light on the street and the parked cars. Red is parked half in a circle of light, half out. Bryan and me stand in the dark.

On the porch, Deb's body and Daddy's body are close, too close.

"Are they kissing?" Bryan says.

"I can't see," I say.

Deb moves her hair around with her fingers and Daddy touches her arm.

"There," Bryan says. "That was definitely a kiss."

"Why is he kissing her?" I say.

Bryan clears his throat and he pushes his body off Red.

"Just shut up," Bryan says.

"What?" I say.

Bryan opens the car door and his chin is tucked low to his chest.

"I didn't do anything," I say.

"Just get in," Bryan says.

Inside Red is quiet and I climb into the back, look out the back window.

Daddy comes down the steep steps and he moves fast and easy, a big smile on his face.

I shift around and Bryan slouches low in his seat. Daddy gets in, shuts the door, and he's all out of breath.

"That went really well, don't you think?" Daddy says.

Daddy rubs his hands together palm to palm.

"Did you like her?" Daddy says. "I mean, I really want you guys to like her."

Bryan looks at me, looks at Daddy, looks out the window, and then he shrugs one shoulder.

"Well," Daddy says, "you do like her, don't you?"

It's quiet in the car and it feels like that space between what is and what will be. I can say, "No way," I can say, "I do not like Deb," I can say, "Let's drive away from this terrible house and that terrible woman and those terrible twins. Let's never come back." I can say anything, but the things I want to say are trapped in that wide open space so I don't say anything at all.

"She's nice," Bryan says, "I guess."

Daddy breathes out and looks at the ceiling of the car.

"That's great," Daddy says, "I'm really glad."

Just like that, I know my chance is gone and Daddy never even looks at me. He starts Red, drives away from Deb's big house.

nine

Two months later and we are living with Deb. There's no reason, that's just the way it is.

Daddy says Deb's house is home now.

I'll never call her house home. Never.

The sky over Deb's house is more gray than blue, like you're looking at it through a screen door. Daddy says the sky is full of smog.

Deb's house has lots of rooms, down for living, up for sleep. There are bedrooms for everyone except Daddy, who shares with Deb. The rule is no kids in that room. Bryan calls that room the off-limits room and I hate how Deb is the one who closes the door, her on the inside with Daddy, me on the outside.

Bryan has a room in the attic, but it's not really a room since the walls aren't finished and the floor is bare wood too. The smell up there is old dust and dry wood, but Bryan says it's fine with him since he finally has a place all his own.

My room is the old guest room and it has a big metal bed painted white. There is a dresser and it's painted white too. Out the window, under the smog, are black tar rooftops, antennas, and chimneys too. The houses are built so close together, you could jump from rooftop to rooftop and never touch the ground. I think about that sometimes, think how I could crawl out the window, walk over the rooftops, jump from house to house and never come back. I think how I could do it, but I never do.

❧

On my eighth birthday, Daddy and me go to Disneyland.

There's the Haunted House, Future World, Pirates of the Caribbean, and then we eat lunch in the Pirates of the Caribbean restaurant. After rides and lunch, Daddy and me hold hands and walk up the Magic Kingdom sidewalk. We don't talk, just walk, and it's nice to have him all to myself.

At the edge of the sidewalk, a man draws on a square sheet of white paper and around his feet are jars of pencils and paint-brushes and paints. In front of the man is a boy with green eyes. The boy looks serious. His mother says he should smile.

We stand behind the man who draws and our shadows are long on the sidewalk, a shadow of me and Daddy holding hands.

"You want to do that?" Daddy says.

The man draws the boy's face without a smile and the boy's mother rolls her eyes.

"Why won't you smile?" the mother says.

Daddy squeezes my hand a little, the warm of his skin into my skin, and I look at his face.

"Go on," Daddy says, "it'll be nice to have a souvenir."

"Souvenir?" I say.

"Something to remember your birthday by," Daddy says.

The boy gets out of the chair and smiles at me. He has a nice smile except there are braces on his teeth, lots of silver in his smile.

Daddy opens his fingers and my hand is my hand again, cool where he touched me. He takes out his wallet and nods his head.

"Go on, Juniper," Daddy says.

Daddy hands money to the man, who smiles at me and his eyes wrinkle around the edges with his smile.

"Happy birthday," the man says.

"Thanks," I say.

The man waves his hand to the chair and I tuck my dress under my legs, sit down. I have on a long dress with little puffy sleeves and elastic around the waist, a ruffle around the bottom. It's brown with some green and blue in it too. I have a blue scarf tied over my hair and the blue matches the blue in the dress.

The man looks at me for a long time. His eyes are a deep clear blue, the kind of blue you want to keep looking at even when you should look away. I wish I had blue eyes like that.

Daddy stands with his arms crossed and then he presses his fingers against his mouth, presses a smile on his lips. I make my mouth smile.

The man takes a deep breath, picks up a pencil, and draws on the white paper.

I wonder if I can scratch my nose, wonder if I can move at all.

Daddy has his hand on his chin the way he does when he concentrates. His eyes are serious and there's a little crease at the top of his nose.

"Makes her look pretty grown-up," Daddy says.

"I just draw what I see," the man says.

I stay still and stiff, watch the man draw. He takes the pencil off the paper and looks at me again.

"You can relax now," the man says.

The man moves his paintbrush in some colors and paints. I scratch my nose, scratch my ear, rub my eye.

Just like that, the man is done and he leans back in his chair.

I come around to where Daddy stands, look at me in pencil and paint.

My face is round cheeks, thin lips but not too thin, and light brown freckles squirted over my nose. It looks like me except the eyes, which look grown-up and serious and sad and there's no way I look that way, not really.

Daddy puts his hand on my shoulder and I look at his face, at his eyes. There's something sad in his eyes too, and just like that, I know there are sad secrets inside both of us. Daddy puts his hand out and I put my hand into his palm, my fingers warm again.

The man signs his name to my painting and it says "Keith—1971."

After Disneyland, I go to my space in Deb's house, Keith's painting under my arm. Daddy says there is going to be cake and ice cream later, but I don't care about that.

Alone in the old guest room, I lean against the door. Everything is like it was before. Inside is white bed, white dresser. Outside the window, rooftops and smog.

Under the window is a big cardboard box with *Jenny's Room* written out in Auntie Carol's curvy handwriting. All my clothes and toys are in the box and I can reach inside without looking, can feel exactly where each thing is.

Next to the cardboard box is a brand-new pink trunk with a silver lock and a tiny silver key. The trunk is a birthday present and Daddy says it's to hold all my toys.

All his genius and I know Daddy is wrong again. This trunk is for secrets, that's why there's a lock and a key.

I lay the painting by Keith on the bed and I open the lid to the new pink trunk. Inside it's gray paper and the smell of glue. I put Keith's painting in the bottom of the trunk and look at the watercolor me, look at the eyes that aren't my eyes. It's nice to have a souvenir, but I don't like the way I look in the painting so I don't look for very long.

Off the floor, I push my hand down inside of the *Jenny's Room* box until my fingers touch cool plastic. I feel over the plastic until my fingers get the handle and I hold on tight, pull up the Barbie suitcase.

The Barbie suitcase is packed tight with my treasures and Momma's treasures. There's Malibu Suntan Barbie, Barbie clothes and shoes, the white book of wedding pictures, and the velvet bag of Momma's jewelry. I hug the Barbie suitcase in my arms, the weight of it against my chest, against my heart.

I forget the way Momma smells.

I forget the sound of Momma's voice.

Ever since Deb, it's like there never was Momma at all.

Maybe that's just the way things are.

Maybe you're supposed to forget people who die.

Daddy acts like he forgot. Bryan acts that way too. The thing is, I don't want to forget. I wish I could just reach that place where Momma went so I can be with her again. Sometimes, it's like she is so close I could just touch her fingers with my fingers, but most of the time, she's so far away it's like being at the other edge of the world, valleys and mountains and graffiti and a sky full of smog that keep us apart. That far-apart feeling is the worst thing I know, a deep dull lonely in my body that doesn't go away.

I hate how I cry so easy now. I wish I could be stronger. I wipe my face with the back of my hand, press hard so my face hurts.

I look at the closed door of the old guest room, look out the window at the gray-blue sky. I sniff hard and bend over, lay the Barbie suitcase in the bottom of the trunk, move it so it's right in the middle with the edge of the suitcase touching the edge of Keith's painting.

The Barbie suitcase fits perfect and I dig into the *Jenny's Room* box one more time, pull out *Snow White and the Seven Dwarfs*.

I sit down on Deb's hardwood floor, my back against the pink trunk, and open the book cover. It's been so long since I looked at *Snow White*, the book is stiff when it opens and makes a crack sound down the spine.

I turn the page and the first drawing is of the queen by her ebony-framed window and she sews on a little white hat. The next drawing is of Snow White barefooted in the forest, wild animals all around. The third drawing is of Snow White all grown up with her hair in a white cloth. From the looks of the drawing, the dwarfs are just home and Snow White serves up dinner. The dwarfs stand around, all of them with these old-men faces, and compared to them, Snow White is a giant. You can just tell she doesn't belong there, pretends she belongs since she's afraid the evil stepmother will find her. Even though she's supposed to be safe, the way the drawing looks, you know Snow White isn't safe at all.

From downstairs, Daddy calls my name, says it's time for birthday cake. I shut *Snow White and the Seven Dwarfs*, lay it on the bottom of the pink trunk next to the painting and the Barbie suitcase.

I close the lid to the pink trunk, lock the lock with the little silver key.

In the box that says *Jenny's Room*, there are my shoes and

socks and underwear and clothes. I put the silver key into the center of a pair of white roll-down socks, push the sock ball into a black patent shoe. I hide the shoe at the bottom of the cardboard box and go downstairs for the rest of my birthday.

That spring, Deb and Daddy have their first fight and I hear the whole thing.

The fight is about Deb's church and how she wants Bryan and me to join. Daddy says he doesn't want us in her church and that makes Deb so mad she starts to yell in a voice I've never heard before. Deb's mad voice is low and high at the same time, fingernails on a chalkboard.

I sit on the bottom step of the entryway and lean my head against the wall, cool plaster against my face. Bryan comes around the corner, a baloney sandwich in his hand, his mouth full.

I put my finger to my lips and look at the ceiling.

"They're fighting," I whisper.

Bryan swallows hard and looks at the ceiling too. The voices come in waves, quiet, then loud.

"Deb is trying to get Daddy to put us into her church," I whisper.

Bryan sits on the bottom step and presses the white bread flat between his fingers.

"What church?" I say.

"Be quiet," Bryan says.

"You can't coddle your children," Deb says.

"You don't understand," Daddy says.

"What church?" I whisper.

Deb says Daddy is overindulgent. Daddy says Deb is

overbearing. Daddy says something else I can't hear, his voice deep and low.

Bryan tilts his head to the side, one ear to the ceiling.

They're so quiet, I can't hear any words, and then the quiet is broken into a hundred pieces with Deb's loud scream voice.

"You are an arrogant son of a bitch," Deb yells, "just get the hell out of my house."

"Calm down," Daddy says.

Bryan looks at me and his eyes are wide open round.

"Let's go," Bryan whispers.

B.J. holds the sandwich between his teeth and opens the big front door with both hands. I tiptoe over the hardwood floor and out the door. Bryan closes the big door without any sound and walks to the edge of the porch.

Big bushes grow in front of Deb's house and the leaves are dark green under street dust.

"What church," I say.

"How should I know?" Bryan says.

He throws the rest of his sandwich behind one of Deb's flower bushes and sits down on the top step. Shade from the porch cuts over Bryan's face and L.A. sunshine slides up the steps.

The front door opens and Daddy holds a travel bag in his hand. His face is set up more mad than I can remember.

"Let's go," Daddy says.

Bryan twists around, his dark eyes wide open.

"Where?" Bryan says.

"No questions," Daddy says, "just go."

Daddy puts one hand on my shoulder, his other hand with the bag against Bryan's back.

I run down the steps and jump from the last step to the sidewalk. Daddy walks fast steps and Bryan runs to the car.

From the big house, Deb yells something at Daddy and Daddy pretends he doesn't hear her.

"Shut the door, Bryan," Daddy says.

I turn around and look at Deb through the back window. She has on one of Daddy's work shirts and her legs are bare, her feet are bare, and I can see her naked shape under Daddy's shirt. Deb is all curvy and skinny at the same time, hands curled into fists, fists pressed into her hips.

"Bud Lauck," Deb yells. "You are a goddamned coward."

"Shut the door, Bryan," Daddy says.

Bryan pulls the door closed and it's us on the inside, Deb on the outside.

Deb yells something, shakes her fist, and flips her long hair back over her shoulders.

I want to tell Daddy to drive as fast as he can, drive us anywhere, drive forever so we never have to come back to Deb or her terrible house again.

Half an hour later, we check into a Holiday Inn.

Our room is on the main level and there are two big beds and one bathroom. Bryan opens the drapes and on the other side is a slider door made out of glass.

"Cool," Bryan says. "A pool."

Daddy throws his travel bag on the bed.

I turn on the light in the bathroom, open and close the drawers around the sink. Except for an extra roll of toilet paper, the drawers are empty.

"Can we go swimming?" Bryan says.

Daddy rubs his face in his big hands and he looks around like he forgot something.

"Sure," Daddy says, "why not. I don't care."

"Cool," Bryan says.

I turn the light off in the bathroom and stand in the space between the two rooms.

"What about our swimsuits?" I say.

"What?" Daddy says.

"We don't have our swimsuits," I say.

Daddy and Bryan look at me, both of them with the same eyes, the same look.

"I can just wear my shorts," Bryan says.

"Fine," Daddy says, "why not. You can swim in your shirt and your underwear, Juniper."

Daddy pushes his hand into his pocket, digs out some change, and hands the change to Bryan.

"Here," Daddy says, "get a couple of sodas and give me some time to sort things out."

Bryan takes the money, pulls the sliding door open, and runs outside.

Daddy sits on the edge of a big bed and puts his face in his hands again, rubs up and down.

"Are we going to stay here?" I say.

Daddy sits up straight again and smiles.

"Go on out and play with your brother," Daddy says, "and let me figure out what we are going to do."

I have never played with Bryan, never. I want to tell Daddy that and I want to say how I don't like Deb or her kids or her house. I want to say something, but I don't. I just stay quiet and go out to where Bryan is.

The Holiday Inn is built around the pool and there are twenty sets of sliding glass doors, some with drapes open, most with drapes closed. Between each room are planters with tall spiky bushes and in the bottom of the planters are white decorative rocks over black plastic. If you look up, there's a balcony and more sliding glass doors.

"It's empty," Bryan says.

Bryan is at the edge of the pool and his voice is loud around the empty patio.

The pool without water is a big circle of cement painted white. Some of the paint pulls off the walls and there are long cracks all the way from the shallow end to the deep end. At the deep end is a small pool of dirty water, not enough for a birdbath, and it looks like someone threw a handful of white decorative rocks down there.

"Figures," Bryan says.

Bryan blows his lips out with a bunch of held-in air and looks around like he is looking for something. He walks lazy steps to a soda machine that's up against a concrete wall and stands in front of it with his hands in his pockets.

"I'm getting a root beer," Bryan says.

He takes the money out of his pocket, feeds in the coins, and pushes a button. A can of root beer rolls to the end of the dispenser and Bryan takes it out.

"What do you want?" Bryan says.

I point to the green button for lemon lime. Bryan feeds more coins in, presses the green button, and I take out the cold can of soda.

Bryan walks back to the edge of the pool and stands with his feet hanging halfway over the edge.

Daddy stands in front of the sliding glass door with the telephone in one hand, the receiver in the other. He smiles and waves, his head leaned into the telephone. I wave back and then I stop waving.

"I wonder who he's talking to?" I say.

Bryan pushes his hand into his pocket and moves the change around.

I walk to the shallow end of the empty pool, sit on the edge where the steps lead down. I put my feet on the top step and pop my lemon lime. The soda is sweet and sour and there are bubbles around my mouth and down my throat.

Even though it's sunny, it's not hot today. It's like the world is in between seasons, not spring, not winter.

Bryan tips his soda can all the way up, his neck with a little bump that moves when he drinks. Then he steps back from the edge of the pool, drops the can on the concrete, and stomps until it's a flat mashed-up can. He pulls his foot back and kicks, the can flies off the concrete and down into the pool of dirty water.

There's something funny about the can in the muddy water and I laugh. Bryan laughs too. I drink the rest of my soda until the can is empty and I hold the can up toward him.

Bryan walks around the pool and takes my can. He drops it on the concrete, stomps it flat, and kicks the can all the way from the shallow end to the deep end. The can drops into the puddle of water and rolls up against the smashed root beer can. Bryan puts his arms up, makes this silent cheer, and drops his hands again.

I pull my knees to my chest, arms around so I make a little ball. Bryan sits next to me, his foot on the top step, his elbows on his knees. This close, he smells like root beer.

It's nice like this, just Bryan and me, and how he took the can and kicked it. It's nice how we laugh at the same thing. From the side, Bryan's face is a long line from his cheek to his chin, a straight line for his nose, the beauty mark over his lip. Bryan looks at me and I look away from his face, my eyes on the muddy water at the bottom of the empty pool.

"What?" Bryan says.

"I hope we never go back," I say.

Bryan leans back, his hands on the concrete.

"We're going back," Bryan says.

"How do you know?" I say.

"I just know," Bryan says.

I have to twist my head to see Bryan's face.

"How?" I say.

Bryan looks into the pool and squints his eyes.

"Just forget it," Bryan says.

My arms and legs are goose-bumpy and I bite my lip between my teeth.

"Come on," I say, "just tell me."

Bryan looks at me again, looks at the sliding glass door, and then he leans his face to my ear.

"Dad and Deb aren't just friends," Bryan whispers. "You know what I mean?"

I lean back from Bryan's face, look at his dark brown eyes, at how his eyebrows are all bushy over his eyes.

"No," I say. "I don't."

"Jesus," Bryan says. "Think about it. What do you think they're doing in the off-limits room? Do you think they just sleep in there?"

I look at Bryan's mouth and Bryan licks his lips.

"Christopher says it's been going on for a while too," Bryan says. "He says Dad was here last year."

"Why?" I say.

Bryan rolls his eyes.

"God," Bryan says, "you're so stupid."

Bryan twists around, his face to where Daddy stands on the other side of the sliding glass doors. Bryan twists back around and kicks his heel against the side of the pool.

Part of me knows what Bryan means and part of me doesn't. It's like understanding how letters make words and words make sentences, but you still don't know how to read.

Bryan picks his finger on the edge of the pool, wiggles out a loose piece of concrete, and he throws it into the muddy water. I know Bryan isn't going to say anything else and I wish he never said all the things he did.

Way up in the sky, a jet flies somewhere and it's the far-off sound of engines. I tilt my head all the way back, but all I can see is a silver shine and a line of white engine smoke.

ten

We have a brown car now, one of those fancy Mercedes types that's supposed to be expensive and important.

I hate the brown car.

Daddy and Deb sit up front, Kenny in between. Christopher, Bryan, Ronny, and me are crammed in the back and Ronny and me are shoulder to shoulder. Ronny has her mouth open and her breath stinks.

I hate Ronny.

Deb's all dolled up today, her hair rolled up in a french twist under a black and white polka-dot scarf, her body squeezed into a white sleeveless dress with big red and yellow flowers. She stretches her arms like a cat and she puts one arm over the back of Daddy's seat, touches her fingers on Daddy's neck.

"I am just so happy," Deb says.

I hate Deb.

Daddy and Deb got married in Las Vegas, just like that, no explanation. That's just the way it is now.

I cross my arms and stare all of my mad at the back of Daddy's head, his neck, the line of his sunglasses on the side of his face.

Ronny shoves against my side, freckly face in my face.

"Move over," Ronny says.

"I can't," I say.

Ronny shoves me again, her back into my shoulder, and she is all edges and corners, her body cold and hard.

"Yes, you can," Ronny says.

"Quit shoving," Bryan says.

Deb twists around and the seat belt pulls her neck skin. Her thin lips have frosted lipstick spread on and when she smiles, there's lipstick on the ends of her front teeth.

"No fighting now, kids," Deb says.

Bryan rolls his eyes like Deb is too stupid to talk.

"We're not fighting," Bryan says.

Deb waves her hand over the seat.

"Just settle down," Deb says, "we're almost there."

Deb turns around, looks at Daddy, smiles. Daddy looks at Deb, smiles back.

Ronny wiggles around, stretches out her legs. I cross my arms tighter, try not to touch any of Ronny with my body, even though that's impossible.

Tall twisted trees grow in an arch over the road and it's like driving through a tunnel of green. The only sign of sunlight is the white cuts that make it through the canopy of leaves. I look out Bryan's window, look at how the sunlight moves over his arms, his face, his legs.

Daddy slows the brown car down and turns off the main road.

"This looks really nice," Deb says, "you kids will have a great summer here."

"I don't want to go to some stupid summer camp," Ronny says.

"Me either," Kenny says.

Deb takes her arm from the back of the seat, her happy face turns serious. Daddy looks at Deb and Deb looks at Daddy.

"Kendall, Veronica," Deb says. "Try to cooperate."

Ronny moves her butt around in the seat, shoves against my shoulder again.

Daddy drives up a hill covered in gravel and it's the sound of rocks bouncing under the car. Out the window is a rail fence and past the fence are fields of green grass and horses with their heads down in the grass.

At the top of the hill is a circle of black asphalt, a big house, and past the house is more fenced-in field. Other cars are parked up the driveway and moms and dads unload luggage and say good-bye to their kids. One kid looks like he's going to cry and his mother tells him to knock it off.

Around the back of the big brown car, Daddy and Deb unload bags. There are five backpacks, each with one of our names on the outside, white iron-on letters, all capitals. Deb hands backpacks to Christopher, Kenny, and Ronny. Daddy hands Bryan a pack and holds the other one out to me.

I look at Daddy's hand, just his hand, and take the pack. Daddy doesn't let go and smiles at me. I pull the pack out of his hand, looking away from his face, and walk to the edge of the driveway where the asphalt turns to gravel.

Behind me are grown-up voices and kid voices and past the voices is the sound of the wind through the tall trees. All the trees have round green leaves and white bark that peels off. The wind blows through the tops of the trees, makes them move together in a silent secret dance.

Deb fusses with her kids, says stuff I can't hear. Christopher leans on one leg, then the other. Kenny stays close to Deb, her hand in Deb's hand. Ronny stands on her toes, looks around.

Daddy talks to Bryan, puts his hand on Bryan's shoulder, and Bryan nods. Daddy looks my way and I look away fast, watch the trees dance.

"Bud, honey," Deb yells, "we have to get going."

"Hold on," Daddy yells.

"Hey, Juniper," Daddy says.

I turn all the way around so I can't see any of him. Behind me is the sound of his feet on the driveway, on the gravel, the feel of his body close to mine. Daddy puts his hands on my shoulders and his fingers are cool through my shirt.

We stand like that for a long time, I don't know how long, and he clears his throat.

"Pretty nice place," Daddy says, "it looks nice, doesn't it?"

I look at the field, the white fence, the trees.

Daddy squeezes easy around my neck and his fingers make goose bumps down my arms and legs. I shrug his hands away, twist my body so he doesn't touch anymore. Daddy stands up tall, puts his hands in his pockets.

"You can't stay mad forever," Daddy says.

I look up at Daddy, squint one eye, and bite my lower lip. All his genius and he's wrong. I can stay mad forever.

"I want you to have a good summer," Daddy says, "I want you to learn how to swim and ride horses. You know, be a kid, have fun."

I don't know anything about being a kid. I look at the empty field, the white fence, the trees.

"I don't want to stay here," I say.

"Come on now," Daddy says, "you'll have fun."

"I don't know why I have to stay here," I say. "I don't know why you have to go on some stupid honeymoon. I don't know why you even have to be married to her anyway."

The words are out of my mouth before I know it and then it's quiet between me and Daddy. Too quiet and I hold still.

Daddy moves me so we are face to face, eye to eye, and the way he looks, I know he doesn't know what to say.

"Look," Daddy says, "I know it's hard now, but everything is going to be fine. I promise."

My throat hurts, my chest hurts, and I blink my eyes to hold the tears.

"But what about Momma?" I say.

Daddy leans his forehead against my forehead and his voice is low and quiet.

"Deb's not as bad as you think," Daddy whispers, "if you just give her a chance."

His head against my head and there's a heavy weight in my stomach, on my shoulders, a heavy weight all around, and there's nothing I can do to lift it off.

Daddy leans back and I look at his face again.

"Bud, honey," Deb yells. "Let's go."

Deb stands with her hands on her flowered hips, feet in black high heel pumps, straw purse off her arm. Daddy lifts his hand and waves at Deb. She shifts her weight and points her finger at her wristwatch.

"Looks like we have to get going," Daddy says.

He reaches for the backpack and holds it in the space between us. I wipe my face with the back of my hand, my head low so Deb can't see me cry.

"Are we okay?" Daddy says.

I can't make any more words. I nod my head like yes, we're okay, even though I know it's not okay, nothing is okay.

Daddy smiles and puts his hand on my head like he used to do when I was little.

"That's my girl," Daddy says.

I sniff one more time and stand up tall, shoulders straight, chin tucked. I put the pack over my shoulder, the weight of it between my shoulders, and I walk to the front gate.

"Have a great summer, Juniper," Daddy yells.

It's called the Jolly Roger Pirate Ranch, which is pretty stupid since pirates are on the ocean, not on a ranch, and there aren't any pirates here anyway, just horses and cows and some goats. There's a swimming pool, a bunch of little white cabins for sleeping, and a barn where all the animals go at night.

Elizabeth is in charge of the Jolly Roger Pirate Ranch and she doesn't look anything like a pirate. Elizabeth is just a regular lady with summer shorts and a summer top and mirror sunglasses over her eyes.

Elizabeth stands on a concrete porch and behind her is the big main house with a sliding glass door. There are three white plastic chairs on the concrete porch and a man sits in one of the chairs, has on summer shorts and a tank top.

Elizabeth talks at us about the Ranch and how it is part of something called the Freedom Community Church and how Freedom Community helps people contemplate life differently. The man behind Elizabeth nods his head up and down, hands together like a prayer.

The Freedom Community Church is Deb's church and right away I know something is wrong about this place except I don't know what. I look around and everyone else acts normal, like everything is fine. I act normal too, that bad feeling up the back of my neck and over the top of my head.

Elizabeth talks and talks and her face doesn't have any kind of expression, just looks flat. She says there are rules and if we don't break the rules, we should all have a great summer, if we do break the rules, then we will have trouble. Elizabeth doesn't say what the rules are and I wonder if you can ask questions. I keep my hand down just in case questions are against the rules.

"This is John," Elizabeth says. "John is in charge of day activities and swim events."

Elizabeth looks at us, looks at John. John nods and stands up.

John is blond hair beautiful, square face, square jaw. He doesn't look a thing like a pirate either. He talks about how each day is structured with time to eat, time to swim, time to be quiet and contemplate life differently.

After Elizabeth and John, we get a white T-shirt with a cartoon of a pirate on the front. The pirate has one eye covered with a patch and his face is all unshaved and he smiles except a couple of his teeth are black. I roll the T-shirt up and put it in the bottom of my backpack, no way I'm wearing a shirt of a pirate with rotten teeth.

Swimming lessons are an hour after lunch and they last until an hour before dinner.

The pool is like any other pool, backyard size, maybe a little bigger. There's a deep end, a shallow end, a diving board on the deep end, and a set of steps in the shallow end.

There are big kids, little kids, boys, girls, all of us around the pool. I have a brand-new bathing suit, one piece, little bird stitched over my heart. I like how the bird is pointed up, how it looks like it's about to fly away.

John-in-charge-of-swimming is almost naked. He has on

one of those little tiny red swimsuits, all of him tan, his stomach flat and his legs all muscley. John doesn't look like a real
person, looks like a statue, looks like a picture in a magazine.

John stands on the diving board, walks one, two, three
steps and jumps on the end of the diving board, arms over his
head. His dive is no splash, just a wave of water around his
body and he swims the whole length of the pool underwater.
At the other end he comes up, makes a sharp turn, pushes off,
and this time swims the length of the pool on top of the water.

Bryan stands close behind me and he has on a pair of baggy
swim trunks like surfers wear. Bryan nudges his shoulder
against the back of my head.

"That guy is a show-off," Bryan says.

Bryan has his chin tucked and his arms crossed and I cross
my arms too.

"Why?" I whisper.

"Just look at him," Bryan says. "What a goofball."

The way he says goofball makes me laugh and I put my
hand over my mouth to keep from laughing out loud.

John swims three full laps and then he stops, pulls himself
out, a sheet of water off his back. All the kids step back to
make room for John to get his towel. Bryan and me step back
too. John wipes the towel over his face, down his chest, puts it
around his neck like a rope.

"That's how I swim," John yells. "Now show me how *you*
can swim."

John waves his arm around, finger pointing where to go.

"I want four lines spaced two feet apart," John says, "five
of you per line, oldest to youngest."

All the kids move into lines and I end up behind Kenny and
Ronny.

John gives directions, says he is going to blow a whistle and time the swimmers on his watch. Four kids line up at the edge of the pool, Bryan in the first group, and John blows his whistle. The first four kids jump into the pool and it's arms and legs and splashing. The four kids swim across the pool and Bryan comes in second place.

John clicks his watch.

"Not bad," John yells. "Next line, step up."

Last in line isn't such a good place to be since you have more time to wait and worry and there are goose bumps up my arms. Kenny and Ronny have on matching bathing suits with bright pink zigzags on neon green. They both wait in line, arms crossed the exact same way over their tomboy bodies. They have freckles everywhere, on their arms, their legs, their backs.

"Are you guys nervous?" I say.

Kenny and Ronny look at each other and then they look at me, Ronny's mouth open like she forgot to close it.

"No," Ronny says.

"I'm nervous," I say.

John blows his whistle and the next line dives into the water.

"I mean," I say, "I can't really swim yet, I thought this was swim lessons."

Ronny squints her eyes, mouth open, freckles everywhere, even on her lips. She looks at Kenny and Kenny looks at her and there's a secret between them, talking without words. Ronny looks at me again, her hands on her hips.

"What kind of kid lives by the ocean and doesn't know how to swim?" Ronny says.

"Yeah," Kenny says.

Kenny laughs at Ronny and Ronny laughs too, like the two of them have a secret joke. I cross my arms over my chest.

"I don't like the ocean," I say.

Ronny looks at me like I smell bad and turns away. Kenny looks at me too, and then she shrugs her shoulders and turns away too.

"Line up," John yells.

Ronny shoves her elbow against her sister.

"Come on," Ronny says, "you're next."

Kenny stands on the edge of the pool.

John blows his whistle and the sound is too loud, like a scream. Kenny jumps in and swims to the other end of the pool. She doesn't win but the way she swims makes it look easy.

Ronny's turn is next and she puts her fingers around the legs of her swimsuit to tug it away from her tomboy butt.

"Line up," John yells.

The whistle screams and Ronny dives. She is a fast streak of neon green and pink, a perfect swimmer, way better than Kenny, way better than everyone.

I never wished I was someone else before, except when I wished I was Samantha on *Bewitched*. Right now, I wish I was Ronny, minus all the freckles.

Ronny pulls out of the pool on the other side and her red hair is slick on her head. Kenny and Ronny hit hands together and they laugh about something.

"Line up," John yells.

Sunlight shines on the choppy pool water, makes it look like broken glass. I'm one of four other kids and I wonder if this is how you're supposed to learn how to swim. All the other kids act normal. I act normal too.

John pushes his whistle into his mouth and blows a scream into the air.

I close my eyes and jump off the edge. My body slaps

against the water, stings against my stomach, and I sink down feet first.

Cold water all around, the muffled sound of voices at the surface, my eyes closed tight, and just like that my legs kick and my arms paddle. I open my eyes and I can see under the water too, a sunny bright blue all around and it's not that bad. I paddle and kick until my head is above the surface of the water and I swim to the other side of the pool.

"Hey, hey, *hey*," John yells. "What are you doing there?"

John comes to Kenny and Ronny's line and pushes them out of the way.

My hand reaches for the concrete edge and John puts his fingers on my wrist, tugs me out of the water. His touch on my body is the worst thing and when he lets go, I rub his touch off my skin.

"I said, what are you doing?" John says.

John bends at his waist, hands on his knees, me in his mirror sunglasses.

"Swimming," I say.

"Swimming?" John says.

All the kids laugh, their voices one loud voice.

"Hey," Bryan yells. "She doesn't know how to swim."

John stands up, red swim trunks in my face, his thingy a little round ball stuffed in there, and it almost hits me in the nose. I turn my face away from his thingy, away from John.

Bryan is up on his toes so he can see over the other kids and I like how it is for him to be there, for him to help explain.

"Was I talking to you?" John says. "Get back in line."

Bryan's dark eyes are wide open and his face gets the red color under his tan cheeks. Bryan looks at me, at John, and then he stands flat on his feet again, just like all the other kids.

John is quiet, all the kids are quiet, and the water in the pool is smooth and quiet too.

"Well, I think this is a learning opportunity for everyone," John says.

John leans over from his waist, me in his mirrors, and I'm all wet, my eyes wide open and round.

"Do you believe you can swim?" John says.

I step back from John, my arms crossed over myself.

"I did swim," I say.

John paws his hands in the air like a cat paws at a ball of string.

"What you were doing was some kind of ugly dog paddle," John says.

The kids laugh at John, laugh at me, and I look at their faces, kids I don't know, who don't know me, everyone a stranger.

"We'll run the drill again," John says, "and I want you to try to conceive of swimming."

John tries to put his hand on my shoulder, but I step back so he can't touch me again. John looks at me for a long time, his mouth pressed tight. He smiles and puts the whistle in his mouth.

All the kids move into lines again like nothing happened. I get in line behind Kenny and Ronny, wish I could get out of here.

Kenny looks at me one time and then she looks away like I'm not even here. Ronny tugs her swimsuit out of her butt, keeps her back to me the whole time.

"Line up," John yells.

It's the same thing all over again: The whistle blows, kids dive and cross the pool, and I still don't know how to swim the way you're supposed to swim.

"All right, little doggy," John yells, "show us how to swim."

There are three kids on my side and they laugh. Across the pool, all the other kids laugh too. I shut my eyes, try to see me swimming in there, but all I see is dark.

John blows his whistle.

I jump into the pool.

When I come to the surface, I paddle-swim the way I did before, the only way I know how to swim, I guess.

John jogs around the pool.

"Swim," John yells, "swim."

I stretch my arms and lie out flat on the water, try to swim like everyone else can. Pool water stings up my nose and down my throat. I put my head up and paddle until I reach the other side. John walks over and pushes his toes over my fingers.

"I don't think you are seeing it," John says. "Try it again."

I move my hand over and hold on to the side of the pool.

"I can't," I say.

John puts his foot on my fingers again, his toes pushing me off the edge of the pool. I let go and grab another part of the edge and hold on.

"There's no such thing as *can't* in the Freedom Community," John says, "you can and you will."

John puts his hands on my wrists and his fingers are hard and strong. He pulls me out of the pool like I'm nothing.

"This is a lesson you'll thank me for later," John says.

John swings my body in the air and pushes me out to the center of the deep end of the pool. He lets me go then and it's just me in the air. All of me is down and under the water with bubbles pushed against my face and in my nose.

The whole idea of swimming is lost in knowing something

worse than terrible is happening to me. I have to get out and get away, no matter what, and that's all there is inside my head. I kick my legs and paddle my arms. My head breaks the surface and I paddle to the side of the pool.

"Swim," John yells, "swim now."

I paddle to the shallow end of the pool, touch my feet to the bottom of the pool, and try to run through the water.

John dives into the pool.

My foot is on the first step and my hand touches the silver handrail.

John puts his arms around my middle and pulls my body against his chest.

I kick my legs and swing my arms.

"Let me go," I yell.

"I don't think you get the concept," John says, his mouth against my ear.

The kids are in a clump at the edge of the steps and my eyes look for Bryan. I know he's in there, but I can't see him.

"Get the hell out of my way," John says.

The clump of kids moves apart and John carries me up the steps and across to the deep side of the pool again. I know he is going to throw me in, I just know it, and I kick and yell and hit. I scratch John's face and he drops me on the concrete instead, a sting of pain in my knees.

"Goddammit," John yells.

John's face is red lines where I scratched him and he touches where the blood comes up.

On my behind, I crab-walk back until there's a wide space between John and me. My fingers touch the edge of the grass and I roll over, push up, and it's freedom around my legs and arms.

John's weight is against my back again, his arm around my

stomach, and all my air is out of my body as he pulls me against his chest again.

"Let go," I yell.

His hand slaps the side of my head and there is a sting behind my eyes, up along my jaw.

"You will swim," John says.

My eyes hurt, my head hurts, my body hurts. Everyone stands there, no one does anything, and John throws me in the deep end again.

Over and over and over again, I can't remember how many times. No matter how hard I try, the rest is lost in being so scared I can't think, I can't swim, I can't get away.

On the gravel driveway that leads to the Jolly Roger Pirate Ranch are two rows of tall white paper bark trees. The branches are heavy with thin round leaves and when the wind blows, the round leaves sound like a very polite audience that gives very quiet applause. The trees grow in a wide cut of dirt between the gravel driveway and the rail fence. Under the trees, weeds grow taller than I stand and all the weeds have these long thorns that get stuck in my hands.

It's twenty demerits for dog paddling. Twenty more for having the kind of mind that cannot contemplate life differently, whatever that means.

Forty demerits is forty hours of hard labor and hard labor at the Jolly Roger Pirate Ranch means you pick weeds.

The worst part is all the thorns.

The best part of being in the weeds is how I'm alone.

I bend over, put both hands low around a weed stalk, and the thorns push sharp into my hands. I hold my breath, pull up, and the weed comes out of the soft dirt, root and all.

Elizabeth says I have to pull the roots out too or she'll make me dig them with a shovel.

I shake the dirt off the roots, earth dust in my nose, my mouth. I throw the weed into a pile with the other dead weeds.

At night, the pool light is turned on and the water is a blue fog.

Nighttime is free swim time and all the kids get to use the inner tubes, underwater masks, and diving fins.

After ten hours of demerits, I'm allowed into the pool for free swim too.

No one talks to me, not Bryan, not Kenny and Ronny.

Everyone watches me, though, I can feel their eyes. When I look, they look away, but I know they watch.

At the shallow end, I press my back against the concrete wall, squeeze my fingers over my nose, take a big deep breath, and go under.

All the kid noise is quiet under the water and I count to thirty.

I stand and the kid sounds are loud again.

No one looks at me, no one talks to me.

I hold my nose, take a deep breath, and go under.

I count forty seconds, come back up.

I hold my nose, take a deep breath, go under.

Sixty seconds.

Up.

Deep breath.

Under.

Seventy seconds.

Up.

Over and over until I can count to one hundred seconds. I

think it's a good idea to know how to hold your breath under water.

Two weeks into the Jolly Roger Pirate Ranch, half my demerits are gone and I can hold my breath under water for one hundred and eighty seconds—three whole minutes. I can open my eyes under the water too and when I do that, I can see all the way to the other end of the pool.

It's nighttime free swim like all the other free swims, except tonight John is out here and that's different. John has on his tight red swim trunks and he walks around the pool. John makes me nervous when he does that.

There's a line of kids waiting to get on the diving board. Kenny and Ronny are in line, their arms hugged around their bodies while they wait. Bryan stands in line too.

John doesn't wait in line. He waves his arms and everyone steps back. John goes to the head of the line, climbs up the ladder, and walks to the end of the diving board. John stands there like he's the most important person in the world and he wants everyone to know he knows it.

I hate John.

I hold my nose, take a deep breath, and go under.

It's quiet under the water and I float down until I sit down on the bottom on the pool, count one thousand one, one thousand two.

Across the pool, John slices the quiet with his dive and there are white bubbles around his head, his arms, his legs. John stays under water and he kicks around at something.

My hair floats around my face and I push it out of the way.

John underwater is zombie-white legs, zombie-white arms, zombie-white butt too, and that's when I see how he doesn't have his red swimsuit on anymore.

I lose count and push up to the surface.

It's just like it always is, all the kids play and laugh and splash. No one looks at me, no one except John. John looks right at me.

My heart beats in my ears and I go under the water again, push my feet against the pool wall and swim like a fish to the shallow steps. At the steps, I push up and wipe the water out of my eyes.

John is already at the top of the steps and he has his red swimsuit on again. His blond hair is slick to his head and his face is set hard, lips in a line, eyes narrow.

"Going somewhere?" John says.

I look around the pool, look at John.

"Me?" I say.

"Yes, you," John says.

John puts his hand like he's going to grab. I step back so he can't touch me.

"Get out of the damn pool," John says.

My legs shake, my arms shake, my stomach shakes, prickles all over the place.

"I didn't do anything," I say.

"Just get out," John says.

At the deep end of the pool, Bryan pulls out of the pool and he's close enough for me to call for help. Bryan's face is different, flat and empty, and the look in his eyes says all the trouble I have is my own fault anyway.

I get out of the pool and water drips on the concrete around my feet.

John throws a towel and it hits me in the face, falls at my feet.

"Dry off," John says. "Hurry up."

It's quiet around the pool now and all the other kids look at us.

There is a raw feeling inside my body, like I swallowed broken glass and it cuts from the inside out. I bend over, take the towel, and put it around my body.

"Let's go," John says.

The Jolly Roger Pirate Ranch is full of night sounds and night shadows. John and me go past the white cabins, past the big house, down a dirt path that goes past the barn. There's the smell of hay and horses and cows. A goat bell rings and then it stops. A tall light by the barn makes a rectangle of light on the dirt.

I hold the towel around my shoulders, the edges of the towel in my fist. My bare feet walk over the soft dirt and I stop in the middle of the rectangle of light.

"Where are we going?" I say.

"Just come on," John says.

I don't want to go with John, but I don't know what else to do.

There is the faraway sound of kids in the pool and I think about screaming, think about running. John reaches to touch and I walk ahead of his hand.

A small house is on the other side of the barn and out front is a bare lightbulb that makes a triangle of light on the front door. John opens the door, flips a switch, and in front of us is a flight of steep stairs.

"Go," John says.

I push my heels into the dirt.

"No way," I say.

I look around, dark and shadows, the corral, the barn, more dark. John pushes against my back and I stumble up the step.

"Go," John says.

I start up the steps and John is right behind, his body against my back, the top of my head to the ripple part of his stomach. It's twenty-seven steps and at the top, I stop. John reaches over my head, pushes open another door, and inside that room is dark too. I stay outside the door and John goes in past me, moves around in the dark.

My fingers hold the handrail and I look down the twenty-seven steps. I look at John in there, me out here. All I have to do is go down the steps, out the door, and run into the night. All I have to do is go, right now.

A light goes on in the dark room, just a bulb and a chain. The light swings back and forth, lightbulb shadow on the white walls, lightbulb light on John.

I look down the stairs.

All I have to do is go, now.

I move my bare foot over the wood step and John runs across the room, fingers pressed into the soft under my arm.

"No, you don't," John says.

He pulls me all the way into the room and shuts the door, the sound loud in my head. He takes his hand off my arm and I rub where he touched me.

There's a mattress on the floor with a sheet over and another sheet messed up in the middle. Clothes are piled against the wall: shorts, shirts, underwear, socks. I look at the floor, at the walls, at John's shadow on the wall.

John stands with his feet wide and his towel is around his waist, over his swimsuit.

"You can leave," John says, "after we clear something up."

John pushes his hand through his blond hair and it's all dry and short around his head.

My hair is wet on my head and my suit is still wet too. I

hold my towel around my shoulders, the edges in my fist and my fist under my chin and I'm cold all over.

"You were watching me under the water," John says.

"I wasn't," I say.

"Don't deny it," John says. "I know you saw me without my suit and I know you laughed."

"I didn't," I say.

"You did," John says. "Now you have to take off your suit in front of me so we are even."

"What?" I say.

"You saw me," John says. "I get to see you."

John's shadow on the white wall looks like he is slanted, like his shadow is falling. My head is dizzy and I feel like I am going to fall down.

"I'm going to make it easy on you," John says. "I'll turn off the light and you'll take off your suit. I'll turn the light back on and that will be it."

My arms shake, my legs shake. All of me shakes and tears are hot down my face. I hold my towel tight around my shoulders, the cold of the towel against my back and my legs.

John pulls the chain and it's black dark all around. I hold my breath and it's quiet. There is the sound of the chain pull, the light on again, and I blink in the bright light.

"Let's try again," John says.

I wish I was stronger, wish I wouldn't cry, and at the same time, maybe if I cry hard enough, he will let me go.

John pulls the chain and the room is dark.

John pulls the chain and the room is bright white light.

John's face is blank wait and I cry so hard it hurts.

I don't know how one person can watch another person cry like that. I don't know how John can be a real person, and that's when I know tears aren't going to get me out of this place.

"Calm down," John says, "and we'll try it again."

John's voice is low and quiet. He tilts his head back, squints his eyes, and pulls the chain one more time.

Calm moves through my arms and legs, quiet calm, clear calm.

I drop the towel, the wet weight of it on my feet.

One strap, two straps, and I pull the navy swimsuit off my body, that suck sound of wet against skin.

Cool air moves around my body, but I'm not cold. I close my eyes tight and stand up tall, shoulders straight, chin tucked.

I know what I look like without clothes. I'm a skinny body with scars on my knees from when I fell off my bike a couple years ago and it's almost funny since I know John is going to turn on the light and probably laugh at how I am nothing. Right then I wish I had a fancy body, something worth seeing so he wouldn't laugh.

The light clicks and it's orange through my eyelids. I keep my eyes closed tight, don't breathe, don't move. It's quiet for a long time, quiet like this is just a nightmare I can open my eyes and wake up from. But when I open my eyes, John is still here and he's naked now too. John's thingy there in a nest of blond hair, his thingy right at me, and that's the last thing I remember. John naked and me naked, white light all around and I'm scared in a way I've never been scared before.

❧

It's the hottest part of the day, hot even in the shade. The dirt is dusty dry and it blows in my face, up my nose, in my eyes and mouth.

I've picked almost half the weeds on this side of the drive-way, another two weeks and I'll have the rest done and start up the other side. My hands are sore and thorns are stuck under my skin like slivers.

I hate weeds, I hate thorns. I bite a thorn on my palm, pull back with my teeth, and spit it out. A bird screams overhead and the sound makes my heart jump, makes me shake like someone said "boo."

Down at the main road, a car turns up the driveway. I step behind a tree and press my face against the white paper bark of the trunk.

The car is painted red. The car has a sputter spit engine. The car is Red.

Just like that all my scared disappears and I walk out of the weeds. I stand on the edge of the gravel and put my hands on my hips like "Look, it's me."

Red slows down and I can see Daddy's shape behind the dusty windshield, can see how he sits low and leans back and how he steers one-handed the way he always does. No one sits in the passenger seat.

I wave my arm over my head. Daddy honks three short beeps.

Daddy pulls Red up and stops on the hill. There is a cloud of dust behind the car and it lifts around us, the taste of dirt in my nose and mouth. I put my hands in the space where the window is rolled down.

"Daddy?" I say.

"Jenny?" Daddy says.

"You look different," I say.

"So do you," Daddy says.

"But your face," I say.

Daddy moves his hand over his chin and he has a beard now, a mustache too.

"You like it?" Daddy says.

"No," I say.

Daddy drops his hand and clears his throat.

"Well, it was Deb's idea," Daddy says.

"You have glasses too," I say.

Daddy touches the frames of his glasses and they are gold and glass, a shine over his eyes.

"Deb says they make me look distinguished," Daddy says.

"Distinguished?" I say.

Daddy takes a deep breath, and he pushes his hand through his hair. His whiskers make his lips look too thick, like earthworms on his face.

"Enough about me, look at you," he says, "you're a mess."

My T-shirt is dirty, my jeans are dirty, my hands are dirty. I try to wipe some dirt off, but it's no use.

"What are you doing out here?" Daddy says. "Why are you such a mess?"

I wipe my face with the back of my hand.

"I'm in trouble," I say.

"Trouble?" Daddy says.

"Isn't that why you're here?" I say.

"No," Daddy says, "I had some business up here so I stopped in to surprise you kids."

Red's engine is a low sound all around the quiet driveway.

"What kind of trouble are you in?" Daddy says.

How can I say about the swimming? How can I explain about John? I don't know what to say, where to begin, and I am too scared anyway.

"Jenny?" Daddy says.

I can't see past the shine on his new glasses and I sniff hard, the back of my hand over my nose.

"Just tell me," he says.

I look at my feet, just my feet on the gravel and dirt stains in my shoes.

"I can't," I say.

"Get in the car," Daddy says, "and we'll go up and figure this out."

I look to the top of the driveway, one side without any weeds, the other side thick with weeds.

"Are we going home?" I say.

"What?" Daddy says.

"Are we leaving," I say. "Today?"

"No," Daddy says, "of course not."

"I can't get in the car then," I say. "I'll get in more trouble."

Daddy gets that look like he's mad, his lips pressed tight. He takes a deep breath and looks at me again.

"All right," Daddy says, "I'll go on up and figure this out."

I look at him and he looks at me and I sniff hard.

Daddy shakes his head side to side like I'm a mystery and I don't know what to do.

"See you in a little bit," he says.

He shifts Red and drives up the hill, sputter and spit and a cloud of gravel dust behind the car. I want to run and follow Daddy, want to tell him everything, want to know he's going to make it right for me, but I stay right where I am, look at the weeds left to pick.

I put my hands around the bottom of a thick weed stalk, bend my knees, and pull up. There are dirt clods around the roots and I hit the weed against the white fence until all the dirt falls off. I throw the weed into the pile of weeds, wipe my face off with the back of my arm, bend over again.

All the kids are in the big house for dinner and it's just Daddy and me at the pool before he has to go. Daddy says all my demerits are gone and I shouldn't have any more trouble.

It's that time between day and night, just a little bit of the sun left in the sunset. I'm in the shallow end of the pool and Daddy is at the edge. He has one knee on the concrete and his whisker face is in his hand.

"Ready?" I say.

"Ready," Daddy says.

I like how it's just Daddy and me and how he made everything better just like that. I back against the pool wall and stand up tall, shoulders straight, chin tucked.

Daddy smiles when I do that and his face is soft the way it gets when he remembers. He nods his head one time and I nod back at him.

I hold my nose, take a deep breath, and float down until I reach the bottom of the pool. I push my feet against the pool wall and swim underwater. At the opposite side of the shallow end, I push up with arms over my head.

"Ta da," I say.

Drops of water spill on the dry concrete and splash around Daddy's pant cuffs.

"That's good," Daddy says, "but that's not swimming. Not really."

My arms drop to my sides and I blink the water out of my eyes.

"I mean it's good and everything, Juniper," Daddy says, "but I thought you learned how to swim."

"I can hold my breath for a hundred and eighty seconds," I say. "That's almost three minutes."

Daddy presses his hands together, palm to palm, finger to finger.

"But you need to learn how to swim too," Daddy says.

"Why?" I say.

Daddy puts his hands wide, fingers wide, shoulders up.

"For safety," he says, "for fun."

"Fun?" I say.

"Right," Daddy says.

The water is a wavy mirror and I can see Daddy's face and body move in the reflection, like he's here but he's not really here.

"Jenny?" Daddy says. "Do you understand what I'm trying to say?"

I walk to the steps where you get out of the pool and Daddy hands me a towel. I take it out of his hands, but I don't look up at him, just keep my eyes on my feet.

"Well," Daddy says, "you have the rest of the summer."

I wrap the towel around my shoulders and look at my feet on the concrete, just my feet.

Daddy stands there, hands in his pockets, and he makes keys jingle. He puts his hand on my shoulder and the weight is heavy. He says something about how he has to go, but he'll be back, how I'm going to have a great summer and how he really wants me to try to learn how to swim.

I tip my head back as far as it will go, look at the sunset pink sky. A wide V of birds fly together and they all move exactly the same, all going to the same place.

Daddy lifts his hand off my shoulder and looks up too. I look at Daddy, really look, but his new glasses are too shiny in front of his eyes. I don't know how, but I know nothing will ever be the same and it's that all-alone feeling even though I'm not alone.

Daddy smiles a nice smile with whiskers and big lips. I hold my towel tight and smile back, but I know it's not the real thing, just something on my face to push the all-alone feeling away.

eleven

We live in Fountain Valley now, but there's no fountain here, not even a water fountain.

Deb says Fountain Valley is the suburbs.

Daddy says Fountain Valley is temporary.

The house is like this: front door, living room, two long hallways to the back of the house. Down each hall are three bedrooms, six bedrooms altogether. Both hallways end in the kitchen and it's one big room made for cooking and for eating. On the far side of the kitchen, sliding glass doors open to a backyard of concrete and a pool. No grass.

It's a nice house, a nice pool, everything is nice, but it's the kind of nice that's on the outside, not on the inside. When things are wrong on the inside, it doesn't matter how nice things look.

I shut the door to my new room and it's new-house quiet in here, the far-off sound of Deb, Christopher, Kenny, and Ronny, their voices like one voice.

I pick my fingernail under the tape on the *Jenny's Room* box and peel the tape back. The box is the same, but the stuff inside is all different. Someone went through my stuff and folded it up, moved it around.

My heart beats in my head, in my ears. I dig to the bottom of the box and my hands feel for the black patent leather shoes that don't fit anymore. My hands can't feel anything and I take them out, put my arms around the big box, and turn it upside down. All my folded-up stuff falls out on the floor, no shoes, no socks, no key hidden inside.

I sit back on my heels, my stuff in a pile on the floor.

"Looking for this?"

It's quiet all around and Deb stands in the doorway, her hand open, my key in her palm.

"That's mine," I say.

Deb closes her fingers over the key and she shuts the door so we are both inside the new room.

"I thought we could have a little chat," Deb says.

Deb has on a blue and white striped shirt and a pair of jeans. Her red hair is long and straight around her face and she flips it over her shoulder all dramatic. Deb stands with one foot back, one foot forward, hips at an angle so she looks like some kind of mannequin in a store window.

I stand up tall, shoulders straight, chin tucked, and put my hand out to Deb.

"May I have it," I say. "Please."

Deb moves her green eyes to my hand and then my face.

"You don't like me very much," Deb says, "do you?"

"I like you," I say, "I just want my key."

"I can appreciate that you don't like me," Deb says. "I can even understand it."

I close my fingers into my palm, drop my hand on my leg.

"But whether you like me or not," Deb says, "you will respect me."

My eyes shift to the pink trunk and I roll my lips together. Daddy says Deb isn't so bad, says I should give her a chance. I wish Daddy were here right now so he could see the Deb I see.

"Can I have the key," I say again. "Please."

Deb looks at her hand with the key, then she looks her cat eyes at me and makes a little click noise with her tongue like she is thinking about it. Then she lets out a deep breath and holds her hand out.

"Fine," she says.

I put my hand under her fist and she opens her hand, the silver key falling from her to me.

Deb leans back and crosses her arms over her chest.

"I know what you have in there," Deb says.

"You went into my trunk?" I say.

"And I think it's important to have memories of your first mother," Deb says.

"That's my stuff," I say.

"But you can't live in the past, Jenny," Deb says. "Your mother is gone and I'm here now."

It's quiet in the new room, empty walls, empty closet. I look at Deb and she watches me and we stand like that for a long time, I don't know how long. Deb looks away first and she steps out of my room, her hand on the doorknob. Deb says something about a family meeting in ten minutes, but I just hold so still, so still it's like I'm not here at all.

My arms and legs are stiff from being so still and when I can't hear Deb anymore, I let out my breath and close the door quiet so it's just me again. On my knees, I open my pink trunk with the silver key and inside is the painting by Keith, the Barbie suitcase, the Our Wedding photo album on top. The wedding album was inside the Barbie suitcase and I know Deb took it out, know Deb had her hands and eyes on my mother and father and the way they were before.

I lift out the Barbie suitcase and open the cover. Malibu Suntan Barbie is in her special slot, still dressed in the black velvet dress and the black high heel shoes.

Careful, careful, I pull open the drawer in the bottom of the Barbie suitcase and it's packed tight with Barbie shoes, Barbie clothes. I tug the little drawer all the way out and everything falls on the carpet—Barbie shoes, Barbie clothes, the rolled-up, wrinkled, black velvet bag.

Just like that, I know Deb never found this secret.

I pick up the bag, hold it between my hands, and it's heavy the way important things are heavy. I press my lips together and untie the knot. The pearls and ring are just like they were, just like always, perfect.

When you get away with something, it's like a second chance.

I put the pearls and the ring back into the black velvet bag, tie the strings, roll the whole thing into a tiny ball. I tuck the ball into the drawer of my Barbie suitcase, pack the drawer with Barbie shoes and clothes, push the drawer back the way it was. I put the Barbie suitcase in the pink trunk, shut the lid, and lock the silver lock with the silver key.

I have a pocket in my shorts, but it's a loose pocket. I don't have any other pockets, not today.

Maybe I could sew the key into my pocket.

Maybe I could hide the key on the top shelf of the closet.

Maybe I could put the key into my shoe.

I untie my shoe, drop the key under the heel, put my shoe on again.

Under my heel, I can feel the shape of the key. I walk around and the key slips to the front of my shoe, the key against my big toe.

I take off my right shoe again and take the lace out of

all the holes. I put the lace through the hole in the silver key and lace up my shoe the way it was. The little silver key points up at me and I turn the key around, tuck it under the flap where you lace the shoe up. You can barely see the key at all, not unless you look close, really look. I move my foot side to side, wiggle it around, and the key stays put, stays hidden.

❧

Family meeting is where everyone sits around and Deb talks. Deb says family meeting is a vital component of successful communication, but I don't know what that means.

Deb and her kids, Daddy and us, we are all in the new living room of the Fountain Valley house. Christopher sits in a big chair and reads a book like he's all alone. Kenny, Ronny, and Bryan are on the sofa and they play rock, paper, scissors, that stupid game with fists you make into objects. When Kenny or Ronny win, they spit on her fingers and slap. When Bryan wins, he gives them Indian burns.

I sit on the floor, my feet tucked under so you can't see my key at all. I stretch my legs, turn my foot, and there is a little flash of silver key. Then, I cross my legs again, hide the key so I can't see it at all.

Daddy and Deb sit on the long green sofa and Daddy looks out the window. His face is whiskers and thick lips and glasses over his eyes.

"I have you all signed up for school, which starts on Monday," Deb says. "Now let's talk about chores.

"Kenny, you're in charge of making lunches during the week," Deb says, "Christopher, you handle the yard, weeds, raking, that kind of thing."

Deb looks at Daddy and pats his leg.

"Bud will do the mowing," Deb says. "Bryan, you're in charge of trash, get it all to the curb on Wednesdays."

Bryan has his finger in his ear and he moves it around and around.

"Ronny is in charge of keeping the inside of the house tidy," Deb says.

Ronny sticks her pinky finger up her nose, looks at the end of her finger, and sticks it into her mouth.

"Jenny is in charge of bathrooms," Deb says.

"In charge of them?" I say.

Deb has a yellow notepad on her lap and she must have everything she wants to say all written there. She puts her finger on a line like she doesn't want to lose her place.

"Excuse me?" Deb says.

"What am I supposed to do?" I say.

"Bathrooms, dipshit," Ronny says.

Kenny laughs at Ronny and Ronny looks at Kenny and laughs too.

"Veronica," Deb says.

Daddy sits forward the way he does when he's giving you all his attention. He looks at Deb, at Ronny.

"What did she say?" Daddy says. "What did you just say?"

Ronny sinks low into the sofa and pushes her hands under her butt.

"Nothing," Ronny says.

"She called Jenny a dipshit," Bryan says.

"Dipshit?" Daddy says.

Christopher smiles and I smile too, since it's funny how everyone says "dipshit."

Daddy sits back and he takes a deep breath through his nose.

"Dipshit," Daddy says. "Well, that's quite impressive."

"Bud," Deb says. "You don't have to speak that way to her."

Daddy looks at Deb and his whisker jaw moves side to side the way he does when he's angry.

"Oh, really?" Daddy says. "And you have a better way?"

Daddy looks at Deb and Deb looks at Daddy and something is between them, something I don't understand. Deb clears her throat and tilts her head to the side.

"Why don't we talk about this later," Deb says, her voice high and sweet.

"Fine," Daddy says.

The air in the room is thick and heavy and when Deb finally starts up again, her voice is wrong. Deb talks high and loud, words about the family unit, the spirit of cooperation, effective communication, and then, just like that, Deb stands up, walks to the hall closet, and opens the door. It's like TV the way she waves her arm at a bunch of shoe boxes stacked inside the closet.

"So we are going to try something the whole unit can participate in," Deb says.

Deb moves her hand at Christopher and he folds over the corner of the page in his book, sets it on the arm of the chair, and starts handing out boxes to each of us, even Daddy. Inside my box is a pair of white shoes with a red stripe up the side and the laces hang from one hole. Inside the shoe is a wadded-up bunch of paper and I pull the paper out, squish it in my fist.

Bryan has a pair of blue shoes with a white stripe and he holds the shoe in his hand like it smells bad. That low red color is up his neck and he looks at Deb with his chin tucked down.

"Let me get this straight," Bryan says. "We are all going to run, like a sport?"

"Right," Deb says. "Isn't that great?"

Deb sits on the edge of the sofa and her shoulders are bunched up around her ears.

"You kids will really benefit from the discipline of being on a team," Deb says.

"What if I don't want to," Bryan says.

Deb slaps her legs with her hands.

"That's the spirit," Deb says.

Daddy puts his hand on Deb's arm and Deb looks at his hand.

"He should at least give it a try," Deb says.

"It's normal to be reluctant," Daddy says. "Give him a chance."

Deb pulls her arm away and the way she moves is big and dramatic.

"So that's the way it is," Deb says. "One way with your children, another way with my children?"

The room gets quiet, and they just look at each other. Daddy looks away first and then he nods at me and Bryan.

"We're done here," Daddy says.

Bryan picks up his box and stands up. I put my shoes into the shoebox with *Jenny* written on the outside.

"Hold on," Deb says. "You don't say when my family meeting is over."

"It's over," Daddy says.

Deb turns her head side to side, like an animal in a cage, and she makes a sound in the back of her throat like she can't believe what is going on.

I don't know what to do, stay or go, say something or stay quiet. Daddy nods again at me and Bryan and when Daddy

BLACKBIRD 243

nods like that, you get up and leave, that's just the way it is. Christopher, Kenny, and Ronny stay sitting and I can feel them watch us walk out of the living room.

I go down the long hall and put my hand on my doorknob. Bryan stops at his door and looks back to the living room and then he looks at me. I shrug and he shrugs and then I go into my room and close the door. I lean against the door and look at my foot, the shine of the key just under the laces, and I move my foot side to side. Outside my door, I hear voices, Deb's high, Daddy's low, and I hear Ronny yell something too.

Part of me wants to be out there and see what is going on, another part of me wants to stay where I am.

I push off the closed door and pick up my clothes and shoes off the floor. I fold my shirts up and make a pile, fold my pants up and make another pile.

It's quiet in the new house, no voices, and then I hear Deb yell again, but I can't hear what.

There is a door slam and it sounds like the door to the garage.

I pick up the piles of shirts and pants and put them on Deb's white dresser.

Red starts up and Deb yells how Daddy is a coward.

The sputter spit sound of Red moves out of the garage and the gears grind around. Whenever there is a fight, Daddy leaves, that's just the way it is. I hate how he leaves like that and for the first time, maybe the only time, I think I agree with Deb. Maybe Daddy is a coward.

Daddy says I should trust Deb.

Daddy says I should give Deb a chance.

Daddy says I'll really like Deb once I get to know her.

And I'm trying to like Deb, I really am.

From first thing in the morning to last thing at night, Deb tells me what to do and I do it. Deb says I should eat oatmeal instead of toast so I eat oatmeal even though I never want anything but toast for breakfast. Deb says I should brush my teeth in a circular pattern instead of side to side so I do it. Deb says I should keep my hair loose rather than put it into ponytails or barrettes so I keep my hair loose.

The thing about Deb is how her way is the only way and there is no me in anything I do. It's like I'm a visitor in my own life.

I don't even get to pick out my own clothes.

Deb threw away almost everything I used to wear and ordered new stuff out of the Sears catalogue. Now I have three skirts, three turtleneck shirts, and three pairs of leotards and they are in white, purple, and green. She picks out what I should wear and lays it on my bed and I can't believe how Deb's got me dressed in mix-and-match fashion.

One day Deb set out a pair of green tights, a green turtleneck, and a green skirt, said I looked just great. I told Deb no way I was wearing all the same color, but she didn't listen to me.

Kenny and Ronny and all the other kids in my new class called me the jolly green giant and none of the girls would even let me play hopscotch or jump rope during recess.

I don't care what Daddy says about Deb. She has no sense of style and there's no way she says what I wear after that, not ever again.

Mile Square Park is low hills, fresh-cut grass, and tall pine trees.

Christopher, Kenny, Ronny, Bryan, and me are Blue Angels now and Blue Angels practice every day in Mile Square Park.

"You have to run eight miles a day to run one good mile in a race," Coach Don says.

Coach Don has on a gray sweat suit, a dark blue baseball cap, and there's a whistle around his neck. He walks in a circle and looks at each kid straight on.

"Am I right?" Coach Don says and looks at me.

"Right," I say.

Coach Don drops his chin, walks five steps, and looks at a different kid.

"You have to practice hard to win races," Coach Don says. "Am I right?"

"Right," the kid says.

Coach Don stands with his feet wide and he hits his fist into his hand like making a point.

"You have to be tough, you have to be lean, you have to be mean," Coach Don says. "Am I right?"

Warm wind blows the smell of fresh-cut grass around and all of us have our eyes on Coach Don.

"Right," we say.

Deb stands with a bunch of other moms and waves her hands around in the air the way she does when she talks.

I wish Deb would just go home.

"We've got eight miles ahead of us, team," Coach Don says, "four long distance, four in wind sprints."

I stand up and cross my arms over my chest even though it's not cold.

"Do your best," Coach Don says, "and I'll meet you back here."

Coach Don puts his whistle into his mouth. I put my hands over my ears and close my eyes tight.

The whistle scream bleeds through to my ears and when I open my eyes, all the Blue Angels are running to the edge of the park.

Coach Don looks at me with his eyebrows up on his forehead like "What are you doing?"

"Sorry," I say.

I sprint as fast as I can, my chin all the way down to my chest and my arms close to my sides. I run until I am up with the other kids and then I slow down to a regular jog.

If you were a bird looking down, Mile Square Park would be a patch of green in the middle of black asphalt. Each side of the park is one mile long and there is a dirt path around the edge of the park where you're supposed to run.

At the first corner of Mile Square Park, my side cramps like a knife is pushed in under my ribs. I pinch at the pain, but the knife pushes deeper.

I slow down to a jog, but the pain stays.

I walk, and finally, the pain pulls out.

Up ahead, all the Blue Angels are far-off dots and I can't tell who is who.

One other kid walks up there, looks like a boy, looks like Bryan.

I jog again and the pain stays away.

I jog to the kid and it is Bryan. His chin is low to his chest and his hands pinch his sides.

"Hey," I yell.

Bryan looks over his shoulder and walks faster.

"It's me," I yell. "Hold up."

Bryan jogs faster and I try to catch him. Bryan runs faster, the space between us wider and wider.

The knife pushes into my side and the one thing I know

about the knife pain in your side, you can't run through it. You have to walk.

I'm the last one to finish the run around Mile Square Park, dead last.

Deb's cat eyes watch me come in last and I don't have to look at her to know she's mad. Deb says one of us is a reflection on all of us.

I jog past Deb, past the other mothers. I can hear them whisper and someone laughs. I jog to Coach Don and my face is hot.

"Tough going, huh?" Coach Don says.

"I ran out of air," I say.

"It happens," Coach Don says. "We'll work on your breathing technique, you'll beat this thing. Am I right?"

"Right," I say.

Coach Don pats his hand on my shoulder and it's nice how he treats you like he's your friend.

"All right, then," Coach Don says, "get in line and let's try some sprints."

Coach Don blows his whistle and a row of kids runs down one hill and up the other hill. When they stop, Coach Don blows his whistle again and the next row goes. It's row after row until the rows are done and then you do it all again. Wind sprints.

I get in line behind Bryan and he looks down at me, blinks, and looks away like I'm not there.

Bryan is different since Deb. He tries to be like she is, like her kids are, and he does a good job fitting in, except when you look in his eyes, really look, you can tell something inside is flat. It's like Bryan stomped himself flat.

"Hey," I say, "didn't you hear me?"

Bryan turns away and his face is red, except I can't tell if it's from running or from being mad.

"I saw you," I say. "I was trying to catch up."

Bryan looks right at me then, his chin low and his eyes in the shadows under his eyebrows. I step away from Bryan and put my hands behind my back.

"I don't care if you walk," I say. "I walk. Running is hard. Even Coach Don said it's hard."

"Why don't you just go away," Bryan says, his voice low and deep.

"You don't have to be mad," I say. "I didn't do anything."

Bryan turns his back on me and he stands with his hands on his sides.

"I'm just trying to be nice," I say.

Bryan turns halfway, looks at me and then past me, and I hate that look since it makes me feel like I'm nothing.

Coach Don blows his whistle and the scream of it is in my head, in my bones. Bryan runs down the hill and his arms pump hard, he runs up to the other side, and when he stops, he has to bend over to catch his breath.

When practice is over, the Blue Angels meet in the middle of the park one more time. Coach Don talks about how it was a good day and how everyone gave one hundred percent.

I lie on the grass and stretch my legs.

Deb stands by the car and holds a brown paper bag. I know there are five apples in that bag and I know she will give each of us an apple for the drive home. I know Deb will talk the whole way home and she'll say how Ronny is just a natural athlete, how Kenny runs like a gazelle, and how Christopher is the very essence of a runner. Then Deb will say how I am a lazy runner since I came in last and she will say Bryan is a lazy runner too since he came in close to last. Deb will talk about how one of us is a reflection on all of us and how a chain is only as strong as its weakest link and how you must work harder when you lack natural ability.

It's hard to like Deb when she talks like that and I wish I could ask Daddy what to do. The thing is, I don't see Daddy much anymore. He has his own business and he says you have to work days and nights when you have your own business. Daddy says Deb is in charge anyway and what Deb says goes.

The wind blows through Mile Square Park and I'm cold all the way through. I look at my foot and the silver of the key shines up at me. I move my foot back and forth, make the silver shine move around my face.

"The Blue Angels are number one," Coach Don says. "Am I right?"

Everyone yells, "Right," and the sound of our voices lifts into the wind and disappears.

Deb cuts up carrots, broccoli, potatoes, every kind of vegetable. Christopher boils water in a big silver pan. My job is to slice the bread, put margarine between the slices, and warm it up in the oven. It's either Kenny or Ronny's turn to set the table, I can't keep them straight, and anyway, they're just sitting on the floor. Ronny has her legs out and she pushes herself into the splits.

"Am I almost touching?" Ronny says.

"Almost," Kenny says.

"Well, push me down," Ronny says.

Kenny gets up on her knees, her hands on Ronny's shoulders.

Deb holds the knife in the air, the silver blade over the cutting board.

"Don't push her, Kendall, that could damage her legs," Deb says.

Kenny shrugs her shoulders and takes her hands off Ronny. Ronny tries to push herself down one more time, her breath held in and her freckled face all red.

"Jenny," Deb says, "wash your hands before you touch any food."

Deb shakes her knife at me and I push up my shirtsleeves, wash my hands in the sink.

Ronny sits up and pulls her legs in to her chest. "I'm going to do it," Ronny says, "I am going to make myself do the splits."

"Let me try," Kenny says.

"You guys are runners," Christopher says, "you don't have to do the splits."

Kenny pushes her legs out, balances her hands on the floor, and tries to make a split.

"Am I close?" Kenny says.

"Coach Don says it's important to be flexible," Ronny says.

"Coach Don is right," Deb says.

Deb puts her vegetables into a bowl and slides the cutting board and knife over to me. I take the bread out of the paper and it's one of those long loaves you can cut any way you want. I put the bread on the cutting board.

"Don't use that cutting board until you wipe it off first," Deb says. "My god, where did you learn to cook?"

It's quiet in the kitchen, the kind of quiet where everyone looks at you and you wish something would happen so it wasn't quiet anymore.

I roll my lips together, bite hard on the insides. I wipe off the cutting board with a wash rag, dry the cutting board with a paper towel.

Christopher opens a bag of pasta noodles, dumps them into the boiling water, and steam lifts into his face.

Deb washes her hands in the sink and I can feel her eyes on me, on the knife in my hand, on the bread on the cutting board.

"Those slices are too big," Deb says.

I look at the bread, look at Deb, look at the bread again.

"Well, don't stop," Deb says, "just do it right."

Deb turns off the water and dries her hands on a dish-towel.

"How big do you want them?" I say.

Deb looks at the ceiling. I look at the ceiling too.

"Christopher," Deb says, "you just do it."

Christopher's face is red and steamy, the blond curls damp on his forehead, and he rolls his dark eyes at Deb. He reaches to take the knife out of my hand but I step back so he can't reach.

"I can do it," I say, "just tell me."

"Forget it," Deb says, "Christopher will do it."

Deb takes a pan out of the cupboard and puts it on the stove, pours oil into the pan like I'm not here at all.

"Look," Kenny says from the floor again, "am I close?"

"Pretty close," Deb says.

Christopher looks at me and I look at Christopher and I don't know what to do. Christopher is different than Deb and the twins. Bryan says he's a momma's boy but I don't think that's true. There's just something quiet and thoughtful about him like he's here but not here at the same time. I like that about Christopher.

He puts his hand out again and I give him the knife, han-dle first.

"Why don't you set the table," he whispers.

"It's Kenny or Ronny's turn," I say.

Kenny gives up on her splits.

"No it's not," Kenny says.

"No it's not," Ronny says.

I stand up, shoulders straight, and I look right at the twins.

"Yes, it is," I say.

Deb turns the dial on the stove, rubs her hands over her skinny hips, and stands with her whole body to me, her eyes on my face.

"Your attitude is unacceptable," Deb says.

"My attitude?" I say.

"I am going to speak to your father about this lack of cooperation," Deb says, "this whole entitlement thing you have going is a little old."

"Entitlement?" I say.

Kenny and Ronny sit exactly the same way, their knees to their chests, arms around, and Ronny has a look on her face like she is going to start laughing.

Christopher takes a deep breath and takes margarine out of the refrigerator, spreads it on the bread. Deb stands in her mannequin pose, one foot forward, one foot back, fingers wide on her hips. She looks at me like it's my turn to say or do something and she's waiting.

"Fine," I say, "I'll set the table."

Deb pulls her head back.

"No," Deb says, "go to your room and think about cooperation."

"But . . . ," I say.

"Now," Deb says.

Deb never talks to her kids the way she talks to me, never sends them to their room, never tells them they don't do things right. It's them and it's me, them on the inside, me on the outside, and it doesn't matter how hard I try, that's just the way it is.

I go down the hall and open the door to my room. Deb, Christopher, Kenny, and Ronny are talking again, their voices mixed together. Down the hall the door to Bryan's room is closed, the muffled sound of music behind, and I know he's in there just like always.

I stand in my room with the door halfway open, halfway closed. I look at the door for a long time, just look, and then I slam it closed so hard it hurts my hand and my arm.

It's dead quiet and I stand still, the slam from the door up my arm and into my body.

"You just bought yourself a night without dinner," Deb yells.

Deb's voice is under my skin and up the back of my neck, Deb's voice like fingernails on a chalkboard.

I hold my hand to the door, middle finger up.

Fuck you, Deb.

Missing a dinner that Deb cooks isn't missing much since she only makes health food. There's no white sugar, just honey. No white bread, just wheat bread. No cheese, no salt, no butter.

I kick my shoes off and sit down on the floor. I unlace the silver key and throw my shoe against the closet door.

Inside my pink trunk is the Barbie suitcase, the painting by Keith, and a bunch of books. I dig down the pile of books and pull out *Snow White and the Seven Dwarfs* with its black cover and copper writing.

I look at the door to my room, me in, them out.

I lean against the cool of my pink trunk, a deep breath in and out again, and I open the book and look at the drawings the way I used to before I could read.

The first drawing is of the queen by her window, the second drawing is of Snow White barefooted in the forest, the third drawing is of Snow White cooking and cleaning for the dwarfs.

The fourth drawing is of the kingdom at sunset, mist over the forests, over the fields, over the castles. A white path cuts from the forest to the kingdom and disappears into the horizon. In the corner is another drawing and Snow White is on the ground like she's dead and a woman wearing a black dress runs away.

Snow White hides out in the dwarfs' house, safe but not really safe, and then the mirror tells the evil stepmother that Snow White is really alive and really the most beautiful. The evil stepmother just can't stand it, can't let Snow White be who she is, can't let her live in peace. No, the evil stepmother tries to kill Snow White by pretending to be a nice peasant lady who then laces up Snow White's dress so tight, she passes out like she's dead. The drawing tells the whole story, the kingdom at dusk, the stepmother disguised as a nice peasant lady, Snow White passed out on the ground outside the little house.

You're never safe, not when you have something someone else wants, even if that thing isn't really a thing but is just you inside, who you are.

Snow White and the Seven Dwarfs isn't a fairy tale, it's a true story, and I bet whoever wrote it had an evil stepmother.

My stomach is hungry, empty sounds from deep inside, dinner sounds and smells coming through the door. I close the book and hold it between my hands, the idea of the story around in my head.

My apple from after running is on the dresser and the red apple skin shines. Off the floor, I take the apple in my hand, bounce it up and down, the weight of it in my fingers.

I look at the closed door again, me inside, them outside.

Across my room is a metal trash can and it's painted white and gold. I walk across, hold the apple over the trash can, and open my fingers. Deb's red apple falls, the weight of it a loud thud in the can.

❧

The Blue Angels is one team in a league with a bunch of other teams.

Every Saturday is a race between the Blue Angels and all the other teams.

Weekend races lead up to Divisionals. Divisionals lead up to Nationals. If you run in the Nationals, it means you might be someone they pick for the Olympic team.

I don't care about being a great runner. I don't care about the Saturday races or the Divisionals or Nationals or the Olympics. I run because Daddy says I should. I run so he can see how hard I'm trying to get along with Deb, how hard I'm trying to fit in.

This Saturday morning, Daddy has already gone to work when I get out of bed.

I'm all alone in my room and I put on the Blue Angels uniform and brush my hair into two ponytails.

The Blue Angels uniform is blue short shorts and a blue tank top with a white and pink diagonal stripe over the middle of my chest. The stripe is like a Miss America banner and I always put pink ribbons on my ponytails so I match with the pink and white stripe. Deb says it's not a beauty contest, says I should worry more about running than my hair, but I just ignore Deb since she has no sense of style.

Christopher, Kenny, Ronny, Bryan, and me are in our Blue Angels uniforms and Deb drives us to Long Beach. The radio is on and Sly and the Family Stone sing "It's a Family Affair."

Bryan looks out his window and I bite the fingernail on my thumb until there isn't any fingernail left. Deb talks the whole way, just like she always does. Her talk is for *her* kids, telling them how great they are, how well they are going to do today, how proud she is.

Deb turns into the parking lot and stops the big brown car. Across the lot, Daddy leans against Red and he has his arms crossed like he's been waiting for a long time. Deb honks her horn and waves.

Bryan opens his door and I climb over his legs.

"Hey," Bryan says.

"Get out of the way," I say.

"Settle down," Deb says.

"Daddy," I yell.

Daddy's whisker face has a smile and I run across the parking lot. Daddy bends down, puts his arms around my back, and I wish he would pick me up the way he used to. I put my arms around his neck and he smells like cigarettes even though he was supposed to stop smoking since Deb says it's bad for him. Daddy hugs me once, just once, and he lets go before I let go. Daddy stands up, flicks one of my ponytails.

"Great ponytails," he says.

"I did them myself," I say.

"Nice," Daddy says.

"Deb says it's not a beauty contest," I say, "but I think you need ponytails when you run."

"You bet you need ponytails," Daddy says, "keeps your hair out of your face."

"I know," I say. "And besides, you can see the Miss America stripe on my uniform better too."

Deb flips her hair over her shoulder and locks her car door. Daddy's face is off me, his eyes across the parking lot, and I know he doesn't listen anymore. I put my hand on his belt, hold on.

"Are you staying for the whole day?" I say.

Daddy walks to Deb and I walk with him.

"Are you coming home after?" I say.

Deb puts her hands on Daddy's face, kisses him on the mouth, and I pull his back pocket.

"I was wondering where you were," Daddy says.

"We got a late start," Deb says.

"Daddy?" I say. "Are you coming home after?"

Daddy looks at me and Deb looks at me. Deb takes a deep breath, crosses her arms, and puts her cat eyes on the sky. I look up too, but it's nothing but clouds up there.

"What, Juniper?" Daddy says.

"Tonight?" I say. "Do you have to work tonight?"

"I do have to work," Daddy says.

"Come on, Jenny," Deb says, "everyone else is already down with Coach Don, it's time to start thinking about your race."

Deb reaches to me and I pull back, move behind Daddy, his body between us.

"See what I'm dealing with here," Deb says.

Daddy laughs and he takes a hold of my arm, pulls me around so I am between him and Deb.

"Jenny," Daddy says, "go with Deb."

"I want to stay with you," I say.

Deb crosses her arms over her chest.

"You have a race to think about, go get stretched out," Daddy says. "I'll be down in just a minute."

Deb looks at me and I look at Deb and I wish I could kick her in the leg with my foot, kick her hard.

"Okay," I say, "but I can go myself."

Daddy lets go of my arm and he smiles like everything is good again.

"That's a big girl," Daddy says.

Deb stands in her mannequin pose, face pinched up at the lips the way she does when she's mad. I walk to the other Blue Angels, but I can feel her watch me. As soon as I get far enough away, I bet Deb is going to tell Daddy how I'm not cooperative, how I'm disruptive, how something should be done.

I hate Deb.

Race day is hundreds of kids and that many parents, coaches with stopwatches and whistles, parents with stopwatches and whistles, officials with stopwatches and whistles. I hate all those whistles.

Kenny, Ronny, and me run in the nine-year-old and under group. We're called nine-and-unders and our race is one mile. Christopher and Bryan run in other classes, run other distances. All day long it's different classes running until all the kids are done and medals are passed out. You always get a medal, even if you come in last place. First, second, and third place get a medal and a trophy.

Ronny says medals are for losers and trophies are for winners.

I have a bunch of medals, no trophies.

Both Kenny and Ronny have a bunch of medals and a bunch of trophies, except Ronny has the most.

Kenny, Ronny, and me are on the start line with all the other nine-and-unders. Coach Don is there too and he makes it a point to give every Blue Angel what he calls a pep talk.

"All the hard work pays off right here," Coach Don says to me. "Am I right?"

"Right," I say.

"All you can do is go out there and do your best," Coach Don says. "Am I right?"

"Right," I say.

Coach Don pats me on the back.

"Stretch out good," Coach Don says, "and keep your sweats on until the two-minute warning."

"Okay," I say.

Coach Don pats me again, his hand squeezed on my shoulder, and he walks down the line, stops to pep-talk Kenny and Ronny.

Long Beach is cloudy sky, wet sand, and a fast wind that blows salt sting up your nose. The ocean is loud, sounds like traffic on the freeway, and the waves are white foam that crash down and pull back.

I stand up tall, look over the heads of all the kids, look for Daddy in the crowd of coaches and parents and runners. Deb is down on the sideline, Christopher right next to where she stands. Daddy is still up in the parking lot with Bryan, has his arm around Bryan's shoulder, and I wonder what Daddy says.

I bend over, stretch my legs the way you are supposed to, try to think about the race. Part of me hopes Daddy will miss my race since I know I'm not going to win anyway. Ronny is the fastest and she always wins, and Kenny always comes in right behind her.

"Two minutes," yells an official.

Daddy talks to Bryan and I take off my sweat pants, my sweat top. I hold them in my arms, my legs bare, my arms bare, and it's cold wind on my skin. Deb comes down to the start line, takes my sweats out of my hand.

"Are you ready?" Deb says.

"I guess," I say.

Deb flips her hair back, eyebrows up like that's not good enough, and I bite my lip between my teeth. Deb takes Kenny's and Ronny's sweats and hugs them both in one big hug.

My stomach waves the way it always does before a race and I hug my arms over my stomach. Coach Don says it's butter-flies, says it's normal, but the wave in my stomach is more like I might throw up.

"One minute," the official yells.

Daddy and Bryan are gone from the parking lot and I look around the faces, my eyes fast over strangers. Daddy is at the sideline and he has his arm around Deb's shoulder, his hand all tangled up in her long hair. Next to each other, Daddy is tall and Deb is short. Daddy starts to wave his arm, but Deb says something in his ear and he drops his arm and listens to her.

"On your mark," the official yells.

The official has a gun and he points it up in the air. I look down the beach, my hands on my knees, my eyes on the wet sand.

"Get set," the official yells.

I look down the line of kids, look at Daddy and Deb, and she is kissing him. I look down the beach again and take a deep breath in my nose.

The start gun pops, and just like that, everyone runs as fast as they can. I run too and the only thing is my arms and legs and the air in and out of my body.

I'm just a couple kids back from Kenny and Ronny and wind blows salt and sting into my eyes. Ronny runs around the flag, then Kenny is around. Two other kids run around the flag, and then me.

Coach Don says you should breathe in and out through your nose, says you should time your breath to a three count with your feet. I breathe one, two, three and pump my arms. A girl passes me and then another and I put my head down low and pump my arms hard.

In my ears is the far-off sound of people who yell and clap and when I look up, the crowd of coaches and parents wave their arms. Ronny is way out in front and she crosses the finish line first. After Ronny, Kenny crosses the line.

I put my head down, pump my arms, run as hard as I can, and when I cross the line, Deb is already down there hugging and kissing the twins.

The best part of running is stopping and I put my hands on my sides, mouth open to the sky like air will just fall into my body.

"Good work," Daddy says, "nice job."

Daddy's hand on my shoulder is too much weight and I bend at the waist, hands on my knees.

"I think that was your best race yet," Daddy says, "you really came on at the end."

The rest of the runners come across the finish line, one after the other, and one girl throws up right there in the sand. Her father picks her up and carries her away from the beach.

Ronny gets the first-place trophy, Kenny gets the second place, and they both walk around holding them in front of their bodies so everyone can see.

My medal for the race is a bronze oval attached to a red and white ribbon. The front of the medal is stamped with AAU for Amateur Athletic Union and on the back it's engraved with "sixth place, Nine and Under Division." There is a pin stuck to the ribbon so you can put the medal on your jacket, like they pin medals to military uniforms.

"Pretty great," Daddy says. "Sixth place."

I hold the medal up between us and Daddy lifts it out of my hand and juggles the weight of it in his palm.

"You can keep it at your office," I say, "you know, to remember me when you're working."

Daddy closes his hand over the medal.

"I always remember you, Juniper," he says.

I look at him then, really look. My eyes are straight on his eyes and there's a quiet between us. Daddy tilts his head like he's thinking and then he nods. He slips the medal into his pocket and puts his hand on my shoulder.

"Thanks," Daddy says.

"Sure," I say.

❧

It's Deb who tells me about the business trip to Catalina Island. It's Deb who says how Daddy wants me, just me out of all the kids, to go with him.

"Me?" I say.

I sit on the front step of the Fountain Valley house, the late afternoon sun hot on my legs and my arms. Deb stands on the sidewalk and her shadow is long and skinny.

"Apparently," Deb says.

"Why didn't he ask me himself?" I say.

Deb shifts her weight and looks up at the sky.

"He's busy working," Deb says.

"Why didn't he ask Bryan?" I say.

"He asked me to ask you," Deb says. "Why do you have to ask so many questions?"

"I'm not asking so many questions," I say, "I just want to understand. That's all."

Deb puts her hands out, shoulders shrugged up to her ears.

"So, do you want to go or not?" Deb says.

"Let me get this straight," I say, "he's going on a sailing trip with a client and he wants me to go?"

"Very good, Jenny," Deb says.

Deb's voice isn't a nice voice and I know she thinks I'm stupid.

"It's not that big of a deal," Deb says. "If you don't want to go, he'll take one of the other kids."

The sun is low behind Deb's head, the color of her hair a deep brown red, and when I look at her face, I have to put my hand up to shade my eyes.

"Why don't you go?" I say.

Deb doesn't say anything, just pushes her lips together in a thin line, and I know she's not going to say anything else. There's only so much of Daddy to go around and I know she wants more of him too.

"So?" Deb says. "Do you want to go or not?"

The way Deb looks at me, I know I have to decide right now. I don't like sailing and I absolutely don't like the ocean. Daddy knows it too. But he asked for me special, and it doesn't seem right to say no since who knows if he'll ever ask me again.

I look at Deb, my hand up to shade my eyes.

"I'll go," I say.

The day of the sailing trip, it's so cloudy it looks like rain. Daddy says it might be rough sailing and my stomach waves around at the idea of being on rough ocean water. Daddy says I should bring a waterproof coat and I get a yellow raincoat out of the closet. We leave before anyone else is awake and the house is full of sleep.

In Red, Daddy is quiet and I'm quiet too. All I want is to be alone with Daddy like this, but now that I am, everything between us is different, like we don't know each other or something. He even looks different, more lines around his eyes, tired lines or maybe wrinkles.

Daddy looks at me looking at him and smiles.

"What?" Daddy says.

"Nothing," I say.

"Are you excited?" he says.

"Excited?" I say.

"For the trip?" Daddy says. "To go on a big sailboat, to see Catalina?"

"Sure," I say.

Daddy looks out the windshield, eyes on the road, and he pulls onto the freeway. It's quiet in Red again, just the sound of the engine, and Daddy reaches and pats on my leg.

"I'm glad you wanted to come with me," he says.

"You are?" I say.

"You bet," Daddy says, "seems like I never see you any-more."

I roll my lips together and my throat is tight. I want to say how I don't ever see him anymore, but I can't say anything, just stay quiet and look out the window. Daddy takes his hand away from my leg and clears his throat.

"This guy is a pretty important client," Daddy says, "so I'll have to talk a lot of business."

Daddy's face is serious the way he gets when he talks about money and business.

"What I'm trying to say," Daddy says, "is that I need you to be on your best behavior while we're on the boat."

Daddy looks at me and looks out at the road again.

"Can you do that?" Daddy says.

I am almost nine years old and Daddy still talks to me like I'm a baby. I sit up straight, shoulders back, chin level.

"Of course I can do that," I say.

Daddy looks at me again and smiles.

"That's my girl," Daddy says.

It's quiet at the marina, sailboats docked and tied. The sky is gray clouds and the air is salty cool.

The important client is just like any other man and he looks at me the way grown-ups look at kids, like you're not really there at all. Daddy introduces me and the important client nods. Daddy and the important client walk ahead of me, talk grown-up talk about boats and sailing and the weather.

The important client's boat is a great big fancy sailboat with lots of masts sticking up and pretty red wood around the cabin area.

"Wow," Daddy says. "What a boat."

"Pretty nice, huh?" the important client says.

"She's gorgeous," Daddy says and his voice is different.

Daddy has that look of someone who wants what he can't have and it's a wide open raw look I never saw on his face before.

"Let's take her out," the important client says.

I put my hand into his hand, my fingers against his fingers, and Daddy looks down at me like he's surprised I'm there at all. He smiles then and takes my hand, helps me get on the big fancy sailboat.

The sailboat is so big you can be on one end and someone else can be on the other end and you could never see the other person. In the middle of the boat is a cabin area and there's a kitchen with a table and benches for sitting. The important client says I can have a soda out of the refrigerator if I want, and I go to the kitchen. Inside the refrigerator are beers and bottles of champagne and fancy cheeses wrapped in colored paper. There are sodas in the door and I take one out.

I can hear the important client talk about how expensive his boat was, how he sails all over the place, how he's going to get a better boat next year. Daddy nods like he listens, but his eyes are far away on the ocean. Wind blows his brown hair back from his face and there's something different about him, something sad and quiet, like he is here but he isn't here at the same time.

I walk to the front of the boat again, sit down on the cushion, and look out at the ocean the way Daddy does. The sailboat moves fast over the water, and I can feel it lift and roll, lift and roll.

Overhead, the heavy clouds split and it's sunshine on the water. Daddy looks down at me and he has a look on his face like he found something he lost a long time ago.

I smile back at him and Daddy looks over the water again.

Momma says when something picks you, that's just the way it is, and the way Daddy looks, I know this is his something. Wind, water, speed, and danger. Being on the boat is like being powerful even though you're really not.

Daddy points his hand into the wind, one finger out, and I look in that direction. Out in the middle of the ocean water is a lump of land that's green and brown and far away.

"Can you see it?" Daddy says. "Can you see the island?"

I nod yes and Daddy drops his arm, his hand on the rail of the boat again.

*

Daddy and me are in an airplane and he lets me sit next to the window so I can see the ocean we just sailed over. Daddy says the important client has more sailing to do and that's why we fly back to Los Angeles. Through the window is choppy ocean water, rain clouds, and Catalina Island. The plane lifts up and up and then the clouds are under us and out the window is blue sky and bright sunshine.

We hold hands, my fingers in his fingers, and his hand is warm and strong and perfect. Daddy's face is close to my face and he looks out the window, his brown cinnamon spice eyes on what's out there. He smells like wind and salt and I squeeze my fingers in his fingers, where I begin and he ends the same place.

I love Daddy right now more than I ever loved him before, and the in-love feeling is good and bad and makes my head all spinny. I wonder if the in-love feeling is what it's like when you meet the man you're going to marry. I wonder if that's how Deb is about Daddy, how Momma was.

Daddy sits back in his seat, his hand still in my hand, and rests his head against the back of his seat.

"What a day," Daddy says, "what an adventure."

He rolls his head on the seatrest and looks at me, his cinnamon spice eyes.

"Jenny?" Daddy says. "Did you have fun?"

I roll my lips together and look at our hands together. The in-love feeling makes my chest hurt and I can't make words. I nod my head yes and look out the airplane window, look at the sunshine and the clouds and the forever-blue sky.

twelve

The day I turn nine years old, Daddy wakes me up by whispering happy birthday in my ear over and over. It's the best thing to get woken up that way, Daddy close and his voice in my ear.

I rub my eyes and sit up in bed. Daddy sits back and his weight makes my bed dip down. His cinnamon brown eyes hold all the stories about me since the day I was born and he smiles like remembering.

"Nine years old," Daddy says, "nine years old!"

"Nine!" I say.

Daddy laughs and shakes his head.

"I just can't believe it," Daddy says.

Outside my room are kitchen sounds and I know Deb's making breakfast.

"Well," Daddy says, "do you have anything special you want this year?"

"Anything?" I say.

"Anything," Daddy says. "Within reason."

I touch my fingers on Daddy's whiskers and they feel springy, like little wires.

"Shave," I whisper.

Daddy blinks and blinks and his smile is gone from his face.

"Shave?" Daddy says.

"You said anything," I say.

"That's true," Daddy says, "but I thought you'd ask for a toy or a book or something like that."

I want to tell Daddy that toys and books are just things and I don't care about money or things or anything like that. I bite my bottom lip between my teeth.

Daddy tilts his head and looks at me for a long time and then he rubs his hand over his whiskers.

"The mustache too?" Daddy says.

"Maybe not the mustache," I say.

Daddy laughs a deep laugh, his head back, bump on his throat up and down. He says he has to go to work, but he'll think about it and get back to me.

When it's your birthday, everyone is supposed to be extra nice and you get to open presents and later you go to Disneyland. This year it's just like any other day except Deb and Christopher say happy birthday at breakfast. Bryan actually forgets and Kenny and Ronny just ignore me like I'm not even here.

Daddy and me can't go to Disneyland, Daddy says he's too busy to get away, there aren't any presents anywhere, and I guess I wasted my one birthday wish on asking Daddy to shave. I bet my whole birthday is going to be like a normal day where you eat Deb's oatmeal, get dressed in mix-and-match, and go to school.

Maybe that's just the way it is when you get older. Maybe that's the way it is when your father works day and night and wants to be a millionaire by the time he's forty. Maybe that's just the way things are now and there isn't a reason, it just is.

By the time I come home from school, I'm the kind of mad where you keep your head down and hold your breath and walk loud, heavy steps.

I stomp, stomp up the sidewalk. Stomp, stomp up the driveway, and I almost fall on top of Red parked in the driveway. Daddy never comes home in the middle of the day, not ever, and I kick my foot hard against the black tire.

Inside the house, it's quiet, too quiet, empty-house feeling all around.

I slam the door and hold extra still, but no one says anything.

When you are this mad, it's best to get to your room and shut the door. I go through the living room and down the hall. The door to my room is pulled shut and I turn the knob and push the door open.

Inside isn't my room at all.

Inside is someone else's room, white and gold furniture, pink curtains, pink bedspread on a canopy bed, with more pink fabric draped over. There's a dresser with a mirror, there's a desk with its own chair, there's two bookcases with my books already stacked in.

I walk into my room, not my room, and I stand there with a wide-open feeling like air blows right through my stomach. All the mad inside me is gone and there's a hot shame instead.

"Happy birthday, Juniper," Daddy says.

Daddy stands in the doorway and his face is the way it was, no whiskers, not even a mustache.

I look at Daddy, at his face, and I don't know what to say, what to do.

Daddy puts his arms wide.

"Surprise," he says. "What do you think?"

How do you tell someone thank you, how can you say you thought they forgot you and there was a hole of loneliness down to your toes all day, how do you say you're sorry for crying when you don't want to cry but it's all you can do, what can you say with the best gift in the world and the best father too.

I wipe my face, and Daddy laughs, says I'm a softy, and then he gives me his handkerchief and hugs me close.

Daddy shows me everything in my new room, the canopy over the canopy bed, the three different shades of pink in the bedspread, how there are six drawers in the dresser and four in the desk, and how there's gold fabric on the chair that goes with the desk.

Daddy says he picked the whole set out himself, with a little help from Deb, and he put the whole thing together too. He says he's sorry about missing Disneyland, says he's sorry I didn't like his beard, says it's high time I had a bedroom nice enough for a princess since that's what I am, his special princess.

Daddy talks, his voice deep and warm through my whole body. I look at him without whiskers and he's like before, boy-next-door drop-dead handsome, like he knows me and I know him and the all-alone feeling is gone.

Daddy looks at me looking at him and he tilts his head to the side.

"What are you looking at?" he says.

"Nothing," I say.

"Are you happy?" Daddy says.

"I am," I say, "I really am."

Christmas, New Year, tax time. Easter, spring break, and then the last day of school. Daddy, Deb, Christopher,

Kenny, Ronny, Bryan, and me, we are more like a family now even if the wrong thing on the inside still lurks around in the shadows. The wrong thing on the inside mostly comes out when there's a fight, and there are lots of fights in our family.

Daddy and Deb fight about money, how she spends it faster than he can make it.

Bryan, Kenny, and Ronny fight over the bathroom and what shows to watch on television.

Christopher is the only one who doesn't fight at all—just stays in his room and reads, sits around the house and reads, goes outside and reads some more. I like that about Christopher, how he is in his own world of words.

I read a lot too. *Mary Poppins, Oz*, all the books by Laura Ingalls Wilder. For Christmas, I got a tape player and the tape from *West Side Story* and I can sit in my princess room all day, listen to *West Side Story* music and read *Little House on the Prairie*.

Deb says I'm antisocial, but I don't care what Deb says, I just close my door, push the play button on my cassette player, and just like that, there's no Deb.

Then, everything changes the day Daddy comes home from work and says we are going to move into a new house.

That same day, Daddy, Bryan, and me drive over to see the new house.

Deb and her kids follow in the big brown car. Daddy says it's better that way since Deb can explain in her own way.

Daddy says the new house is right on a marina where, one day, he's going to have his own sailboat right across the street just like he always dreamed.

"Cool," Bryan says.

Daddy turns Red into a neighborhood of wide streets and

big houses. Daddy moves his face close to the windshield, reads the names of the streets out loud.

"We're looking for Marina," Daddy says, "Marina Drive."

Daddy drives slow, turns right, right again.

"There," Bryan says, "Marina."

"Good eye," Daddy says.

Daddy makes a right turn and there is the edge of the water, sailboats parked across the street, houses on the other side.

"Far out," Bryan says.

"There it is," Daddy says, points to the house with the real estate sign stuck in the grass. The house is one of those non-colors, like brown mixed with a lot of white, light beige or tan. It's got lots of big windows and a perfect green lawn that runs absolutely flat all the way to the curb.

Daddy pulls into the driveway and turns off the car.

"Wow," Bryan says, "it's really big."

Daddy nods, looks at Bryan, and looks at the house again.

"Yes, sir," Daddy says, "it makes a statement."

"Statement?" I say.

Daddy takes his glasses off and rubs that place where they sit on his nose.

"Status," Daddy says, "says we're moving up in the world."

Daddy cleans his glasses with his sweater, puts them on again.

"Who would have thought," Daddy says, "me in a house like this before I'm forty."

It's quiet in the car and Daddy takes another deep breath. He claps his hands and opens his door.

"Well, let's take a look," Daddy says.

The air is moist and it smells like the ocean. Daddy, Bryan, and me walk over the grass, around the side of the house, and around the back. Daddy has his hands in his pockets, jiggles his change and keys together, says how the real estate market is sluggish and how he's going to get in on the ground floor. Daddy talks about rent-to-own programs and VA mortgages and I don't understand a thing he says.

It's quiet around here, no kids, no grown-ups, no dogs, no cars. All the houses are the same, big with lots of windows, mowed lawns, flowers and bushes in everyone's yard.

I sit down on the front step, my butt on the cool cement, and you can see everything from here, the boats, the other houses, Marina Drive all the way until it runs into some other street. I like the front step, like how it feels so quiet and calm here.

It's nothing like the house on Mary Street, no willow trees, no white fence around the grass, no forever-blue sky over-head and Sierra Nevada Mountains with white runs of snow. It's not like home, but it's pretty nice, almost like it would be to live in one of those fancy magazines Deb likes to read, like living in *Architectural Digest*.

Daddy and Bryan are along the side of the house, their voices in the middle of the calm. Daddy says it's a lot of money, maybe more than he can afford, but what the hell, he'll just work harder.

thirteen

Before Deb, we were Catholics, but the only thing we did when we were Catholics was say prayers before dinner and bed.

Daddy says the Catholics are fine for people who want to follow a bunch of confusing rituals, but he likes the Freedom Community Church better since it's more about how you make your life better by the way you think about things.

Before you can be a full member of the Freedom Community Church, you have to take a test and it has to be given to you by a Freedom Community Church leader, who comes to your house. That's just the way it is.

My test is in the end of November and Deb says if I pass, I can be in the church in 1973. Christopher, Kenny, and Ronny are full members and Bryan just passed his test too. I could care less about being in the church, but Deb is all worked up about it, like my examination is her examination. She has on a pair of brown slacks, a tan sweater pulled low around her thin hips and there's even makeup on her face. Deb's face with makeup is all wrong, makes her look like a clown.

I have on my school clothes, a purple and green sweater, a matching purple skirt, and white tights. Deb got me a new pair of shoes, black Mary Jane shoes without any laces. I have the silver key to my pink trunk inside the shoe and I move my foot around, the key under my heel.

"Quit fidgeting," Deb says, "settle down."

She flips her hair over her shoulder, walks down the hall, and her heels click on the tiles around the front door. She opens the door, looks out, closes the door again.

"Just sit there and contemplate," Deb says.

"I'm tired of contemplating," I say.

The house on Marina Drive is white walls, high ceilings, and big windows that overlook the marina. Deb has it all decorated in leather couches, glass tables, and lamps made out of silver metal, and it's more like something to look at than to live in.

The doorbell rings like a bunch of bells, each one ringing one at a time. Deb clicks down the hall and waves her hands in the air.

"Sit up," Deb says. "No, stand up. No, come over here."

On the sofa, off the sofa, I walk a couple steps and Deb puts her hand up.

"Right there," Deb says, "just stay right there."

Deb takes a deep breath and turns the knob when the last bell is done ringing.

"Mr. Gray? Welcome," Deb says, "ha ha ha, please come in, ha ha ha."

The church guy has a briefcase and wears a dark suit. Deb closes the door and puts her hands wide.

"Can I take your coat?" Deb says.

The church guy shakes his head. Deb drops her hands and presses them over her stomach, holds herself together.

"Is everything ready?" Mr. Gray says.

"Of course," Deb says, "Jenny is right here. Say hello to Mr. Gray."

"Hello, Mr. Gray," I say.

"Hello," Mr. Gray says.

It's quiet in the house, quiet all around, and Mr. Gray clears his throat.

"Yes, well," Deb says, "all right then. I have a special area ready."

Deb, Mr. Gray, and me go up the stairs to Daddy and Deb's bedroom and I've never been in here before. Against one wall is a big modern bed in a frame built low to the ground, side tables built in on both ends of the bed frame. Across from the bed is a tall window with a view of the marina, the masts of sailboats up and down on the water. Between the bed and the window is a desk with a glass top. Two black chairs sit in front of the desk. Daddy's chair is behind the desk.

Deb stays at the door and Mr. Gray lays his briefcase on the desk and snaps it open.

"Can I bring you anything," Deb says, "coffee, tea, water?"

Mr. Gray shakes his head and sets out blank papers, a pencil, a pen, a clipboard, and a little square clock. Mr. Gray looks up at Deb like he is surprised she's still there.

"Please make sure we are not disturbed," Mr. Gray says.

"Of course," Deb says.

She backs out of the room and her face is red like she's embarrassed. The door closes without any sound, just a little click, and Deb is gone. Mr. Gray nods at me and I sit down in one of the black chairs, the cool of the seat through my tights.

Mr. Gray sits down in Daddy's chair and writes on a blank sheet of paper in handwriting I can't read.

It's quiet in the bedroom and my head is full of Freedom

Community Church information. There's contemplating your life differently, overcoming adversity, visualizing your destiny.

"The examination of Jennifer Lauck will now begin," Mr. Gray says.

Mr. Gray's eyes are light blue, white blue, and I look at him close, but there's nothing to see.

"I will ask you a series of questions," Mr. Gray says. "Please answer immediately and without thought."

"Name?" Mr. Gray says.

"You know my name," I say, "you just said it."

Mr. Gray writes something on the paper.

"Age?" Mr. Gray says.

"Nine, almost ten, ten in two weeks."

Mr. Gray lifts his pen in the air, a line up and down.

"Concise answers, please," Mr. Gray says.

"Concise?" I say.

"Short," Mr. Gray says, "to the point. You are nine, not ten, correct?"

"But I'm almost ten," I say.

Mr. Gray looks at me and blinks.

"But you are nine today," Mr. Gray says, "yes or no?"

"Yes," I say, "but."

"No but," Mr. Gray says.

Mr. Gray writes on his paper.

Out the window, Marina Drive is empty street, houses, boats on the water. Down the street is a red car that looks like Red, except I know it's not Red, no way Daddy is home in the middle of the day.

"Date and year of birth," Mr. Gray says.

"What?" I say.

Mr. Gray writes on his paper.

The red car swerves on Marina Drive, S swerve back and forth.

"Address," Mr. Gray says.

Over my chair, I lean close to the window and it is Red. Red out of control.

"Address," Mr. Gray says.

Red makes a wide turn into the driveway, just halfway in, almost hits the mailbox. The door opens and it's Daddy out of Red and on the grass. Daddy down on the grass like he fell.

Out of my chair, up against the window, I press my face against the cool glass.

"Please sit back down," Mr. Gray says.

"Daddy!" I yell.

"Please sit down," Mr. Gray says.

"Something's wrong," I say.

Daddy gets up off the grass, walks away from Red, his hand over his chest. Red is half in the street, half in the driveway, the lights on, the door open.

Mr. Gray stands up by the window and I can hear him breathe.

Downstairs, Deb yells and Daddy talks in a low voice.

I push off the glass, run to the door.

Just like that, Daddy is up the stairs, and he holds his arm like he hurt himself, maybe broke his arm.

"Juniper," Daddy says, "I'm sorry I ruined your examination."

"You didn't," I say. "What's wrong?"

Daddy goes to the bed, sits, leans, falls down. He breathes out his mouth, breathes like he ran, breathes like he can't breathe.

"I need to rest," Daddy says.

Deb is in the doorway, her mouth open, her hand over her chest too.

"What do I do?" Deb yells. "I don't know what to do."

Mr. Gray looks at Daddy.

"Call a doctor," Mr. Gray says, "call an ambulance."

Mr. Gray packs up his briefcase, walks out of the room, and I can hear his heels down the stairs.

Deb looks at Daddy, looks at the door where Mr. Gray was, looks at Daddy again.

"Bud?" Deb says.

When something is wrong, really wrong, my skin knows first.

Deb puts her hand on Daddy's shoulder and Daddy breathes deep low breaths, holds himself tight, eyes shut.

"Bud?" Deb yells.

There are prickles up the back of my neck, over the top of my head, and down into my nose, like a nosebleed coming on.

Deb reaches for the telephone by the bed and looks at me.

"Go downstairs now," Deb says.

"Daddy?" I say.

"Get the hell out of here right now," Deb yells.

There's a sign on Bryan's door that says GO AWAY. I lean my face against the door and there is no sound on the other side.

I open the door and look in. Bryan lies on his bed, eyes closed.

"Bryan?" I say.

Bryan opens his eyes, turns his head.

"Don't you knock?" he says.

Half in, half out, I push the door open a little more.

"Something's wrong," I say, "it's Daddy."

Bryan sits up quick, both hands on the bed, feet on the floor.

"I think he broke his arm," I say.

My hands hold the edge of the door, fingers so tight they start to hurt.

"His arm?" he says.

"I don't know," I say, "I don't know."

Bryan's eyes are on me, in me, through me. I hold my arm against my chest the way Daddy did. I shake the way you do when you're scared, really scared, and I'm cold all over.

"Don't cry," Bryan says.

I sniff and wipe the back of my hand under my nose.

"I can't help it," I say, "it's bad. I think this is really bad."

Bryan crosses his room, takes the door, and opens it all the way. He looks down the hall and up the hall. He looks at me again and I bite my top lip between my teeth.

"Come on," Bryan says.

It's not a broken arm, it's a broken heart. Heart attack.

Christopher, Kenny, Ronny, Bryan, and me sit around the kitchen table. Deb leans her hip against the kitchen counter and her voice is low and calm, too low, too calm.

"It's too soon to tell," Deb says, "everything that can be done is being done."

Bryan has his elbows on the table, his head between his hands.

"What does that mean?" Bryan says.

Deb takes a deep breath and flips her hair back.

"Exactly what it means," Deb says.

Bryan slaps his hand on the table.

"But you're not telling me anything," Bryan says. "Is he awake? Is he coming home?"

Christopher, Kenny, and Ronny, they line up in a row on the other side of the table. Christopher watches Deb, lips in a tight line. Ronny chews on her lips, makes them all bunched up like a fish face. Kenny wiggles her fingers a little, watches her fingers wiggle.

The clock on the wall is one of those without numbers, just lines and two hands pointing to lines. The hands point to ten o'clock. Ten o'clock on a school night.

Deb uncrosses her arms, hands wide, palms to the ceiling.

"I'm telling you what the doctors told me," Deb says.

"Why are you here?" Bryan says. "Why are we here?"

He stands up and waves at me across the table.

"We should be at the hospital right now," Bryan says. "What if he wakes up and he's alone? We should be there."

Deb looks lost, her face blank.

"Bryan," Deb says, "I'm not at the hospital right now so I can be here with you kids, so I can explain. Please calm down. We need to stay calm right now."

"Calm down?" Bryan yells. "He's my father."

Deb's hands are out to Bryan, palms up.

"Please, Bryan," Deb says.

Bryan looks at her hands and shakes his head, sits down in the chair next to me.

It's quiet, quiet around the table. Them and us.

Deb says how things are going to be, how we need to go on like things are normal. It's time for bed, tomorrow is school, homework, running. Deb says the routine will help us.

Everything is the same except nothing is the same. It's breakfast, brush your teeth, walk to school, walk home, memorize all the presidents of the United States. Washington, Adams, Jefferson. I make a list and another list and another list and I can't remember anything past Jefferson.

Deb makes macaroni and vegetables, sets it on the orange Formica table with a gallon of milk. It's just like any other dinner: Ronny complains about how she hates macaroni and vegetables, Kenny says she really likes macaroni and vegetables, and Christopher just eats without talking, that faraway look in his dark brown eyes. But Bryan doesn't eat, just looks at his plate of food.

"Come on, Bryan," Deb says, "you should eat. You too, Jenny."

"I want to see my father," Bryan says.

The clock says six o'clock.

"Me too," I say.

Deb pulls up a chair, sits down, and leans over the table.

Christopher, Kenny, and Ronny look at Deb.

Them and us.

"I'm sorry, Bryan," Deb says, "the rules say no children allowed. The only one of you old enough is Christopher."

"Christopher?" Bryan says.

"Christopher?" I say at the same time.

Christopher sits back in his chair, like he's surprised anyone said his name.

"What?" he says.

"The hospital," Bryan says, "you're the only one who can go."

"Me?" he says. "I don't want to go to the hospital."

"Me neither," Ronny says, "hospitals are gross."

"Totally gross," Kenny says.

"You don't get to go anyway," Bryan says, "no one is talking to you."

"Everyone calm down," Deb says. "And the hospital really isn't that bad, it's just disturbing to see Bud right now since he has tubes up his nose and down his throat."

"Gross," Kenny and Ronny say together.

"Why don't you both just shut up," Bryan says.

"Tubes?" I say. "What kind of tubes?"

"Tubes to help him breathe, Jenny," Deb says, "and it's not gross, it's saving his life."

"He can't breathe?" I say.

"No, no," Deb says, "he can breathe, it's just the machine helps."

Deb sits up, hands flipping her long red hair back, and she makes her face smile.

"Well, the good news is this," Deb says, "Freedom Community has agreed to send healers to the hospital."

"What?" Bryan says.

"It can't hurt," Deb says.

"The Church can see my father, but I can't," Bryan says. "That is just great."

"The Freedom Community Church is very powerful," Deb says, "they can help Bud contemplate . . ."

"Just shut up," Bryan says. "I can't take this crap."

Deb puts her hand over her chest, her face blank.

"Excuse me?" Deb says.

Bryan gets up from the table, walks away from Deb, from Deb's kids, from me. He slams the door to his room. Deb's eyes are wide and her face is red and it looks like someone threw cold water in her face, she's that surprised.

"I'm not hungry," I say, "can I go too?"

Deb presses her mouth in a tight line.

"Fine," Deb says.

❧

Daddy's been gone two nights and two days and nothing is right. I sit in school, I eat lunch, I stand with my back against the wall at recess. It's like being here and not being here at the same time.

When I come home from school, I sit on the front step and look across the street at the marina. All those sailboats, but no one sails today. Daddy doesn't have a sailboat there, not yet. He says he might get enough money together next year.

There is a sound from the garage, a meow sound.

Off the step, I go along the sidewalk and my shadow is long in front of my body. A gray- and rust-colored cat is against the garage door and it's got green eyes that look like big marbles, much greener than Deb's eyes. The cat lifts up like it might run and its eyes are wide open scared.

I kneel down slow so there are a couple feet between us and she settles down again.

"Hey, kitty," I say, "what are you doing here?"

The cat just looks at me and blinks. I put my hand out, palm up, and rub my fingers together.

"Did you get lost?" I say.

The cat looks at my hand and looks at me. She gets up and walks two steps. The cat stops and that's the way it is with cats, they'll meet you halfway. I lean up and touch my hand on the cat's head, pet between its ears.

It's no time before the cat is in my arms, against my heart, and I know she's supposed to be mine. Her body is swollen in the middle and skinny everywhere else, like she's starved. I carry her into the kitchen and Deb says she's a calico cat, probably just a stray or maybe a runaway.

"I'm going to name her Natasha," I say.

"Natasha?" Deb says.

Holding Natasha against my chest, I pet between her ears, and she closes her green cat eyes.

"Natasha," I say. "She needs some food."

"Wait a minute," Deb says, "just one minute. You can't keep her."

"Why not?" I say. "I found her."

"Why not?" Deb says. "Because she's someone's cat, she has to be someone's cat."

"We have to take care of her," I say, "we have to feed her."

"If you feed her," Deb says, "she'll think she lives here."

I hold Natasha and her cat body is warm and perfect. I look at Deb, just look.

"All right," Deb says, "but she stays in the garage."

"Okay," I say.

"And if someone comes for her," Deb says, "you have to give her back."

"Okay," I say.

"And you better not get too attached because someone will probably come get her," Deb says.

Natasha opens her cat eyes, looks at Deb, and then she blinks her eyes closed again. Cats don't need to talk when they have great big eyes like they do. Natasha is tired and hungry and she's supposed to be my cat, at least for now.

"I'll get some food on my way back from the hospital," Deb says.

"And kitty litter," I say.

"And kitty litter," Deb says.

In the morning, I go to the garage and Natasha stands in a box of kitty litter.

"Hey, kitty, kitty," I say.

Natasha does that paw-kick thing, steps out of the box, and shakes litter off her feet. I rub my hand over her head, down her back and to her tail, and Natasha pushes against my hand, lifts her behind for more petting. There is a box of cat chow and I pour some into a dish, take the other dish and get her some milk.

Deb is in the kitchen, smiles at me like she's really happy and I smile back.

"Thanks for the kitty litter and the food," I say.

"No problem," Deb says.

"I'm going to give her some milk," I say.

"Okay," Deb says. "As soon as you do that come on back because I have news about your dad."

"News?" I say.

"Good news," Deb says.

The way Deb says those words, *good news,* there is a bad feeling up the back of my neck. Deb's voice is down the hall and she tells everyone to get up, to come into the kitchen, says she has good news.

My stomach has the throw-up feeling and my legs shake and I just stand there in the kitchen, Natasha's empty bowl still on the counter.

Christopher, Kenny, Ronny, and Bryan come in and everyone sits down. Deb stands all dramatic, her face with a big smile and she holds her hands over her chest.

"The healing worked," Deb says. "Bud was able to free his mind."

I look at Bryan and Bryan stands up, his hand on the table, his other hand to the countertop.

"What does that mean?" Bryan says.

"It means," Deb says, "he is getting off the respirator, and if all goes well, he'll be home by tomorrow."

"Tomorrow?" I say.

"Tomorrow," Deb says, "maybe the morning, probably the afternoon."

The good news *is* good news and Bryan sits down, puts his

head in his hands. Deb talks about the power of the Freedom Community and the power of contemplation.

That night, the house on Marina Drive is quiet and I can't sleep when I know Natasha is out there in the cold, all alone. I sneak down the hall and turn on the light to the garage. Natasha sits up in her box and blinks her green cat eyes.

I lift her up and hold her with both arms. Natasha rubs her head under my chin and purrs. I pet her head with my whole hand, over and over again.

"Want to sleep with me?" I say.

Natasha's green eyes are half open the way cats do when they are sleepy and I hold her close, turn off the garage light, and carry her into my room.

The best thing about waking up in my room is how the morning sunshine comes through the pink drapes and makes the white walls a golden pink color. It's like being inside a perfect seashell where you're safe and warm and beauty is everywhere you lay your eyes.

Natasha is on top of my bedspread and her cat body is curled up tight. I shift myself up in bed and sit against my pillows, quiet and warm, my hand in Natasha's soft fur.

Outside my door is a sound, maybe a person going by, maybe not. Then the door opens and just like that, Deb looks at me and I look at her.

"I was going to take her right out," I say, "I just brought her in for the night, just one night."

Deb's face is blotchy and red and she doesn't even look at Natasha, just looks at me.

"It's all right," Deb says. She comes all the way into my room and closes the door.

Deb walks across the room and sits down on the edge of my bed. She has never done that, not ever, and there's that bad feeling up the back of my neck, over the top of my head, down into my nose.

Natasha uncurls and stretches out long so her paws push against Deb's hip. Then Deb's hand is on Natasha, her long thin fingers over a little patch of rust color.

"Jenny," Deb says, her voice low and wrong.

Her hair falls around her head like a curtain but I can still see the lines of tears down her face and she looks at her hands, not at me. I know what Deb is going to say next, and when you know something like that, you don't want any more words.

"I'm so sorry," Deb says, "I am just so sorry."

"You said he was coming home," I say, my voice not my voice. "You said he was better."

"Oh, Jenny," Deb says, "I know I said that, and he was better, he really was."

Deb has a wadded-up tissue in her hand and she wipes at her face. Her eyes are wide open and she shakes her head like nothing makes sense.

"It was another heart attack," she says, "they don't know why. It just happened."

Deb looks at me for a long time, her eyes on my eyes like she wants me to make it right for her.

I never hated anyone as much as I hate Deb, and right here, right now, I could hit her with my fists, hit her face and her body and her legs. I bite my lips together and pick up Natasha.

"Go away," I whisper.

"What?" Deb says.

"Leave," I say. "And take the cat too."

I push Natasha against Deb's legs.

"Jenny," she says, "you shouldn't be alone at a time like this."

"Just go," I yell.

I cross my arms over my chest, pull my knees up under the covers, and sit there like a rock. I know Deb watches, I can feel her eyes, but I'm not going to look at her and I'm not going to talk.

Deb clears her throat then, a cough and a cry all mixed up.

I feel her leave my room and hear the small sound of the door close.

If you stay still, if you don't breathe, if you don't even blink, maybe it won't be true. I sit that way, quiet and still and stiff, and I hold what I know away from myself. The thing is, it doesn't really matter, the truth is stronger than me, and pretty soon the tears are down my face, under my chin, and dripping on my bare arms. I cry that way for so long, I don't even know how long.

Time spreads a slow wide path between the way it was before and the way it's going to be. It's an hour, a day, a month, who knows. It's a million years when I come out of the princess bedroom and walk down the long hallway. The light is different, shadows without edges, white walls turned a flat shade of gray.

Through the long hall and into the living room, it's art deco lamps, leather sofas, and Deb, Christopher, Kenny, and Ronny. They sit together, Christopher leaned into Kenny, and Deb with one arm around Ronny and the other arm around Kenny. Deb's hand is in the middle of Kenny's chest and she pats up and down like heartbeats.

They look at me when I come in and then they look away.

It feels like crying in here and I'm on the edge of what is normal and what is crazy. I want to yell at all of them, *You can't cry for my father, you never even loved him.* I don't say anything though, just stand there and make my hands into tight fists to hold the crazy inside.

Bryan stands by the big window and his arms are crossed over his chest. I walk quiet steps to where he stands and he looks down like he knows I'm there. The top of my head almost reaches his shoulder and I can feel the warm from him on my arm. I want to say something except nothing seems right. Bryan tucks his chin and his eyes move in my direction like he looks but he doesn't want to.

"What?" he says.

I put my hands out, palms up like I don't know, and Bryan makes his arms tighter over his chest and looks out the window again.

It's a terrible thing to feel alone when you are with other people, when those other people are supposed to be your family even though they aren't, not really. That kind of being alone makes you feel wrong inside your own body, like your bones don't fit under your skin, like something inside your stomach wants to get out and fly away.

I walk quiet steps away from Bryan and away from the living room. I open the door to the garage and turn on the light. The big brown car is there and Red is backed in. There's a scratch in the paint where Daddy hit the mailbox and even though that was just a couple days ago, it seems like forever.

I touch the paint scratch on Daddy's car and little red flecks of paint fall off on the cement floor.

There is a mew sound, part cat and part cry. I walk around Red and Natasha is in her cat box with her eyes squeezed shut.

I try to pet between her eyes, but she shakes me off, makes a deep sound from inside her cat body. Something pushes out of her like she's going to the bathroom right there in her box, except I know she's not going to the bathroom.

A long time ago, I don't even remember how long, it was Momma and me in the house on Mary Street and we watched Diana have a litter of kittens. Momma made me stand way back, said you have to make room when babies come, even little kittens.

The smell of the garage is all around, oil and cardboard and concrete.

I step back and my butt hits Daddy's car.

Natasha works hard and she pushes out one, two, three, four kittens. They come into the world with their eyes squeezed shut and they move their heads around like they are struggling against something.

Momma told me that every birth is a miracle and I didn't know what she meant. Now I understand and I wish she was here so I could tell her what I know.

Natasha licks each kitten and then she pulls them up to her tummy.

I lean against Red and watch Natasha be a mother. I cry and I laugh and I wipe my nose with the back of my hand. I know nothing will ever be the same.

❧

It's sunny and hot and the air smells clean. It should be stormy today, it should be the kind of day where it's better to just stay in bed.

All of us are outside in the bright perfect sunshine and it's trees and bushes and lots of green grass. We wait by a side door that leads into an old building that's like a chapel or church, except it's not a Freedom Community place, just some place Deb found. We stay outside while everyone else goes in the main doors. Deb says there are seats already reserved for us, says she doesn't want to sit there longer than she has to, says she doesn't want everyone to stare at the back of our heads at a time like this.

A lot of people come to Daddy's funeral, men who wear black, ladies who wear black. No little kids. Bryan says lots of Daddy's family will come too and I look for people I should know, people I forgot.

"There's Aunt Margie," Bryan says.

Bryan points at the front door and squints his dark eyes. A fat lady holds her hand up to her eyes, waves at Bryan like she knows him, and then she stops waving like maybe she doesn't. I don't remember Aunt Margie, not at all.

"Aunt Margie?" I say.

"What a cow," Ronny says.

"A total cow," Kenny says.

Ronny's freckle nose is scrunched up like something smells bad and Kenny laughs.

"Kendall, Veronica, don't say 'cow,'" Deb says, "it's not polite."

Christopher is quiet and he bends close to Ronny's ear.

"She's not a cow anyway," Christopher says, "she's pregnant."

"Gross," Ronny says.

Christopher stands up again and takes a deep breath. He stands still and looks off over the grass, his eyes far away. I like that about Christopher and I stand the way he stands, look over the grass too.

"There's Uncle Larry," Bryan says, "and Aunt Ruth."

Uncle Larry is Daddy's only brother, except he doesn't look a thing like Daddy. Larry has white skin with red splotches high on the sides of his round face. His body is soft and thick and he wears glasses that make his eyes look like big marbles.

"Can we go in?" Bryan says. "Everyone is here."

Deb wears all black, black sunglasses too, and she looks like some kind of witch dressed like that.

"No," Deb says, "not yet. Let people get settled."

Ronny walks up the sidewalk, hits her hands together, turns around, and walks back.

"I'm not going to cry," Ronny says.

"No way," Kenny says. "No crying."

"So what," Bryan says. "Big deal."

"It's all right to cry," Deb says.

"Crying is for babies," Ronny says. "The first one to cry is a baby."

"Yeah," Kenny says.

"Would you two just grow up," Christopher says.

Deb puts her hand on Kenny's and Ronny's shoulders, moves them away from where we all stand and says something only they can hear. Ronny crosses her arms and then Kenny crosses her arms and they both get mad looks on their faces.

"They're just being jerks," Christopher says. "I'm sorry."

Bryan looks down at his shoes, pushes both hands into his pockets, and walks slow steps to the front of the chapel. He stops halfway between the front doors and us.

"Can we go in now?" Bryan says.

Inside the church is the quiet sound of people, lots of people. Deb nods her head and holds her arm like she's showing us the way.

It's me, Bryan, Kenny, Ronny, and Christopher, and Deb walks in last with her head down. I can feel all the people behind us, can feel their eyes.

Up front are white roses, yellow daisies, purple gladiolas. A man walks out and he has a guitar. He sits down on a stool and talks about Daddy, about what kind of man he was, how he loved life and music and the ocean. The man says today shouldn't be a day of mourning but a day of celebration since Daddy's life was a gift.

I turn in my seat, look back at the rows of people, and none of them smile, none of them celebrate. Aunt Margie's eyes are wet and she smiles a sad smile right at me. Uncle Larry sits up tall and I can't tell if he's happy or sad, his eyes lost behind those thick glasses.

I don't care what the man says, it's not right to be happy today and I'm not going to clap my hands or sing along or do anything like that. Daddy is gone and I'm here and right now I would give anything to spend one more day with him.

Down the row of seats, Ronny looks at me and she points one freckly finger. Deb slaps at Ronny's leg and then she opens her purse, takes out a pack of plastic to-go tissue, and passes the little packet down to me. Bryan doesn't cry, Christopher doesn't cry, Kenny doesn't cry, and Ronny looks almost happy.

I hold the pack of tissue between my hands, press down, and it's like a little pillow.

The man plays a Cat Stevens song about listening to the wind of your soul, about not knowing where you're going to end up.

Sometimes, the only thing you can do is cry and I don't care what Ronny or Kenny think of me. I blink the tears out and let them fall down my face. I am going to sit here and cry and maybe I'll never stop.

❧

It's funny when someone dies. I know Daddy's gone, I really do, but it's just in my head. My heart doesn't understand. I wake up, go to school, go to bed, but that's just my body.

At night, I stay awake in case he comes home. In the morning, I open my eyes and listen for the sound of his voice. In the afternoon, I sit on the concrete step in front of the house on Marina Drive and look for Red to turn the corner. I know he's gone, but I can't help it, I have to look.

It's my birthday and then Christmas day, just days you want to be over, but Christmas is the worst since all the presents for Daddy are unwrapped by Deb and stacked in a pile. Daddy's presents and no Daddy makes me so sad, I end up crying in my room all day long.

Finally, it's the new year and that's when Deb says we have to give away Natasha's kittens. Kenny and Ronny pick one of the kittens to keep and they name it Buttermilk. The rest of them go one by one and I think Natasha is sad about it, since she still looks around for her babies the same way I look around for Daddy.

Natasha is smarter than me though. One day she just leaves the house on Marina Drive. Deb says she probably went home, but I know she's looking for her babies.

Deb says it's all decided, says Bryan and me are going to stay with her and her kids. Deb says Aunt Margie, Uncle Larry, and Grandma and Grandpa Lauck decided it was best, but I didn't know it was going to be any other way.

"We are a family," Deb says, "family sticks together."

It's like a family meeting but in the art deco living room, and Bryan sits slouched low in a leather chair, his chin is to his chest.

Deb, Christopher, Kenny, and Ronny sit on the leather sofa.

I sit on the edge of the other leather chair, my hands under my legs.

Deb puts her hands wide, touches the knees of Kenny and Ronny, reaches long to Christopher. She looks at Bryan and me again.

"This is painful for all of us," Deb says, "but we have to move on. It's time to think about the future."

"Future?" I say.

"For example, this house," Deb says. "We can't stay here."

Christopher, Kenny, and Ronny look at Deb like they know what she's talking about.

"We're moving?" I say.

"That's right," Deb says, "we are going to Palo Alto."

"Palo Alto?" Bryan says.

The sound of Bryan's voice cracks high and he coughs.

"That's right," Deb says, "Palo Alto. The Freedom Community Church has a wonderful school for children, an experimental school, and there are plenty of opportunities for me as well."

Deb talks to her kids and they look back at her like they already know.

Bryan sits up in his chair, shifting so he's on the edge. Bright red blotches lift under his skin around the collar of his shirt.

"I found a great house to lease and there's lots of room for a horse, maybe a couple of goats," she says. "It'll be great."

"Hold it," Bryan says, "horses, goats, what are you talking about?"

"We need a fresh start," Deb says, "we need to move on, that's what your father would have wanted."

My eyes are out the big window like Daddy might walk up the sidewalk with his coat over his arm and his briefcase in his hand.

"My father never said anything about Palo Alto," Bryan says, "he never said anything about some experimental school. My father wanted me to go to college here."

Deb blinks and her happy smile is gone.

"Why don't you kids go to your rooms," Deb says. "Let me have a little chat with Bryan and Jenny."

Christopher, Kenny, and Ronny get up fast and leave without looking back. They never take off like that and I get a bad feeling up the back of my neck. Bryan looks at me and I look at Bryan and it's quiet all around.

Deb clears her throat, tosses her hair over her shoulders, and presses down on her knees with her fingers.

"Bryan," Deb says, "I appreciate you are grieving, but now you need to contemplate."

"What?" Bryan says.

Deb puts her hand up, palm up.

"That's right," Deb says, "see your situation differently and you can be free."

"What are you talking about?" Bryan says.

Deb puts her arm up on the back of the sofa, head tilted to the side, and her voice is quiet.

"You might not believe this, but all of this is as hard on me as it is on you," Deb says. "What I mean is, Bud did not make any arrangements for you."

Deb shifts her eyes at me, shifts back to Bryan.

"It breaks my heart to tell you this," Deb says, "but the reason you are here with me, with us . . ."

Deb stops and looks around at the living room like there's a bunch of people, and then she puts her creepy cat eyes right on Bryan.

"Your father's family did not want you," Deb says, "they didn't want either of you."

Bryan sits up tall and turns his head, eyes on me, on Deb, on me again.

Deb sits forward, elbows on her knees, her face on her hands.

"There is almost no money to speak of," Deb says quietly. "I can barely pay the bills and the debt. Don't even get me started about the debt your father left me in. Hell, I'll even have to sell that silly car of his."

Bryan lifts his head, red stain all the way to his ears.

"You can't do that," Bryan says.

Deb laughs a mean hard laugh.

"Your father was not a god, Bryan," Deb says. "He was human, he was even cruel. Did you know he wished one of his clients would die of a heart attack?"

Bryan shakes his head, tears out of his eyes, and he pushes at them fast with the back of his hand.

"It's true," Deb says, "haven't you ever heard of karma? That's why he died of a heart attack the way he did. Negative energy projects and reflects."

"Shut up," Bryan yells.

"In essence, your father killed himself," Deb says.

"Shut up," Bryan yells, his voice loud in my ears, in the living room.

I can't understand Deb, can't believe what she says.

Bryan is out of his chair and he looks like he is going to hit

Deb. He holds his hands in fists and she just looks at him, calm in her green eyes.

It's quiet, a terrible quiet where someone has to do something. I wish Daddy would just come and take us out of here.

"I'm all you've got now," Deb says. "So you better get used to it."

Bryan looks at Deb for a long time and his shoulders drop like a weight is on his back and he sits down again.

part four
Palo Alto and Los Angeles
1974–1975

fourteen

Deb says each of us must solve our own problems.

Deb says individuals who solve problems are self-sufficient.

Deb says self-sufficient individuals who work together make a successful family unit.

"Fuck Deb," Bryan says.

Bryan has his back against my bedroom door and he has his middle finger up in the air.

"You ever notice how you can't understand a thing Deb says?" Bryan says.

"She's going to hear you," I say.

Bryan stabs his middle finger up to the ceiling.

"If she catches you in here," I say, "there's going to be trouble."

"You let me worry about Deb," Bryan says.

Bryan pushes hair out of his eyes and makes a wide smile, a perfect line of white teeth. Bryan is different now, almost nice, and the change makes me nervous.

He helps me put together my canopy bed even though Deb says I am supposed to do it myself, and when we're done with the bed, he even puts together my bookcases.

"What else?" Bryan says.

"That's it," I say.

Bryan looks around and scratches his ear.

"You need tunes," Bryan says. "Where's your radio?"

I point to the pink trunk.

"It's in there," I say.

"Well, get it out," Bryan says, "where's the key?"

I stand still and hold my hands the way I do when I think about something.

"I'll open it," I say, "but you can't look."

"Why?" Bryan says.

"Just turn around," I say.

Bryan turns so his face is to the wall.

I take off my whole shoe, wiggle the key so it sticks out, and open the lock with the key still on the shoelace. I look at Bryan and he turns his head to look over his shoulder.

"Don't look," I say.

I pull my shoe on again, tuck the key under the shoelaces.

"Okay," I say.

Bryan turns around and his dark eyes are on the trunk, on me, on the trunk again. The clock radio is on top of the Our Wedding book. I lift out the clock and Bryan takes it out of my hand.

"What's the big deal?" Bryan says.

"No big deal," I say.

"So why did I have to turn around?" Bryan says.

"Because," I say. "Because it's my room. Okay?"

"Okay," he says, "don't get all snippy."

Bryan sits down on the carpet and holds the clock radio from Number One on his lap.

"I can't believe you still have this thing," he says.

"It works," I say.

He looks into the pink trunk and he nods his chin up.

"What's in there anyway?" Bryan says.

"Nothing," I say.

I close the lid, but Bryan reaches out and holds the lid open.

"It's just books and stuff," I say, "girl stuff."

Bryan looks at me and looks at the trunk again.

"Just forget it," I say. "We need tunes."

Bryan doesn't listen to me and he lifts the lid of the trunk all the way up. All my stuff is small and silly in front of someone else, and I bet he's going to laugh at me. Bryan doesn't laugh though, he just reaches long and takes out the Our Wedding book.

"Where did you get this?" Bryan says.

The room is quiet and I hold my breath. The wedding book is small in his big hands and he just sits there and looks at the cover.

"Auntie Carol gave it to me," I say.

On my knees, I sit with my butt on my heels, and this close Bryan smells like salt and sweat. The heavy weight of memory is all around and I take a deep breath and trace my finger over the gold letters the way Auntie Carol did. My hand shakes, but I don't care. I touch the bottom right corner of the book and lift the cover open. Inside is a black and white picture of Momma in a beautiful white wedding dress. She smiles and stands on her own and she has the prettiest round cheeks and darkest sharpest eyes.

I move my whole hand over the photograph, sad all around.

"She looked like a princess," I whisper.

Bryan looks at the photo and blinks his dark eyes and I never noticed how he has such long dark eyelashes. I bite my lip, move my finger to the bottom right-hand corner, and turn the page.

The picture is Momma with Grandma Rowena and Grandpa Ivan in front of some house and a cat is asleep in the shadow of Momma's dress.

"The wedding was in Reno," I say.

Bryan looks at me and I look at him and it's quiet in the room, so quiet it's like time has stopped. I move my whole hand over the photograph, touch the bottom right-hand corner, and turn again.

Momma stands next to a car and some man holds the door. The wind blows Momma's veil the wrong way and she smiles and has her arm up to keep it from blowing away.

"It was a sunny day," I say. "Windy too."

Bryan watches me and he makes a sound, like a laugh except it's a hard short sound like a cough too. I clear my throat, make my hand steady, and turn the page again.

The photo is Daddy in a white tuxedo with three other men in white tuxedos too. Momma is in her beautiful white wedding dress with three women in short light-colored dresses. Everyone smiles.

"Uncle Charles was an usher," I say, "and Aunt Ruth was a bridesmaid."

Bryan nods and I know he recognizes all the people.

I move my hand over the photograph, touch the bottom right-hand corner, and turn again.

The photo is of Momma and Daddy up the aisle. Daddy's eyes are happy, his nose wrinkled, and his squared-up jaw has a little dent right in the middle.

It's so hard to look at Momma and Daddy the way they used to be, I have to close my eyes and swallow tears that lift up in my throat. I remember how Auntie Carol said Daddy was lucky and I wonder if I should say it. I sniff and look right at Bryan, right at his dark eyes.

"Daddy used to say how lucky he was to marry her," I whisper.

Tears roll down my face and drop on the plastic photo cover. I wish I wouldn't cry, wish I was stronger, and I look down and blink fast.

"Lucky?" Bryan says.

Bryan's eyes are wide open and his mouth is just a straight line of lips on his face, so serious. I wipe my face with the back of my hand and nod my head.

"That's what Auntie Carol told me," I say.

There are more pictures, lots more, but the way I feel and the way Bryan looks, I know it's enough. I take the Our Wedding book off his lap and close the cover.

"It's not good to look at too many at one time," I say. "So many memories can hurt."

I put the Our Wedding book into the pink trunk and I can feel Bryan watch.

"They're not really mine," I say. "I mean, you can look at them whenever you want."

I close the lid and push the lock closed with my palm.

Bryan's eyes are full of tears, but I know he won't cry in front of me.

"You just shouldn't look at too many at one time," I say, "okay?"

Bryan nods his head and he pulls his knees to his chest, puts his arms around his legs, and lays his head on his knees. He closes his eyes then and we sit in the quiet of my room.

Palo Alto is curvy roads and steep hills. Our new house is built in the middle of one of those steep hills. It's like someone just came along, carved out a big hunk of hill, and built the house right in there. A steep driveway curves to the house and in the middle of the curving driveway is what Deb calls a corral.

Our house is one of those Spanish-style houses with stucco walls and dark wood beams along the ceilings. Out back is a pool with a diving board and past the pool is the rest of the hill. If you bend back and look up, another house is built up there, and if our hill gave way, it looks like that house would slide right down.

Deb buys a horse and Ronny names it Chiquita. The rule is, one kid, one week, oldest to youngest, and when it's your week you're in charge of everything, riding, feeding, brushing, cleaning. I have to wait a month before I ride Chiquita.

Deb buys two baby goats and she says we're going to make goat cheese and drink goat milk. The rule is, one week, one kid, youngest to oldest, Ronny before Kenny, and when it's your week you are in charge of everything. I have to take care of the goats now.

When the goats are hungry, they baa like babies and you have to feed them with these wine bottles full of gross-smelling milk and molasses.

This morning, it's rain and wind and my clothes are soaked from being in the corral and trying to feed the stupid goats their bottles of milk.

In the house again, I stand at the sink and rinse the bottles with hot water. The window over the sink steams up and I stand there until the steam is so thick you can't see outside. Then I stand on my tiptoes, make my hand into a fist, and press the side of my hand into the steamy window. The side of my fist makes a print like a baby's foot and then I use my pinkie finger and make five baby toes.

"Don't do that," Deb says, "you're making a mess."

Deb's voice makes me jump and I put my hands behind my back like I have something to hide. Deb has on her bathrobe and her hair is mashed against her head. She moves her fingers through her hair and yawns without covering her mouth.

"Jesus," Deb says, "you didn't wipe your feet off either. Look at all the mud you tracked in."

My shoes and jeans are wet and muddy, little puddles of dirty water on the floor.

"Sorry," I say, "it was wet out there."

"I don't care if it was wet out there," Deb says, "you wipe your feet off when you come in here."

"All I can say is I'm sorry," I say, "I'll clean it up."

Deb doesn't say anything, just looks at me like I'm too stupid for words. That's the way it is with Deb now, she doesn't try to hide her feelings the way she did when Daddy was here. Now it's in her eyes and in her voice and I know there isn't any room for me here.

When you have a feeling about someone and you find out the feeling is true, it's a good thing and bad thing too. It's nice to know your gut is right, but it's terrible to know you're not wanted, especially when there's nowhere else to go.

Deb turns around and acts like I'm not here at all. She takes out a measuring cup and a pan and she puts water in the pan.

I carry my shoes down the steps and use an old towel to clean up the floor.

Every morning, it's breakfast in the dining room and we use the old dining set from the house on Mary Street. It used to be in storage, but Deb took it out when we moved to Palo Alto. It's the table, the hutch, and the buffet with dark wood and tulips and vines.

I sit at the end of the table and trace from one red tulip to the next red tulip and there are twenty tulips altogether.

Deb puts six bowls, six spoons, milk, and a pot of hot wheat cereal in the middle of the table. She makes a plate of toast, puts it in the middle of the table too.

I take a piece of toast, put it on a napkin, and turn the honey bear upside down.

When Deb comes back to the dining room table, she holds a bunch of white plastic pill bottles against her chest.

A line of honey threads around on my toast and I pretend there is no Deb.

"Where is everyone?" Deb says.

I tip the honey bear right side up and put him on the table, my eyes on the toast, just the toast.

"BREAKFAST," Deb yells.

"There is mud on the stairs too," Deb says. "Clean it up before you leave this morning."

Fuck you, Deb.

"Sorry," I say.

Deb sits at the other end of Momma's table and opens a book that says *Vitamins* on the cover. I chew with my mouth closed and look at Deb. She looks at me and I look down. One by one it's Christopher, Kenny, Ronny, and Bryan out of their rooms and into the dining room.

"What took you guys so long?" Deb says.

"Christopher was hogging the bathroom," Ronny says.

"No, I wasn't," Christopher says.

"We have three bathrooms," Deb says.

"Bryan stunk up the other one," Ronny says.

"Shut up," Bryan says.

Bryan's face is red and he looks at me, looks away.

Christopher takes one of the pill bottles, turns it to the side, and the pills inside rattle.

"What are you doing with all this stuff?" Christopher says.

Deb closes her vitamin book and puts her hand over the cover.

"Vitamins are the key to good health and longevity," Deb says.

Christopher takes a deep breath and shrugs his shoulder like who cares.

Deb unscrews a vitamin bottle and shakes out a handful of pills.

"We are going to start taking vitamins," Deb says.

Deb makes six piles of yellow pills, white pills, green pills, names like kelp and A and E and C. When Deb is done, there are so many pills it looks like a vitamin overdose.

I look at Bryan and Bryan looks at me.

"We have to take all of those?" I say.

"Just your pile," Deb says, "one pile each."

Deb slides vitamin piles down the table and she fills six glasses with orange juice, puts the glasses around the table too.

Deb says vitamins are the latest breakthrough, how modern medicine is a conspiracy against good health, how the Freedom Community endorses the breakaway from the medical establishment. Christopher, Kenny, and Ronny pop vitamins into their mouths and swallow them down.

Bryan pushes the pile of pills away.

"I'm not taking these," Bryan says.

Christopher, Kenny, Ronny and Deb, everyone looks at Bryan.

Deb sits down again and she adjusts her bathrobe around her legs.

"Are you trying to undermine my authority?" Deb says.

"No," Bryan says, "I'm just not taking them."

I look at Bryan, just a quick look, my eyes on the pills in front of me again.

Deb puts her elbows on Momma's table, on the red tulips and brown vines. She holds her hands together and looks at Bryan.

"You really don't have a choice," Deb says. "Remember, I'm your only option these days."

Bryan watches Deb, the red stain up his neck to his cheeks. He moves his eyes to the pills and bites his bottom lip with his top teeth.

I wish Bryan would hold his hand up and flip Deb his middle finger.

Bryan reaches his hand, pulls the pill pile close again, and takes the pills one by one, his face with a look like he might throw up.

Deb clears her throat and looks at her children, smiles like Bryan and me are long gone. Deb says she met a wealthy widower who lives up the hill, says he is the most charming, interesting man, says they are going to meet later in the week for a glass of wine and won't that be wonderful.

Bryan won't look at me, just sits there with his eyes somewhere else.

After breakfast, I go into the bathroom and lock the door. One by one, I take the vitamins out of the little pocket of my jeans and drop them into the toilet bowl. I hold my hand on the silver handle and it's the loud sound of water rushing in a circle to take the pills away. I wait until the flush is done to make sure no pills are left behind and when the toilet is quiet again, I hold my middle finger out and point it at the toilet.

Fuck you, Deb.

There's no Blue Angels team in Palo Alto, but Deb says we should all keep in shape anyway. There is a running schedule all set up and it's a mile and a half on Mondays and Fridays, three miles on Tuesdays and Thursdays, five miles on Wednesdays. Deb says our incentive to run is the forty-five cents she pays in allowance, but money or not, you still have to run.

That's the rule.

Bryan says rules are made to be broken.

Today is a three-mile day and I run down the long drive-way. I make a right turn on the main road and look back to make sure no one's following me.

It's empty road, tall trees, and shifting shadows behind me, and I stop running.

My shadow angles on the road and I zigzag. The shadow zigzags too and I laugh out loud, my voice the only sound.

I know Daddy's gone, I really do, but I look down the road like he is going to be around the next corner. I know exactly how he'll look, what he'll wear, the way his face will smile when I jog up and hold his hand. That's what I would do too, I would just catch up to Daddy and curl my fingers into his.

Deb says the mile and a half mark is where the main road makes a sharp left. At the mark, I turn around and walk back home. If Deb asks, I'll just tell her I went three miles and it won't be a lie, not really.

When I get to our driveway, I jog in case someone watches. At the top of the driveway is a brown UPS truck and a UPS man who unloads tubes from the back end. He squints when he sees me and waves his arm. I wave back and let my arm fall to my side.

The UPS guy comes over and he carries one tube under his arm, a clipboard in the other hand.

"Can you sign for these?" the UPS guy says.

"I don't know," I say. "I guess."

The UPS guy is dressed in brown pants, a brown shirt, a brown hat, and all you see of him is brown. He turns the clipboard to me and points at the paper.

"All you have to do is write your name," the UPS guy says, "right here on the line."

I take the pen out of his hand, spell my name in cursive letters, and then the UPS guy turns the clipboard around again.

"Jennifer Lauck?" he says.

"Right," I say.

He holds the cardboard tube out and I take it in both hands.

"Here you go, Jennifer Lauck," he says.

I like the way he says my full name. He takes out three more tubes and I balance them against my chest.

"What are they?" I say.

The UPS man shrugs and looks at his clipboard.

"Something from the Audubon Society," he says, "maybe some bird prints. Pretty pricey ones from the looks of all the insurance."

The tubes are cardboard and I have to bend back to hold all four in my arms.

"Hey," the UPS guy says, "you want a little help with those?"

"That's okay," I say, "I got it."

He touches his hat with his hand.

"Have a good day, Jennifer Lauck," he says.

"Thanks," I say.

The house is quiet the way it gets when no one is home and I put the cardboard tubes on the dining room table. I go into the kitchen, open the refrigerator, and stand there with the cool air on my legs, my arms, my face.

Deb says you should never eat between meals.

I take out a container of tuna fish and a loaf of bread. I

make a sandwich on the counter and wipe off all the crumbs, just in case.

"Hey," Bryan says.

The sound of his voice is cold water over my head and goose bumps lift down my arms and legs.

"You scared me," I say.

"If Deb catches you, you're screwed," Bryan says.

"Let me worry about Deb," I say.

Bryan laughs and I laugh.

"You want half?" I say.

"Sure," he says.

Bryan and me go into the dining room and sit down at the table. Bryan pushes at the cardboard tubes.

"What are those?" he says.

I pull the sandwich in half.

"Bird prints," I say, "I think."

Bryan takes the sandwich and bites the half in half.

"The UPS guy says they are expensive too," I say.

Bryan touches his finger to one of the tubes, turns it to read the label.

"Broke, my ass," Bryan says.

"What?" I say.

"Deb said we're broke," Bryan says, "but you ever notice how she spends money?"

I squeeze my fingers on the bread, make it flat, and bite into the flat bread and tuna. Bryan sits back in the chair and crosses his arms over his chest.

"I know Dad had insurance," Bryan says, "and I know she's getting money from the government too."

"What do you mean?" I say.

Bryan rolls his lips together, leans close like he has a secret, and his breath smells like tuna.

"Checks come here in my name and your name and Deb keeps the money," Bryan says. "I saw them, but Deb said it wasn't really for us, it was for her."

"Checks?" I say.

"Right," Bryan says, "Social Security Administration money. It's because of Dad and it's a lot too, I opened one."

No one talks about money around here, not ever. Deb gives us an allowance and she says there's a special account for us to save money, but that's it. Mostly Deb says we're broke and it's Daddy's fault, but I don't know what that means since we have a nice house and everything.

Bryan looks at me and puts his arms on the table.

"I bet that's why we're here," Bryan says, "I mean it makes sense, doesn't it?"

"What do you mean?" I say.

Bryan looks around the dining room and the chair creaks under his weight.

"I mean," Bryan says, "we're Dad's kids and without us, no moolah."

My mouth is dry and my stomach hurts. I don't understand and I do understand at the same time.

"I mean," Bryan says, "she sure doesn't love us. She barely likes us."

I look at Bryan and he looks at me. I'm not hungry, not at all, but I eat the tuna sandwich and it's salty in my mouth.

"What's going to happen to us?" I say.

"When the money runs out, you mean?" Bryan says.

"Will it?" I say.

Bryan moves his hand over his mouth and his eyes don't know any more than I do now. Outside is the sound of voices.

"I'm out of here," Bryan says.

He stands up and pushes in his chair.

"Bryan?" I say.

Downstairs, the front door opens and closes and Deb, Christopher, Kenny, and Ronny laugh and talk.

"See ya," Bryan says.

❧

My inside job is to clean the bathrooms and the rule is no TV until chores are done. I scrub the toilet with the toilet brush and I flush the soap bubbles down.

Everyone is in the TV room and *The Brady Bunch* is on the television.

I love *The Brady Bunch*.

I wipe the mirror off and there are streaks around the top.

The theme song is almost over and that means the show is going to be on any minute.

I hold the paper towel in my fist and go to the TV room, lean against the doorway.

Christopher reads a book and he looks at me over the top.

"I'll finish on the commercial," I say.

Christopher shrugs and looks at his book again.

I look at Bryan and he shrugs too. I push off the doorway and sit on the floor so my back leans against the sofa.

Kenny and Ronny are on the sofa and between them is a dog Deb bought from somewhere in Africa. Deb says the dog is called a basenji and that he cost four hundred dollars.

Broke, my ass.

The Brady Bunch is about how Marsha wants to make Mr. Brady father of the year, but she keeps getting herself into trouble. I've already seen this one, but I stay on the floor, even when it's a commercial. Christopher looks at me and I look at Christopher and he bites his lips together.

"You better finish up," Christopher says.

"I will," I say.

"You should do it now," Christopher says. "That's the way my mom wants it and we should follow her rules right now."

I cross my arms and look at the television. It's a commercial for a candy bar. I don't know why I want to break the rules, I just do.

"Lay off," Bryan says. "Deb's not even here."

It's nice the way he looks at me and smiles, like I count, like we have a secret.

"I'm going to finish, Christopher," I say. "I'm just going to do it later."

"It's not like I make the rules," Christopher says. "Let's just call my mom and let her decide."

Bryan laughs and it's a mean laugh.

"Good luck getting her to answer the telephone, mama's boy," Bryan says, "they're probably getting it on right now."

Christopher's face gets serious fast and he sits up tall.

"Who's getting it on?" Kenny says.

Bryan laughs out his nose and he looks at Kenny like she's too stupid.

"You know," Bryan says, "Deb and her 'special friend.'"

It's funny the way Bryan says that, "special friend," and I laugh out loud.

"Shut up," Ronny says.

"You shut up," I say.

Kenny looks at me, looks at Ronny. Christopher looks at the twins and it's the first time I've ever seen him anything close to being upset, his face all flushed and red.

"Use your head," Bryan says, "what do you think she's doing? Talking? Discussing current events?"

"Shut up," Ronny says. "That's a lie."

"Grow up, Veronica," Bryan says.

"You grow up," Christopher says. "You don't know what you're talking about."

Bryan sits back in his chair and looks all smug like he knows exactly what he's talking about. Right now, it's the best thing being on his side, being on the side that knows. I lean my back against the sofa and try to make my face all smug too.

The only sound is the television and everyone is a mad kind of quiet. Ronny moves around on the sofa and puts her foot on the floor. I look at her freckly toes almost on my arm and I cross my arms so we don't touch. Ronny moves around again and she rubs her foot on me.

"Stop it," I say.

"Get out of the way," Ronny says.

"Yeah," Kenny says, "you're in the way."

"I'm not," I say.

Ronny kicks up and down, kicks me with her heel and Kenny laughs.

"Knock it off," I say.

"I was here first," Ronny says.

"So what," I say.

"So leave," Ronny says.

"Yeah," Kenny says, "just leave."

All the anger in the room is inside my body and it beats against my chest. I have as much right to be here as they do and I'm tired of being the one everyone kicks around, tired of being on the outside, tired of being on the wrong side.

I stand up and look at Ronny, just Ronny, for a long time. She ignores me and then blinks her blue eyes and looks me right in the face.

"Take a picture," Ronny says, "it'll last longer."

I go into the bathroom and there is a broom in the corner. I take the broom in my hand and turn it upside down so the handle is down and the bristles are up. I go back to the living room and stand between Ronny and the TV.

"Get out of my way, you idiot," Ronny says, "I can't see the TV."

I look at Bryan and he looks at me.

"Fuck you, Veronica," I say.

I pull the broom back like a bat and hit the handle across Ronny's legs, the sound of wood on bone, the sound of Ronny's scream in my ears, Kenny screaming too even though I never even hit her. I pull the handle back and swing the other way.

Kenny jumps up so her feet are on the sofa and she holds her knees with her arms. Christopher stands up and starts yelling at us to stop.

Ronny jumps at me and knocks me on the ground so fast, I can't breathe. She pulls the broom out of my hands and lifts it over her head. Ronny's anger is even bigger than mine will ever be and her blue eyes look like an animal. She hits me in the face, one time, two times, three times, and the pain is worse than any pain I know.

Kenny screams. Christopher yells at Bryan to get me out of the room.

Bryan is over Ronny and pulls her off my body.

Ronny screams and struggles against Bryan and then Kenny jumps on Bryan's back, tries to pull him off Ronny.

I roll over and blood is on the carpet. I put my hand up and the blood is out of my mouth.

"Get out of here," Bryan yells, "now."

I get up on my hands and knees, crawl to the bathroom, and shut the door. Ronny screams how she is going to kill me and Kenny sounds like she's crying. Christopher says everyone should calm down, over and over.

My blood is red against the white tile floor, the white countertop, the white porcelain sink. There's blood down my chin, my neck, on my T-shirt and I lean over the sink and spit. One of my teeth rattles around in the sink and then another.

"Open the door," Bryan says.

I lean my ear against the door and it's quiet in the TV room. Bryan hits the door again and I turn the knob. It's just Bryan and he closes the door, locks the lock. I step back and hold my hand over my mouth.

"She knocked out two teeth," I say.

"Shit," Bryan says. "Let me see."

I sniff and it's the taste of blood down my throat.

"They're in the sink," I say.

Bryan looks into the sink and takes the teeth out, holds them up.

"Shit," he says.

Bryan puts the teeth on the counter and runs water in the sink. He takes a white washcloth and soaks it with water.

"Stop crying and come here," Bryan says.

In the mirror is Bryan's back and my face with blood everywhere. He wipes my chin and my neck and the washcloth is cold on my skin.

"It looks worse than it is," Bryan says, "it's just a lot of blood."

He rinses the washcloth out and the white is stained pink. He turns off the water and wipes around my nose.

"Does it hurt anywhere else?" he says. "I mean, do you think she broke your nose?"

"No," I say.

I lean close to the mirror and look at my face and it's purple and red around my nose, my eyes, my lips. I move my mouth around and spit blood into the sink. Bryan leans his hip against the counter and crosses his arms.

"I can't believe you," Bryan says.

"She just made me mad," I say. "I'm sick of her. I'm sick of all of them."

Bryan laughs and shakes his head.

"I guess so," Bryan says.

His dark eyes look like he knows all about being mad and fed up, and for the first time, maybe I know what it's like to be inside of Bryan.

I wipe blood off the counter and sink. I can feel Bryan's eyes and I rinse the washcloth out under the cold water. I look at Bryan in the mirror and he smiles.

"You're a spooky chick," Bryan says.

"I thought I was spunky," I say.

"Spooky and spunky," Bryan says.

He makes a fist and nudges my shoulder, but it's not like a real punch. I turn off the water and look at him looking at me, the two of us on the inside.

Chiquita is a chocolate milk color and she has a patch of white between her milk chocolate eyes. She smells like the goats, only there is a sweet smell too, warm and deep, and I like her special smell.

After I brush her whole horse body, I saddle her up and lead her out of the corral. The goats baa like they are hungry and I lock the gate so they can't get out.

"Baa baa yourself, you stupid goats," I say.

Chiquita lifts her head up and down like she thinks the

goats are stupid too. I rub the side of her face and lead her down to the dirt riding trail.

The thing about horses is how they are big and strong, but when you look at them, you just know they have a whole world of thoughts going on inside. No one has to tell me to be nice to Chiquita, I know from a place deep inside that you have to be nice to animals like horses, or bad things will happen to you.

"I'm going to get on now," I say, "okay, girl?"

Chiquita stands still and I put my foot in the stirrup, pull on top of her body, and adjust my behind in the saddle.

"You go where you want to go," I say, "this is your ride."

Chiquita moves her head around and she walks careful steps up the narrow trail. She always ends up at Windmill Hill, where there's a field of long sweet grass and wildflowers. Windmill Hill is the only place you can see the sky without looking through trees and when we get up there, I get off Chiquita and lie down under the wide blue sky.

The smell is grass and wind and clean and it's like being the only person in the world. Chiquita makes a horse noise and pulls up a mouthful of grass.

The sun is warm on my face and I close my eyes, the color orange behind my eyelids. I used to be able to see Daddy in color, used to be able to smell That Man and cigarettes, used to be able to hear the sound of his voice. When I close my eyes now, he's mostly black and white, like an old movie, and he's mostly the way he was the day we were on the boat trip to Catalina.

I wish he was here so I could tell him how Ronny knocked out two of my teeth, how Deb said it was my fault, and how I was on bread and water for five days as punishment.

A warm puff of horse breath is on my face and I open my eyes, the black and white of Daddy gone. Chiquita sniffs and makes a noise like laughing. I put my hand up to her nose and it's soft like velvet. She sniffs my hand and takes a bite of grass next to my shoulder.

Bryan is at the corral when we get back and he sits on the fence with his feet tucked between one of the slats.

"Where have you been?" he says.

"Why?" I say.

"Deb's on a rampage," he says.

It's funny the way he says that word and I laugh out loud.

Bryan pats Chiquita, his hand on her side.

"I think that old guy dumped her," Bryan says.

"Really?" I say.

Bryan holds Chiquita, I open the gate and push the goats back, and Bryan leads Chiquita into the corral.

"Who knows," Bryan says, "but she's all freaked out and says there's a family meeting. I'm supposed to get you."

He shuts the gate, takes the halter off Chiquita's head, and hangs it in the shed.

"Well, I can't go until I brush her out," I say.

I unbuckle the saddle, slide it off, and carry it to the shed.

"I'll help you," he says.

Bryan and me are quiet. Bryan fills up Chiquita's water trough and puts down a leaf of alfalfa. I brush off her back, her sides, her neck, and down her legs.

"What the hell are you doing?" Deb stands on the porch and holds the rail with both hands.

Bryan shades his eyes with his hand and squints.

"We're coming," Bryan yells.

"Hurry up," Deb yells.

The door slams and Deb is gone inside.

Bryan laughs and shakes his head.

"She's losing it," Bryan says.

I hit my hand against the horse brush and a cloud of dust lifts up in the sunshine. Bryan is right, Deb is losing it. She says we are going back to Los Angeles, says she is going to become a teacher for the Freedom Community Church, says they have agreed to admit her to their special training course for a very attractive price.

Deb talks and it's like watching something on television. Bryan looks at me across the table and his dark eyes have the same look.

Ronny looks like she is going to cry, Kenny is crying, and Christopher's face is white.

"But, Mom," Ronny says, "I don't want to move again."

"Me neither," Kenny says, her hand across her nose.

Deb puts her hand on her chest and her eyes look out the window like she sees the future.

"We have no choice," Deb says, "I've been chosen."

It's quiet like time has stopped right here, right now, and I look around the table. Bryan coughs and time starts again.

"Do you think this is funny?" Deb says.

"No," Bryan says.

"Do you have something to say?" Deb says.

Bryan sits up in his chair and looks at Deb with his smug look.

"What about your friend?" Bryan says.

The look in Deb's eyes is worse than mad and she moves her mouth so her lips are just a thin line.

"That's none of your damn business," Deb says.

Bryan lifts his dark eyebrows and laughs a quiet laugh.

"Excuse me," Bryan says.

I trace my finger from one red tulip to the next red tulip. I look up and Bryan looks at me like we have a secret.

"Mother," Ronny says, "I can't believe we're moving."

"I can't believe it," Kenny says.

"Girls," Deb says, "this is fate and we must follow."

fifteen

L A is hot and gray and dirty. Look up and it's smog. Look down and it's black and brown stains on concrete. Who knows what's on this sidewalk and how it got here.

Deb has a pair of round sunglasses on her face, Mod Squad shades, and she wears high heel boots and a short suede jacket with a belt that ties around her thin waist. Deb looks like a crime fighter from a comic book, long hair flapping around her shoulders.

It's just Deb and me and all around is the noise of buses and cars, horns and sirens.

An old man walks up to us and he has on a long coat, a dirty face, a sunburned nose, and he carries two bags full of shoes. He stops in front of Deb and he smells like trash and pee.

Deb steps back, touches her hand to her Mod Squad shades, and looks down her nose like maybe she's about to reach into her leather purse and pull out a gun to defend the street against bums.

"Spare some change, lady?" the man says, a smile on his face, not one tooth in his mouth.

Deb flips her hair over her shoulder like she never even heard the man.

"Come on," Deb says.

Deb's boot heels tap tap up some concrete steps, but I stay on the sidewalk. At the top of the steps is a big old house with lots of windows. The house is the only one in the middle of all the dirty and gray and noise and all the way around the house is a black iron fence. Outside the fence is some brown grass and a couple of trees.

Deb is at the top of the steps, one hand on the doorknob and the other hand on her thin hip.

"Well, get up here," she says.

My feet make a scraping sound over the concrete and bits of paper and cigarette butts clutter the corners of the steps. At the top of the steps, I look down at the sidewalk again.

I know he's gone, I really do, but I look for Daddy to come around the corner and reach out his hand.

Deb touches my shoulder instead and her hand is cold all the way through to my skin. I move my shoulder and go in the open door.

Inside, the house is quiet and cool and smells the way old houses smell. The ceilings are tall, the walls are painted white, and there's dark wood trim around the doors and windows. The floor is dark wood too.

Down a long hall, it's the sound of voices and I see the shadow of a man. No one comes to meet us.

"What it this place?" I say.

Deb takes off her sunglasses, folds them together, and walks in front of me.

"This is charming," Deb says, "early Victorian, maybe late. I get them confused."

Deb looks into a room off the entry and there's a sofa, a couple of chairs, and a fireplace. She turns around and walks to the entrance of another room.

"This is it," Deb says.

"It?" I say.

Deb puts her sunglasses into the pocket of her jacket and takes out a square of white paper. She reads something, looks at the room again, folds the paper, and shoves it back into her pocket.

"Yes," Deb says, "this is it."

Deb walks into the big room and it's long and wide with light fixtures built into the walls. The room is empty except for one rug and some mattresses on the floor. It's ten mattresses, singles and doubles, and some have sheets and blankets. A couple of the mattresses are bare and there are dark stains in the blue and white mattress material.

At the far end of the room is a circle of windows and daylight shines in at an angle, makes a rectangle of light on the dark wood floor. Deb walks to the circle of windows, the sound of her heels tap tap. I stand in the gray shadow where the sun doesn't shine and I look at Deb.

"This is just delightful," Deb says, "like a bay window except it's a bay room."

When something is wrong, my skin knows.

"Is this where we are going to live?" I whisper.

Deb moves her face down and puts her green eyes on my face.

"Not we," Deb says, "you."

"What?" I say.

Deb holds her arms up to the windows and smiles.

"Home sweet home," Deb says. "Your home."

"You're leaving me here?" I say.

Deb moves one foot forward, one foot back, and it's her mannequin pose, all hips and elbows.

"It's what you want," Deb says, "to be alone. You're getting what you want."

"What do you mean?" I say.

Deb bends at the waist and she looks at me a long time, just looks. There's a whole world inside Deb's green cat eyes, things I will never know, don't want to know. I look at my feet on the floor, but I can still feel her eyes on my head.

She stands up straight again and tugs at the belt around her waist.

"You are going to school at Hoover Street Elementary," Deb says. "It's within walking distance."

Deb moves her foot over a piece of something stuck to the floor, maybe gum.

"You are going to work to pay your way," Deb says, "here in the kitchen and at the Freedom Community after school."

"What about Bryan?" I say.

Deb walks in a circle and her boots tap tap on the wood floor.

"You are expected to be somewhere every day," Deb says, "and I will be informed if you neglect your responsibilities."

"Where is Bryan?" I say.

Deb stops walking and holds her hands behind her back.

"You always ask too many questions," Deb says.

Nothing is real, nothing makes sense, and I look around. Inside my head is a line of questions and they push against each other, push to get out.

"But," I say, "how long do I have to stay here?"

"That is up to you," Deb says.

"Me?" I say.

Deb looks out the window and puts her hands on her hips, fingers splayed out wide over her hipbones.

"How?" I say. "How is it up to me?"

Deb won't look at me, acts like she doesn't hear my voice.

"How will I know where to go?" I say.

Deb snaps her fingers in the air.

"Figure it out," Deb says. "It's called survival."

She reaches into the pocket of her coat, takes out a ten-dollar bill, and lays it on the windowsill.

"This is for expenses," Deb says, "incidentals."

"Deb?" I say. "You can't do this."

Deb presses her lips together in a line, thin eyebrows low over her creepy cat eyes, and I know she's done. She walks away, her heels tap tap all the way to the front door. Deb never looks back, not one time.

"You can't just leave me here," I yell.

Deb stops at the door, takes out her Mod Squad shades, and puts them on.

"You'll thank me later," Deb says.

She opens the door, walks out, and closes the door behind her.

It's just me and the rectangle of sun and old house quiet all around. I run to the window, stand on my tiptoes, and it's the back of Deb's head until she turns the corner and is gone.

I lean against the wall and slide down until my behind hits the wood floor. I pull my knees to my chest, the smell of dust in my nose. I press my hands hard against my eyes, but it's too late. Hot tears push through my fingers, roll down my arms, and drip off my elbows.

I don't know how long I sit there like that, seems like forever, and then someone calls my name. There's a lightness in my chest, in my heart, and I know its Daddy.

I take my hands off my face and a man in orange coveralls looks at me.

"Hey," the guy says, "you expecting some furniture?"

My arms and my legs are heavy and I push off the floor. There's a big circle left where I sat in the dust and I wipe my hands over my butt.

"Are you okay?" the guy says.

I sniff and push my wet hands over my jeans. Deep inside is flat and empty.

"Sure," I say, "I'm just great."

The guy looks at his clipboard and he looks at me again.

"This can't be right," the guy says, "but I got a bunch of furniture for Jennifer Lauck."

"That's me," I say.

I push my hands into my pockets and look at the guy. The guy looks at his clipboard again and shrugs his shoulders.

"Okay," he says, "where do you want the stuff?"

The moving guys are Darryl and Chuck. Darryl wears the orange coveralls and Chuck has on jeans and a sweatshirt that says *Keep on Truckin'*. They carry all my stuff into the half-circle of a room: the headboard, the mattress, the box spring, the dresser, the desk, the mirror, the chair with the gold seat, and all the posts for the canopy bed.

The last thing is my pink trunk and Darryl carries it against his chest.

"Be careful," I say, "stuff in there can break."

Darryl lowers the pink trunk to the floor and I can hear the stuff move around inside. He wipes his hands together, steps back, and Chuck says that's it.

Darryl checks something off his clipboard and hands the board to me.

"Sign here," Darryl says.

I write my name in cursive letters and Darryl turns his head to the side, reads my name. Chuck and Darryl look at each other, look at me, and Chuck puts his hands into his pockets.

"Is anyone here to help put this stuff together?" Darryl says.

I look at the pieces of my room and lick my lips.

"I don't need any help," I say, "I can do it."

Chuck laughs and he pushes his hands deeper into his pockets like he's reaching for his knees. Darryl scratches his head.

"Shit," Darryl says, "I can't just let a little kid put all this junk together. How about we get your bed set up, maybe move things the way you want them?"

Individuals who solve problems are self-sufficient.

Fuck you, Deb.

"That's okay," I say. "I've got it."

Darryl looks at me, eyes steady.

"Okay," Darryl says, "I guess."

"Really," I say, "I can do it."

Deb thinks she's so smart, thinks she knows all about me, but one thing is for sure, Deb doesn't know shit about me and I'm going to show her how I don't need anything, I don't need anyone.

I slide the bookcase, the dresser, and the other bookcase in a row so the back sides face out and the front sides face in. My princess furniture makes a wall between me and the rest of the big room and you can only see out if you look between the cracks.

My canopy bed goes between the wall of furniture and the

windows and I balance the headboard against the wall. The metal bars for the mattress are on the floor and I lay them between the headboard and the end board.

Bryan says my bed is like a puzzle, so I fit it together the way he did, one piece at a time. Sweat is down my back and over my stomach and I wipe my face with my arm.

There are no sheets on the bed and it looks naked and raw that way. I sit on the edge of the mattress and outside the window is the faraway sound of horns, a siren, and then someone yells something in Spanish.

I push the toe of one shoe against the heel of the other, push until the shoe is off and it hits against the wall under the window. I pull the key from under the laces and hold the shoe in my hand. I unlock the pink trunk, and open the lid.

My sheets, bedspread, and pillows are packed tight with my books, the clock radio, and all my other secret things.

I tuck the sheets and blanket tight, shake out the bedspread, and pull until it's flat. I punch my pillow three times and put it at the top of the bed. I carry my desk chair to the edge of the bed, climb up, and shake out the pink canopy fabric. Each corner goes up over the poles and it stays in place with a decorative knob that fits into the pole. I put each knob in and the canopy hangs over my bed, like pink safety.

There's the Sleeping Beauty lamp, the lamp for the bookcase, my clock radio, and the cassette player with the *West Side Story* cassette tape. *Mary Poppins, Ferdinand the Bull, Snow White and the Seven Dwarfs* all go into the bookcase. I put everything out like this is normal and then I sit on my bed with my old copy of *Snow White and the Seven Dwarfs*.

My body is tired and the all-alone feeling feels like someone knocking inside my body. My room is nice though, as nice as any room, and that'll show Deb.

The black cloth cover is embossed with a raven and a dove and between the birds is a flower in full bloom. I never noticed that before and I move my fingers over, feeling the birds and the flower. Inside, I turn the pages and just look at the drawings.

The first drawing is of the queen by her ebony-framed window.

The second drawing is Snow White barefoot in the forest.

The third drawing is Snow White with the dwarfs.

The fourth drawing is of the whole kingdom at sunset.

The fifth drawing is a full moon through a window and the evil stepmother holds an apple to the moonlight. There is a wood table and on top are roots and herbs and flowers and a book that's open to a page with a recipe for poison. A black widow spider weaves her web in the corner and three tarot cards are face up, the death card on top.

The stepmother plans death because it's not enough to have a castle and be a queen, she has to be the most beautiful woman too. That's just the way it is with some people, they can have so much and they're still miserable.

There is sound in the big room and I open my eyes. It's cold and dark in my part of the room, circles of light from the big room. *Snow White and the Seven Dwarfs* is on the floor, so I pick it up and close the cover.

I look through the crack between my dresser and bookcase and a lady with a braided ponytail sits under one of the lights. The lady reads a Freedom Community Church book with birds all over the cover and there are dirty clothes around her mattress. A couple of mattresses down is a man with a back-pack and he stands and looks at the mattress on the floor, just looks.

I walk into the big room and stand there. The lady doesn't look at me, just reads. I walk by the man with the backpack and he looks at me, nods, and puts his eyes on the mattress again.

In the entryway, I turn around and look at my corner of the big room. All you can see is the back of the bookcases and the dresser and then it's just dark.

A staircase leads up and it's twenty-two steps, a sharp turn, and twenty-two more steps to the second floor. At the top of the stairs is a bathroom and inside is an old-fashioned bathtub with feet. I shut the door and feel my hand along on the wall for a lightswitch. The light comes on over the mirror and it's just a bare bulb.

Streaks of dirt are down my cheeks to my chin and I turn on the water, lean over the sink, and wash the dirty lines of tears away. I turn off the water and make a smile. I stop smiling and look at my eyes. I don't know what there is inside of me that makes Deb hate me so much. I don't know what it is that makes everything so hard. All there is in the mirror is me and the way I look, I'm just like any other kid.

I dry my face with toilet paper, blow my nose, and throw the tissue in the trash. I take another wad of tissue, wipe the extra water off around the sink, and throw that tissue in the trash too.

Out of the bathroom, I look down the hallway, the smell of dust and spices up here. There are closed doors and I can hear people move around in their rooms.

It's twenty-two steps down, turn, twenty-two more, and I'm at the entryway again. There's a dark hall and on the other side I can hear kitchen sounds. I go fifteen steps down the hall and on the other end is a wide kitchen half set up for cooking, the other half for eating. The kitchen is painted a yellow color, the floor is brown linoleum, and there's a big cutting board table between the sink and stove. A wide wire rack hangs over the cutting board table and every kind of cooking thing hangs off: spatulas, pans, bowls, whisks.

A man and a woman are cooking in here. The man stirs something in a pot on the stove and the lady cuts bread at the cutting board table. The man looks at me, looks at his pot, and looks at me again.

"Who are you?" he says.

The lady looks at me too and she has on a white apron.

"I'm Jenny," I say.

The lady smiles a nice smile, a welcome smile, and she has the best hair I've ever seen, blond and red and brown mixed together and it's long and curly around her shoulders.

The lady comes around the cutting board table and she has a big round stomach pushed way out. She tucks curls behind her ears and smiles her nice smile.

"That must be all your pretty bedroom furniture in the front room," she says, "I had to sneak a peek. I'm Karen."

Karen holds her hand out the way grown-ups do when they say hello for the first time. I put my hand into her hand and her skin is soft.

"That's Max," Karen says.

Max moves his face around like he has to scratch or something and he holds his hand out too. Max's hand is a give-me-five hand and I don't know what to do, give him five or not. I look at his hand, look at Max. He has black eyes and black hair and black whiskers. Max takes his hand back before I figure out what to do and puts his hands on his hips behind his back.

"We've been expecting you," Max says.

"You knew I was coming?" I say.

Karen puts her hands over her stomach and moves them around and around.

"We need the help," she says.

Max leans his hip against the cutting board table and looks at me up and down.

"I thought you were a little older," Max says. "Do you know anything about cooking?"

I stand up tall, shoulders straight, chin tucked, and I hold my hands behind my back.

"I can make toast," I say, "and sandwiches. And I can scramble eggs."

Karen laughs, the sound light and high. Max laughs too and he rubs his hand over his chin.

"I'm almost eleven," I say.

"Eleven?" Karen says.

Karen stops smiling and she looks at Max, looks at me. They talk without words and I know something is wrong.

"I'm a tall eleven," I say, "I think."

Karen looks at me again and she has a sad look all of a sudden.

"Well, Jenny," Karen says, "welcome."

Karen ties a white apron around my waist and up close she smells like the upstairs spices. My apron goes all the way to the floor and over my shoes and Karen stands back, laughs at how I look. Max laughs too.

I wash my hands at the big sink and the soap smells bitter and sharp, stings my skin. Karen says it's homemade soap. Max says it's strong to kill the germs. Even when my hands are rinsed off and dry, I can still smell the soap and Max laughs at the way I sniff my fingers, says I'll get used to the smell.

Max shows me where all the dishes are for setting up the

table and says I can just pile them up on one end so people can serve themselves.

There's no rule about eating in the kitchen or eating in your room, the only rule is that people in the house have to help pay for the food. Max says no one eats unless they put money in a jar at the end of the table, but he says I don't put money in because I'm a kitchen helper.

I set the table with a pile of plates, a pile of bowls, a pile of spoons and knives.

I'm the most hungry I can remember and my stomach makes hungry sounds. Karen dishes out a bowl of stew from the pot on the stove and says I can have a slice of bread too.

Karen and Max make themselves a bowl of stew too and sit down at the table, Karen across from me and Max next to Karen.

They eat and I eat and it's quiet in the kitchen. The stew is carrots and potatoes and broccoli in brown gravy and it's good, really good.

People come into the kitchen, put money in the jar, serve up a bowl of stew, take bread. Some leave, some stay. The woman with the braid comes in and sits at the other end of the table. She doesn't look at Max or Karen or me, just eats with her eyes on her food.

When I look up Karen looks at me, a little smile on her face.

"Where is your family?" Karen says.

The table has three pots of tall plants, red flowers on the tops, big leaves around the middle. I reach out and touch my fingers to one of the pots, cool clay against my fingertip.

"It's kind of complicated," I say.

The lady with the braid looks at me and looks down again. I take my hand off the pot and put both hands in my lap.

"You don't have to tell us anything, man," Max says, "none of our business, right?"

"Are you in the Freedom Community?" Karen says.

"Karen," Max says.

"I'm just curious," Karen says, "I mean I never heard of such a thing, a child here."

"No other kids have been here before?" I say.

"Karen," Max says.

Karen and Max look at each other and Max pulls off a piece of his bread and dips at his stew.

"Well," Karen says, "there was a little boy, but his mother was here too."

"It's okay, man," Max says, "your old lady told me how she's a little busted and you're a good worker, so it's cool."

"My old lady?" I say.

"Deb?" Max says. "Something like that. Isn't she your mother?"

"No," I say and I look down at my stew.

"My mother is dead," I say. "My father is dead too."

It's a terrible quiet, just the sound of my voice in my ears and those words on the table around the pots of red flowers.

The lady with the braided hair gets up, takes her bowl to the sink, washes it out, and dries it off.

Karen leans over and reaches her hand out palm up.

"I'm so sorry," Karen says.

I look at Karen's hand, how it's so soft and white inside, and I wish I didn't say anything now, stupid, stupid, stupid in my head.

Karen clears her throat and takes her hand back.

"It's okay," I say.

Karen tilts her head and smiles a sad smile.

"Old soul," Max says.

"Definitely," Karen says.

It's quiet for a long time, Max and Karen and me, and then Max clears his throat, explains how things are.

Max says the house is part Freedom Community Church, part commune, says people who just pass through stay in the big front room. Max and Karen live upstairs and another couple lives up there too. Max says I need to help with breakfast and dinner, six-thirty and five-thirty, says I just show up and he'll tell me what to do.

When Max stops talking, it's quiet in the kitchen, and I know I should get up and leave. I want to stay with Max and Karen, the flowers and the quiet. They look at me and I look at them, but I don't have any words to say.

I get up from the table, clean out my bowl, and dry it with a dish towel. I take off my white apron and fold it in a little square.

"Do you know what time it is?" I say.

Karen and Max look at me, smiles on their faces, and Max looks at his watch.

"Eight-thirty," Max says.

"Thanks," I say. "See ya."

"In the morning," Max says. "Bright and early."

My corner of the room is just like I left it and I sit on the edge of my bed, take the clock radio, and set the time to eight-thirty. I set the radio alarm for six o'clock A.M., and adjust the clock so I can see the numbers from my bed.

A street lamp shines a white light through the top part of the windows and it makes white and black shadows over the top of the pink canopy. The wind blows the bushes against the window and the branches scrape the glass. It's scary here, scary to be alone, but my princess bedroom is nice and somehow it feels safe.

I rub my hands over my face, up and down, and then I take off my shoes, pull back the bedspread, blanket, and sheets. I curl tight in a little ball under the covers and close my eyes. Branches scrape against the window and I open my eyes, look at the dirt smears on the glass. I pull the blankets over my head and close my eyes again.

If someone comes in here, I can run down the hall and scream loud, scream for Max and Karen, and I know they would help me.

I pull my pillow down so it's against my chest and I hold the pillow as tight as I can. Warm moves up my legs and back, that familiar sleepy feeling, and finally, I don't think about anything at all.

sixteen

When you sleep in your clothes, it's not really sleep, it's waiting for dark to be light.

I open my eyes and it's bright morning in the circle of windows. The clock radio says six and the radio automatically turns on. A man on the radio talks about God, about faith, says life is a mystery we cannot understand without the light. I push the button, turn off the voice, put the clock radio on the bookcase again.

It's quiet in the big room, people under covers, under sleeping bags. Five of the mattresses have people on them, the other five are empty.

I walk twenty-five steps through the big room, up the twenty-two steps, turn, twenty-two more, and the bathroom door is open. At the end of the hall is a closed door and music plays on the other side of the door, sad, slow music.

I turn on the light and lock the bathroom door. I put on a pair of jeans, clean underpants, a shirt with a yellow sun face on the front, clean socks, and my shoes with the silver key on the lace.

I brush my teeth and make sure all the sleepy gunk is gone from around my eyes. My hair sticks up here and there and I bring it all around to the side, comb from the bottom up. After the comb, I brush until all my hair is smooth, and then I pull it all back and make one ponytail. I put on my gray sweatshirt, roll my dirty clothes into a pile, and gather all my stuff together.

In the hall, there's a different kind of music, sounds like Beatles music. I love the Beatles, my most favorite music after Michael Jackson. I walk slow steps to the door and listen. My toothbrush soaks wet through my sweatshirt and my T-shirt and I can feel the wet on my skin. The song is "The Long and Winding Road," and I just knew it was the Beatles.

It's just Max in the kitchen and he breaks eggs into a big pot. He smiles like he's really happy and I don't know what to do, just stand there and rub my hands together.

"Right on time," Max says, "I like that."

"Where's Karen?" I say.

"Karen just helps with dinners now," Max says. "Wash your hands and come on over."

I wash my hands with the stinky soap and Max tosses me the white apron from last night, still folded in a little square.

"I heard music upstairs," I say, "the Beatles."

Max nods, black whiskers and mustache, white teeth.

"Karen digs the Beatles," Max says.

I tie the apron around my middle.

"Okay," Max says. "Come up here and crack a few eggs."

Max slides a step stool to the cutting board table and I climb up. He takes an egg in one hand, hits it on the edge of the pot, pulls the shell back with his fingers, and the egg falls into the pot with all the other eggs. Looks like twenty eggs in there.

"One-handed," Max says, "now you try."

Max puts his hands on his hips, his white apron half folded down, and he smells like coffee and spices, cinnamon and nutmeg.

I take an egg out of the carton, hold it in one hand, hit it like Max did, and pull it apart. Max moves my hand so it's over the middle of the pot, spreads my fingers open from the egg, and the yellow yolk falls out, egg white dripping a long line. Max's hand on my hand is scratchy and dry and he lifts my whole hand up and down, makes the rest of the egg drip out.

"Nice," Max says, "but you have to be quick and confident. Got it?"

I put the eggshell into the carton and take out another egg.

It's the same thing again and I get it right. I look at Max to make sure and he nods and smiles.

"Now do that whole carton and then whip them good," Max says.

Max reaches up, takes a wire whisk off the wire rack, puts it on the cutting board table, and I pick out another egg. Max goes around the table, starts cutting a new loaf of bread, puts four slices in a big toaster by the stove. Max moves around the kitchen like he knows everything about cooking. He takes out a big black pan, throws in a hunk of butter, and turns on the heat. He looks at me cracking eggs, smiles, looks at the big black pan again, and moves the butter around with a spatula.

Max picks up his white mug, makes a sip sound.

"Don't guess you want coffee?" Max says.

I wipe my hands on my apron.

"I never had coffee," I say.

Max takes a new mug off the counter, fills it up halfway, sets it next to me on the cutting board table.

"Let it cool off first," Max says, "then tell me what you think."

I put the last eggshell in the carton, take the whisk, and whip all the separate eggs into a big yellow glob of egg. Max comes around the table, looks into the pot and nods. He takes the pot and whisk, keeps whipping, and carries the whole thing to the stove.

The toaster pops, four slices up, and Max pours the eggs into the pan of melted butter.

"Take that toast," Max says, nods to the toaster, "stack it on a plate, and add four more slices. We'll let folks butter and jam what they want. Butter's in the refrigerator there."

I do like Max says, move toast, slice bread, make more toast, and I hope I'm doing it right. Max never says anything, never really checks on me at all, and I guess I must be doing it okay. I set the table with plates and forks and mugs for coffee. I make a pitcher of frozen orange juice, four cans of juice, sixteen cans of water mixed in.

People come in the kitchen while Max works on the eggs, while I work on the toast, and they sit around the big table eating breakfast. Some people say hi to Max, say "How are you doing, man?" No one talks to me.

When all the people are done taking toast, eating eggs, and drinking coffee, it's just Max and me again.

"Pretty crazy," Max says, "but that's it."

"That's it?" I say.

"Right," Max says. "Breakfast isn't a big deal around here, dinner's the main meal."

Max goes to the table, turns the jar of money around, spills the cash and coins out. He stacks coins, counts the dollar bills.

"You can eat now," Max says, "just help yourself."

Down the hall is the sound of the door opening and closing, the sound of people leaving. I want to eat, maybe some eggs, maybe some toast. The mug of coffee Max poured is still on the cutting board table, but it's cold. I pour it into the sink, fill the mug up again, and look at the steam move over the black. I sip the coffee, just a little sip since it's so hot, and the taste is bitter.

Max walks over, lays three dollars by the coffeepot.

"That's for you," Max says.

"Me?" I say.

"For helping in the kitchen," he says, "last night and today. Not a lot, but you know, it's something."

I look at the money for a long time and then I take the three dollar bills, fold them in half, in half again, push them into my pocket like I know all about getting paid.

"Thanks," I say.

He nods at the counter, where there is a small white bowl and a little carton of something called half and half.

"There's milk and sugar if it's too strong," Max says. Max carries his mug of coffee back to the table, takes a plate, and spoons out eggs. He takes a piece of toast, swings his leg over a chair, and sits down.

I put milk and sugar in the coffee and it makes it taste nice. I carry the mug to the table, sit down a couple chairs away from Max. He eats with his fist holding his fork, his eyes on his food. I take one slice of toast off the pile, put it on a napkin. I take a spoon, stir the honey around, lift the spoon out, and let the honey line fall on my toast.

"Can I ask you something?" I say.

"Sure," Max says.

The honey pools on the toast, sinks in, and I swirl it in a circle.

"I'm supposed to go to school," I say, "Hoover Street."

Max eats a bite of egg, nods his head.

"Where is it?" I say.

Max sits up straight, swallows, eyes wide like he is surprised.

"South Hoover Street? It's about twenty blocks up from here," Max says.

I take a bite of my toast and nod like I knew that. Swallowing the toast, I sip at the coffee like everything is just fine.

"The Freedom Community Church?" I say, "Do you know where that is, you know, from here?"

Max takes a piece of toast, holds it up, and moves it back and forth like drawing a map in the air.

"There's a bus," Max says, "you can catch it by the park and take it across town."

"Right," I say.

It's quiet in the kitchen and I look at my toast, just two bites gone. Max leans over his plate, hands flat on the table.

"You seem like a pretty nice kid," Max says.

"What?" I say.

"Well," Max says, "I'm just saying, it's a heavy load when you have to figure things out all alone."

I trace my fingers through toast crumbs on the table.

"It's supposed to be this way," I say. "That's what Deb says."

Max looks at me and I can't look back at him since I know I'll start to cry and I don't want to cry, not here, not now, not again.

I open the front door and stand at the top of the steps. Everything is the same as yesterday but different at the same time. I'm all alone and no one is here to tell me what to do, no one. I look around for Deb, for Bryan, for anyone I know, but it's just quiet morning, a bus across the street, and some birds that peck at the dry grass in front of the old house.

I go down the steps and there's a bum on the sidewalk with his back against the concrete wall. The man is bunched up under a dark gray coat, head down so his chin is against his chest and he looks like he's sleeping.

I tiptoe around the man and the smell off him is strong and bitter.

He moves his head a little, up and down, and I turn around fast, walk away fast, and push my hands deep into my pockets.

It's forty-two steps per block, ten to get across the street, and each section of sidewalk is three steps. If Deb is supposed to be my mother, I don't care about the cracks. I walk three steps over the section of sidewalk and stop, jump with both feet on the crack.

Fuck you, Deb.

Whenever you come to a street, the rule is look both ways. If there is a red light, you wait until it turns green and the sign says WALK. The light is red and the sign says DON'T WALK. No one is behind me, no one is across the street, no traffic is between me and the other side. The light stays red. I look around again and it seems like a pretty stupid rule when no one is here.

I run across against the DON'T WALK sign, run down the next block, run across the next street, cross all the streets against the DON'T WALK and nothing happens to me. Stupid rule.

I stop running and just walk without counting anything. Everywhere I look is sidewalk and street, buses and cars, and I think I'm lost. A man waits at a bus stop with a newspaper under his arm. He says Hoover Street is just a couple more blocks.

A couple more blocks and I hear kid sounds. I walk another block and I can see a playground with kids inside.

Deb says I have to go to school, says it's all worked out.

I cross on the DON'T WALK and walk along the outside of the playground, touch my hand to the chain link fence.

Inside the playground, kids bounce balls, play hopscotch, chase each other, kid stuff. There's every kind of kid too, black, white, brown, and they talk and yell in lots of different languages.

A bell rings and all the kids run off the playground until it's just empty asphalt and a couple balls that roll against the fence.

No one is here to tell me to go in and I wonder if Deb watches from some secret hiding place. I look around and bite my bottom lip. No one is here, just me, and I walk around the school and pull open a double door. Inside is dark hall and shiny floor. There are doors all the way down the hall and some doors are open, some of the doors are closed.

In the hall, it's like I'm outside the real world and I take a deep breath. Every room is the same, kids at desks, a teacher who talks and writes on the chalkboard. There is a water fountain and I turn the silver handle, just a wet dribble of water and it's no use drinking off that.

The office is halfway down the hall and inside a lady with glasses on her face talks on the telephone and another lady types at a typewriter. I wonder if these ladies know I'm supposed to be here and now I'm late. The lady with glasses hangs up the telephone and looks at me. The lady on the typewriter just keeps typing.

"May I help you?" says the lady with the glasses.

"I'm supposed to go to school here," I say.

She takes my name, goes to a file cabinet, pulls out a little card, and I know she doesn't know me and she doesn't know I'm late. She reads something, says how I am going to be in Mrs. Greene's fifth grade class, says how Mrs. Greene is room eight.

I walk out of the office like I know where to go and what to do.

Just like that, I'm back in a school again. The thing is, when you aren't like everyone else, when you aren't normal, school isn't real, and that's how I feel here, like it's not real at all. There are other kids and there is a teacher, but I don't see them, don't become part of what they are a part of. They belong here and I don't, and that's just the way it is.

After school, I walk back the way I came, afternoon sunshine warm on everything. I carry a brown bag with books and papers and homework.

At the big house, my canopy bed is made up like I left it, but there is a butt dent in the middle of the bedspread and a note by the dent. The note says *JENNY* and the writing is Deb's.

I look around and wonder if Deb is hiding somewhere. The note says that I should go to the Freedom Community Church and meet someone named Ray, that I have a cleaning job and Ray will explain. Deb wrote the address down, wrote how I have to take a crosstown bus.

She's not here, but it's like she is here, and I hate how she was in my room, how she sat on my bed and messed it up with her skinny butt. I smooth out my bedspread so there is no proof of Deb.

There are lots of buses, none of them called crosstown, and I can't figure out which one I should be on. A lady waits for a bus by the park and I ask her about the crosstown bus, where it is. She smiles and points to the bus stop across the street.

You have to have exact change for the bus and you can't get on if you don't. I go to a 7-Eleven store to get change for a dollar. The man in the store says he can't give me change unless I buy something.

I look around the store, down the aisles of toilet paper, potato chips, and candy. I go down the candy aisle and get a Butterfinger, a crunch bar, and twenty Tootsie Rolls and lay them on the counter. The man rings up my candy, says forty cents, and I give him a dollar. The man puts my candy in a brown bag, presses his lips together and nods. I take the bag and my change, nod my head back. I fold the top over and over, all the way down until I can't fold it anymore, and go back to the bus.

The Freedom Community Church is in a building that looks like an old warehouse. There's a sign out front and it says *Freedom Community* and under is a rainbow with birds that fly through the colors.

I stand in front of the glass double doors, see my reflection in the glass. My sweatshirt is around my waist and my hair is still in a ponytail. I pull to make the rubber band tighter and look side to side for Deb or Bryan or someone I know. No one is here, so I open the door and go inside.

Ray is a black man and he has chocolate eyes, red in the white part, and he swings his arms when he walks, bends his knees deep too. Ray says I'm in charge of emptying the trash and cleaning the big lady's office. That's the way he says it, "big lady," and the big lady is the person in charge of everything.

Ray walks slow, talks slow, and he shows me where the

empty trash bags are, where to put the full trash bags, where all the cleaning supplies are. Then Ray takes me to the big lady's office, where I'm supposed to dust everything, empty the trash, and once a week, shine the silver tea set that sits behind her desk.

Ray says I clean only when the big lady is gone, never go in when she's there, that's the rule.

I do what Ray tells me to do, empty trash, wipe down around books on the bookshelf, behind the desk, around the typewriter next to the desk. I wipe down the desk, around the telephone and around the one photograph. It might be the big lady in the picture, except she isn't that big, she's just a small person with white hair, pink cheeks, and a happy smile.

After I'm done, I look all over for Ray and I tell him I'm all done. Ray smiles, teeth more yellow than white, and says, "See you later, alligator."

I laugh at how he says that, but Ray says you're supposed to say, "In a while, crocodile."

I laugh so hard I can't say anything. Ray says it's not really that funny, but that makes me laugh harder. I laugh so hard I have to pinch my sides and cross my legs. Ray watches me, rubs his hand over the top of his head, and says I'm a crazy white girl.

I like the way he says "crazy white girl" and he's right, I am crazy, going crazy, gone crazy, who knows.

It's almost dark when I get off the crosstown bus at the park. I run across the street on the DON'T WALK, run along the sidewalk, run up the steps to the big house.

Inside it's the same as it was when I left and I look in the big room, all my stuff back in the shadows. I make myself walk to the kitchen, even though I want to run.

Max and Karen are already there.

"I'm sorry," I say. "I'm sorry I'm late."

"You're not," Max says, "you're right on time."

I bend over and put my hands on my knees, all out of breath.

Karen moves around the table and stands close. She smells like flowers and something sweet.

"It's okay," Karen says, "you don't have to be right on time anyway, we're cool around here."

Karen's eyes are green and brown and her great hair is piled up on top of her head.

"Sorry," I say.

Karen puts her hand on my shoulder, touches so light it's like she isn't touching at all.

"No need for sorry," Karen says, "let's get you an apron."

❧

I don't know how long it's just me in the big house, a couple days, a week, maybe a month, when I wake up in the darkest part of night with a terrible itch in my hands. The itch is so bad, I can't sleep, and I have to go upstairs and put cold water on my palms until the itch goes away. If you look close, there are bumps on the soft part of my palms, too many bumps to count, and inside the bumps are tiny blisters. If you push on the blisters, they pop and clear fluid runs out.

Then it's my eyes.

One morning I wake up and my eyes are stuck shut.

Hands into fists, I rub into my eyes, but they won't open and my whole body is pins and needles. I sit up in bed, eyes stuck shut, dark all I can see.

"I'm blind," I yell, "I'm blind."

No one says anything, no one comes. I know people are out there, I know someone had to hear me.

"Help," I yell, "I'm blind."

It's quiet, my voice the only sound, and no one comes.

When you wake up and you need help, someone should come, that's the way it should be, but that's not the way it is here. When no one cares that I'm blind, no one comes to help, that's when I start to cry, hands over my face. I cry and cry and the wet melts the crusty gunk just enough so that my eyes start to open, just enough so I can see light out there.

I stop crying, get out of bed, feel my way along the wall of the big room. It's twenty-five steps to the hall, ten steps to the staircase. I can see my feet on the floor and if I tilt my head back, I can see the steps. My hand out to the handrail, I hold on tight and go slow up the stairs. Twenty-two steps, turn, twenty-two more. At the top of the steps, I tilt my head back, the door is open, and I walk five steps into the dark bathroom.

I feel along the wall to the toilet and then to the sink, turn on the hot and cold water. I put my hands under the water and rub around my eyes. The rest of the gunk melts away and my eyes open all the way.

My eyes are wet and red, gunk all over the lashes and in the corners. I clean and clean all the gunk off so they are just like they always are, but the red doesn't go away and they itch.

I walk slow steps down the staircase, go into the big room, and there are lots of people in here, people who heard me yell for help, who heard me say I was blind. No one in this house cares about you, everyone just pretends you're not even here, just like Deb.

I stand up straight, shoulders back, chin tucked, and I don't need any help anyway. I don't need anybody. I walk fast through the big room, go to my part of the room, and make my bed.

My hands don't heal, my eyes stay red, and then one day, the worst thing happens.

I come back from work at the Freedom Community Church and my room is all wrong. My books are on the floor, my clock radio is unplugged, my lamps are on the bed, and my cassette player is gone. The tape for *West Side Story* is gone and my wood jewelry box is empty. All the stuff in my drawers is messed up, like someone moved my things around. Even my comb is gone. I can't believe someone stole my comb.

Two people are in the big room, new people I don't know, a guy and a woman. They sit on a bed facing each other, but their eyes are closed. I want to scream at them, but I don't do anything, just stand there.

My heart beats in my ears and I turn around in my room. The pink trunk is pulled out a little and there are scratches in the metal around the lock. On the floor, I kick off my shoe and open the lock with my key. Inside, my trunk is the way it was: Barbie suitcase, Our Wedding book, the black velvet bag of Momma's pearls and her wedding ring, the drawing by Keith, 1971. I sit back on my heels, my hands over my heart, and it beats hard against my fingers.

Quiet, quiet, just the sound of my breathing, and nothing is the same here, never was. I go around my room and take my things off my dresser, out of my bookcases, off the desk, and I pile everything into the pink trunk. My books, my clock radio, my jewelry box, everything is in danger. I push the lock closed with my whole hand and push the pink trunk under my bed. My room is empty without my things, but I don't care about that anymore. No way anyone is going to take what's mine, not ever again.

I put my shoe on my foot and tie the lace with the key into a double knot.

I hate everyone here, everyone. I know someone in this house stole my stuff.

In the kitchen, Max cuts onions on the cutting board table.

"Hey," Max says.

Maybe Max stole my stuff and I look at him, look away, and nod. Karen is at the big table and she sips a mug of something. She looks at me, smiles, and I quickly smile back and stop smiling. I wash my hands with the stinky soap, take an apron out of the drawer by the sink, and put it over my head. I feel Max and Karen looking at me, but I don't care. I tie the apron around my middle.

"Everything okay?" Max says.

"Yeah," I say, "everything is just great. What do you want me to do?"

Max looks at Karen, looks at me.

"Spaghetti tonight," Max says, "so how about you fill that pan with water for the noodles."

I pull the big pan off the shelf under the cutting board table and lift it with both hands.

"Why don't you help her lift that big pan?" Karen says.

"I don't need any help," I say.

I put the pan in the sink and it makes a bang sound. Max reaches for the step stool and I shake my head.

"I said I got it," I say.

I push the stool to the sink, climb up, and turn on the water. Karen comes to the sink, pours out what's left in her cup, and it's the smell of mint.

I look at the running water, just the water, and then I turn off the tap. Karen and her big stomach stay right next to me and I can feel her eyes watch.

"How are you doing today?" Karen says.

Karen's voice is soft and nice and it's hard to be so mad when she's so close, the smell of her flowery perfume all over.

"It's a bad day," I say.

"Really?" Karen says. "Want to tell me why?"

Max comes to the sink then, both hands on the big pot full of water, and he makes a grunt noise when he lifts it up. I watch Max and take a deep breath.

"We should cook," I say. "What should I do?"

Karen looks around the kitchen, hands on her hips, stomach pushed out.

"You can slice the bread," Karen says, "and put butter between the slices, how about that?"

At the cutting board table, I slice long loaves of French bread and put butter between the slices.

Max says something to Karen about the hot water running out this morning and Karen says she called someone to fix the hot water heater. Max says this old house needs new plumbing and Karen says this old house needs just about everything. They talk and talk and the mad in me smoothes out as we work.

Max cooks onions in a big black pan and Karen opens six big cans of tomatoes. Max takes a package out of the refrigerator, opens it up, and inside is ground beef. Max puts the beef in the pan, breaks it up with the onions.

There is a roll of aluminum foil on the rack next to the stove and I take the foil out, one long piece, roll the bread up in a long tube. At the stove, I look at Max and pull the handle so the oven door opens. Max steps out of my way, leans over, and turns on the heat.

"Your eyes are all red," Max says, "they've been like that for a while now, haven't they?"

I slice the other loaf of bread and keep my eyes down.

"They're not that red," I say, "they're fine."

Karen bends a little, big stomach pointing to the ground. She looks at me and I look away.

"Do they itch?" Karen says.

"No," I say, "not really. Maybe a little."

Karen stands back up.

"How long have they been red and itchy?" Karen says.

"I don't know," I say, "a while, not too long."

Karen looks at Max. Max looks at Karen.

"You might have an infection," Max says.

"Infection?" I say.

"Maybe," Karen says.

"Maybe not," I say.

Max takes the cans of tomatoes, dumps them into the pan of hamburger and onion, and it's a sizzle sound. Max and Karen are quiet and I look at them, look down, hands down over my apron.

"It's nothing," I say, "my eyes are just a little itchy, I mean, it's nothing."

Max smiles, not much of a smile, and takes a deep breath.

Karen comes back to the cutting board table and pulls a head of lettuce apart. Max stirs the meat sauce, looks into the spaghetti pot with steam up in his face. I roll up the bread in the aluminum foil, put it into the oven next to the other loaf. Closing the oven door, I turn around and take a deep breath. I know the spaghetti noodles are in the pantry cupboard so I take them out and put them on the corner of the cutting board table. Max takes the noodles and opens the package.

Max won't look at me, and I get a bad feeling.

"Am I in trouble?" I say.

Max empties the whole package of spaghetti into the pan and squints in the steam.

"You're not in trouble," Max says, "but you should have those eyes looked at and get some medicine if you have an infection."

Karen wipes her hands off and tilts her head to the side.

"You might be contagious," Karen says.

"Contagious?" I say.

"Sick," she says, "if you're contagious, that means some- one else can get sick."

I rub my palms up and down over the white apron and I never thought about someone else getting itchy eyes, maybe itchy hands too.

It's quiet and I look at my feet on the brown floor.

"I should leave," I say, "I guess I shouldn't be here."

"No," Karen says, "you shouldn't leave."

"No," Max says, "just let us finish up dinner."

I untie the apron, fold it up, and lay it on the cutting board table. There could be itchy germs all over the apron, all over me, my germs could make Karen sick, make her baby sick. I hold the apron between my hands.

"I'll just put this in the laundry," I say.

"Okay," Karen says.

The laundry is downstairs in the basement and I go down the long flight of wood steps. The basement is damp and cold and I put the apron in the hamper of dirty clothes and lean back against the washing machine. There are lots of shadows here, dark corners, and I bet there are spiders in the corners.

I hug my arms around myself and that wrong feeling is all over my skin.

Up the stairs, I close the door quiet, look both ways, and go down the hall and into the big room. No one is in here and I bet everyone is in the kitchen now eating dinner. I go to the back of the room, go into my corner, and sit on my bed in the dark.

"Jenny?" Karen says, her voice a whisper. In the dark, I know she can't see me even though I can see her. Karen has a bottle in one hand, a plate in the other, spaghetti on the plate and some bread too.

I turn on the lamp that's next to my bookcase and a warm yellow light pools on the floor and the bed. Karen's stomach moves between the space of the desk chair and the wall, barely enough room for her to come in.

"This is really pretty," she says, "and so private."

Karen sets the plate of food on my dresser and holds the dark brown plastic bottle in both hands.

"I brought you some dinner," she says.

I stand up next to my bed and I don't know what to do with my hands, how to be with her in here. I look at Karen, at the bed, at the empty shelves of my bookcases.

"All right if I sit?" Karen says.

"Sure," I say.

Karen walks two waddle steps, sits down on the bed, and lets out a big breath of air. She pushes her hand over her hair, shifts around on my bed, and all her weight moves the mattress low. Karen pats the bed next to her, hand up and down, the brown bottle in her hand.

"Is it okay if we talk?" Karen says.

"Sure," I say.

I sit down on my bed too, just on the edge, my feet on the

floor. I look at the food on my dresser, the steam from the meat sauce and the noodles against the dirty windows.

"I think you have something called pinkeye," Karen says.

"Pinkeye?"

Karen nods and holds the brown bottle between us.

"This is boric acid," she says.

Karen laughs and the sound is nice.

"It sounds pretty bad," Karen says, "but boric acid is what you use for pinkeye."

"Really?" I say.

Karen smiles and nods and hands me the bottle. The label has blue writing on the front, BORIC ACID in big letters. There is little writing all around the bottom and there are a bunch of warnings. Karen taps her finger on the label.

"I talked to a friend who has kids and she says you just put a little in the cap there," Karen says, "put it over your eye, tip your head back, and let the boric acid move around in your eye. Put it in both eyes, a couple times a day, and that should do the trick."

"Will it hurt?" I say.

Karen shakes her head, hands together on her lap.

"It shouldn't," Karen says, "my friend says it will clear right up, no sweat."

It's quiet in my corner of the room and I look at the brown bottle, the writing on the label blurry. My tears fall on the label and I sniff them back.

Rubbing the back of my hand over my nose, I wish I wasn't such a baby, wish I didn't cry all the time.

"Thanks," I say.

Karen puts her hand on my shoulder and her hand feels good, feels warm.

"It's okay," Karen says.

seventeen

A couple days later my eyes are right again, just like Karen said. I wake up and just open my eyes and I can't remember the last time I could do that.

You don't really know you're happy until you've been unhappy for a long time, and when I can open my eyes, I'm really happy. It's a light and easy feeling and I can't stop myself from smiling.

I want to do something extra nice for Karen, maybe find her some baby clothes or a baby blanket or get her some flowers.

I make my bed, like I always do.

I get my clothes together and go to the upstairs bathroom, like I always do.

I brush my hair, like I always do. Since my comb was ripped off, I can't untangle way in the back and there's a knot of hair back there, too tangled for a ponytail, but I don't care, not this morning. I barrette my hair to the side. I laugh at myself in the mirror and the sound is nice in my ears.

In the kitchen, Max takes a bowl and a whisk off the wire rack, puts the bowl down on the cutting board table. Max nods at me, but I don't just nod back, not today.

"Good morning," I say.

"Well, good morning to you, Sunshine," Max says.

I look at Max and he looks at me and it's goose bumps up my legs and down my arms.

"My mother used to call me that," I say.

Max moves his hands around in front of his body, rubs them together.

"I'm sorry," he says.

"It's okay," I say, "you can call me that too, if you want."

Max moves his hand over his chin and it's all whiskers. He shrugs and smiles.

"You're in a good mood," Max says.

I point to my eyes, my normal eyes.

"All better?" Max says.

"Yep," I say.

"Cool," Max says.

Flour, eggs, milk, and sugar are in a row on the cutting board table and I push the step stool across the kitchen.

"Pancakes?" I say.

"You got it," Max says.

Max goes to the refrigerator, pulls the door open, takes out a package of bacon, and tears open the paper. Max pulls a black pan off a rack of pans next to the stove, puts it down on the stove, turns on the heat.

It's four cups of flour, a half a cup of sugar, six eggs, and a cup of milk. I measure everything out, put it into the silver bowl.

Max peels off bacon one slice at a time, lays it in the hot pan, makes it sizzle and send that bacon smell all around.

I set the table, put out a bottle of syrup, the tray of butter, and then I lay four paper towels on a plate. Max takes the bowl of pancake batter off the cutting board table and he looks at me with the plate of paper towels. He smiles and nods.

"You anticipate me," Max says, "thanks."

"Sure," I say.

I like how Max talks, like he's one step ahead of you all the time.

Max ladles out four pancakes, forks out brown slices of cooked bacon, and lays them on the paper towels.

I take out a clean coffee mug and fill it halfway with black coffee. I add cream and sugar and lean my body against the counter, where I can watch as the people come, eat, leave.

A little girl comes in and she has a light blue dress on like Alice in Wonderland, except it's too big for her, like she plays dress-up. The little girl has long blond hair the color of white sunshine and she moves her head so fast, the blond hair flips side to side. She looks at Max, at me, at the food, at the table.

A woman is behind the little girl and she puts her hands on the little girl's shoulders. The woman is short with plain brown hair pulled back from her face. She has on a flowery skirt and a brown sweater, one of those big sweaters that goes past her hips.

She whispers in the little girl's ear and the little girl reaches out, opens her hand over the money jar, and drops in change and dollar bills.

The woman makes a plate with one pancake, a slice of bacon, butter on the pancake, syrup too. She slices the pancake into little squares and slides the plate to the little girl.

I watch, and just like that, the happy feeling is gone and the old pain is heavy in my chest.

The little girl talks in a light, high voice, says something like Momma, and her mother talks back in a low calm voice, the way moms and kids should be.

I turn around and dump out my coffee, the brown of the coffee against the white sink. I wash my mug and set it in the dish drainer.

"See ya," I say.

"Hey, kiddo," Max says. "No breakfast?"

"I'm not hungry," I say.

I can feel Max watch me and I look down at my foot, the silver key under the laces, and leave the kitchen.

It's cold today and I pull up the hood of my sweatshirt, zip it all the way to the top. I push my hands into my pockets and go down the steps, turn along the concrete wall, and walk toward Hoover Street. I left my books in my room, but it doesn't matter anyway. Nothing matters when you feel like this, sad and mad and everything wrong in between.

I walk head down into the wind, one block, three blocks, ten blocks. Up ahead another person walks with his head down too and across the street, a guy wearing an army surplus coat stands at the bus stop. He walks in small circles and weaves around like he drank too much.

The wind blows an old newspaper across the street and it's too cold for Los Angeles. I push my hands deeper into my sweatshirt and tuck my chin down. I count three steps, step on the line with both feet, three more steps, and jump on the crack.

Someone yells, someone screams, and there is a terrible sound, a thud sound.

A bus is stopped where buses never stop, right in the middle of the street, and in front of the bus is the guy who was just weaving around. He's facedown on the asphalt, hands on the street, elbows up. He looks like he might just push up anytime, dust himself off, and start to walk in circles at the stop again.

But he doesn't get up.

The man is bald and there is a zigzag crack in his head. A line of blood comes out of the crack and runs onto the street.

Sirens scream, brakes squeal, and two police cars pull up and stop in the middle of the street. There are people behind me and one of them says the guy jumped.

My eyes won't move away from the crack in the man's head and the blood that spills out. Someone should do something, someone should make the blood stop. Someone should help but the grown-ups who stand around just look and no one does anything.

I push back and bump into a man or a woman, I don't know. I turn around, walk away, and go up the street, three steps, crack, three steps, crack. It's DON'T WALK and a car comes, but I don't wait, just cross against the light. The car honks at me, I hold up my middle finger at the driver.

I walk and walk, I don't know how long, and when I stop I'm in a neighborhood with trees and houses. There is a little kid's tricycle in the front yard of a blue house and I just stand there and look at it for a long time, I don't know how long.

I can hear people talk, voices that laugh and say things, but I can't understand what they say. I turn around and look, but no one is here. I look across the street and there is the far-off sound of a radio. The voices aren't outside, they're inside my head, in my ears. I press my hands against my ears and that makes the voices louder, makes it worse.

I clear my throat and the sound makes the voices in my head quiet down. I start back the way I came, walk and count my steps out loud.

"One, two, three," I say. "Crack."

"Four, five, six. Crack."

"Seven, eight, nine. Crack."

It takes a long time, but I find my way back to the big house. I stand on the sidewalk and look up at the front door and the voices in my head laugh and talk.

"Stop it," I say, my own voice outside of my head.

A man with a paper cup of coffee walks by and he stops and looks down at me.

"Not you," I say. "I wasn't talking to you."

The man shrugs his shoulder and walks away. I go across the street and stand at the crosstown bus stop.

The voices in my head mutter and talk.

"Stop," I say.

Three grown-ups wait too and they all look at me like I did something wrong. I look around, look up at the smog sky, at the park, at my feet, and the silver key.

The voices laugh and talk and I press my hands over my ears, push on my head.

When the bus comes, I go up the steps and put my money in the little box by the bus driver. My coins fall in with the other coins, a bell rings, and the bus driver nods. I walk down the aisle and all the people who sit on the bus look at me. I pretend I don't see anyone, pretend the voices aren't in my head at all, and sit down with my back to the window.

The voices in my head laugh and whisper and talk.

I stomp my foot like there's a bug on the floor and the voices finally stop.

At the Freedom Community Church, I can't find Ray anywhere. I look by the cleaning closet, look by the trash cans outside, look around the offices. There's no Ray and I bet it's too early. I open the cleaning closet myself and take out a bottle of window cleaner, a bunch of paper towels, and the silver polish.

The big lady's office is just like it always is, so clean it's hard to believe it needs cleaning, and I wipe down the shelves of books, the counter behind her desk, the typewriter with the plastic cover on top.

The voices in my head stay quiet.

I take the silver tea set off the counter and put it on the coffee table. The directions on the jar of paste say to rub the polish on, let it dry, and then buff it off with a clean cloth.

Outside the office, a telephone rings, and someone picks up and says hello.

The silver tea set is cool in my hands and I trace my finger over the design of leaves and flowers in the silver. One by one, I polish the pieces, line them up on the coffee table. I buff the silver so shiny I can see my face in the teapot. I put all the pieces back on the tray and screw the lid on the silver polish.

"What are you doing?" a voice says.

A man I don't know stands in the door and he wears a white shirt and a pair of dark blue pants that are too tight and too short.

"I said, what are you doing?" he says.

I stand up and the jar of silver polish falls on the floor, rolls under the coffee table.

"I'm cleaning," I say, "I'm supposed to clean this office."

"I wasn't informed of any cleaning," the man says, "I don't know you. This is a restricted area."

"Ray told me to clean here," I say, "I come every day."

The man crosses his arms and leans back. I know he doesn't believe me, I can tell the way his eyes look at me.

"Are you a member of this Church?" he says.

"Yes," I say, "I mean no, I'm like a member but I work here too, and I'm supposed to clean this office and empty the trash and polish the tea set once a week."

The man comes into the office and stands so close I can smell cigarettes. He squeezes his hand on my shoulder.

"Come with me," he says.

"Why?" I say. "I'm not doing anything, I have to finish."

"You're finished," he says.

The man's hand is hard and he pushes me out of the office and down the hall.

The inside of the Freedom Community Church is all open with freestanding partitions that make separate offices for the people who work here. The man moves me through the maze of partitions and I can barely keep up without tripping on my own feet.

The man pulls me into an empty office area and pushes me into a chair by an empty desk. He picks up a telephone and dials and I know he's going to call Deb and then she'll find out how I cut school and saw the bum kill himself and there's no way I'll ever get out of trouble, not this time.

My voice is in my ears and I scream so loud it hurts inside my head. The man looks at me and his eyes are wide. I stand up and push the telephone off the man's desk, the loud sound of it on the floor.

"What the hell is going on," yells a lady in a mint green suit.

"I don't know," the man says, "she's going crazy."

I squeeze my eyes shut and put my hands over my ears. I scream like I will never stop screaming and then the man picks me up like a football. I open my eyes and he runs with me down the hall, around the maze of partitions, and people look at him and me. The lady in the mint green suit runs behind us and waves her arms around in front of her body.

I scream again and my voice is the worst sound I've ever heard.

The man pushes the big glass doors open and throws me on the sidewalk, and just like that, I'm quiet again.

The man brushes off his arms and legs like he's covered in something. He looks at me like I'm crazy and I hold up my middle finger.

"Don't let me catch you here again," the man says, "because next time I'll call the cops."

He goes back into the Freedom Community Church and I let my middle finger down. There are white scratches on my palms and little dots of blood here and there. I stand up and press my scratched-up hands against my stomach and that makes the sting stop for a second.

Just when you think things can't get any worse, they do, but now things are so bad I really don't know how they can get worse. Somehow it's funny and I laugh out loud.

The street is full of traffic, buses back and forth, car horns honk. A man in a plastic poncho pushes a grocery cart full of cans and bottles and one of the wheels on the cart rattles back and forth.

I walk away from the Freedom Community Church and I know I will never go back to that place. Never.

It's the middle of the day, but I don't care. When I get back to the big house, I lie down on top of my bedspread and close my eyes. The sound inside my head is far away, whispers, murmurs, mumbles. I press my hands together between my knees and curl up tighter. The voices aren't real, I know they aren't real. I look for Daddy inside my head, look for his face, his eyes, his smile.

There is a sound in the big room, like someone who tries to walk slow and careful. I open my eyes and the little girl with blond hair stands in the entrance to my room.

I sit up on my bed and clear my throat.

The little girl tucks her chin and her eyes blink one time.

"Are you sick?" the little girl says.

"Sick?" I say. "No."

"Why are you in bed?" she says.

My eyes are tired and I rub them with my fingers.

"Why not," I say.

I smile, but the little girl doesn't smile. Her eyes are the color of the sky without the smog, forever blue and she looks at me like I'm someone important.

"Is this all your stuff?" she says.

"Yes," I say.

"It's pretty," she says.

I stand up and move my hands to smooth the bedspread.

"It used to be a lot nicer," I say.

"Really?" she says.

"Sure," I say, "there's stuff that goes on the shelves, on the dresser and the desk, but I can't keep it out now."

The little girl's eyes are quiet and serious.

"Why?" she says.

"Just because," I say.

I rub my hands together like it's cold even though I'm not cold.

"Do you like Barbies?" I say.

"Barbies?" she says.

"You never saw a Barbie before?" I say.

She shakes her head side to side and I can't believe that. Everyone knows what a Barbie is.

Her name is Zoë and I say her name out loud over and over, that's how much I like the sound. Zoë and me play with Malibu Suntan Barbie, take turns changing her clothes, and

Zoë comes up with the idea to have Barbie go on an adventure all around the big house. Zoë, Barbie, and me go around the edges of the big room, over all the empty mattresses, stop at the front corner of the room where Zoë and her mom are going to stay.

Zoë's mom has a sad face, mouth down in the corners, eyes down too. Zoë tells her mother that I'm her new long lost friend, says I live in Fairy Princess Land and we're on an adventure.

Zoë's mom does what moms do, tells Zoë to stay close by, not to bother anyone. Zoë does that kid thing, nods like she will be good, except you can tell she isn't really paying any attention to her mother.

Zoë and Barbie and me keep going on the adventure, across the hall, into the side room with the sofa and the fireplace and the two big chairs. I never play in the big house, have never even been in this room, I always just walk by. Zoë walks Barbie on the sofa, across the top, bounces her on the cushions. Off the sofa, on the chair, Zoë keeps going until Barbie has been in every part of the room, in the corner, on the windowsill, in a little built-in cupboard by the fireplace.

People in the house are different around Zoë. They smile when she goes by them with Barbie in her hand. Zoë acts like she doesn't know anyone is around at all, just holds Barbie and looks for the next adventure. The whole time she plays, Zoë talks out loud, says this is the sofa, this is the chair, this is the floor, this is the fireplace, this is the window.

I never had this much fun with Barbie and I just follow Zoë around and listen to her sweet voice say, "These are the stairs, this is the banister, this is the bathroom."

There's the pretend me and there's the real me. The pretend me is the one who gets up in the morning, gets dressed, helps in the kitchen, and leaves the big house like she's going to school.

The real me walks past the street that smells like Chinese food, past the street that smells like Mexican food, past the street where they make fresh bread and donuts and muffins.

Some mornings, I go into the donut shop and buy three donuts for twenty-five cents, all three chocolate glazed. I sit at a booth at the end of the line of booths, my donuts on three napkins. I pretend Daddy and me eat the donuts like we have a breakfast date, except I'm the one who eats all the donuts, one at a time, not one crumb left over. It's that way until school is out for the summer, no more donuts in the summer.

There's pretend me in the afternoon, too. Pretend me going to work at the Freedom Community just like always. Real me going to the movies. Double feature, twenty-five cents plus popcorn and a Coke.

One thing that never changes is how there is always scared me. Scared about getting caught, scared Deb is on her way over, scared everyone will find out I'm not telling the truth.

Saturday is laundry day, no pretend school, no pretend work at the Freedom Community. Saturday is just real me.

Zoë says Saturday is official long skirt day. I find a skirt in the lost and found and it's a forest green velvet with yellow trim. Zoë wears one of her mom's skirts and it has three layers of ruffles in green and blue and purple. Zoë says official long skirt day is the one day when princesses get to show themselves to the whole world and you have to be extra beautiful for people to recognize who you really are.

I don't really feel like a princess, but when Zoë's around, it's like being inside the magic world of her imagination, and I don't mind wearing a long skirt.

Zoë and me get all dressed up in my room since Zoë says it's Fairy Princess Land and then we run over to show Zoë's mom.

Zoë's mom put up three sheets between three chairs around their mattress for a little privacy and it's like a fort in here. Zoë sits on the edge of the mattress, her three-layer skirt all around in a circle, and Zoë's mom combs her long blond hair from the top down.

"Make a braid to go with my long skirt," Zoë says.

"A French braid?" Zoë's mom says. "Or a regular braid?"

"Magic braid," Zoë says. "Make a magic braid for Jenny too."

Zoë's mom smiles, not much of a smile. I don't think Zoë's mom likes me very much, probably thinks I'm too big to play with Zoë, even though she never says anything like that.

I pick little white fluff off my green velvet skirt.

"That's okay," I say. "I don't need a braid."

"Magic braids," Zoë says, "all princesses have magic braids."

Zoë's mom looks at me, really looks, and then she moves her smile to more of a smile.

"I would be glad to do your hair," she says.

"No, no," I say, "that's okay."

"You have to have magic braids," Zoë says, "you have to."

"Zoë, honey," Zoë's mom says, "let's hold still now."

Zoë crosses her arms, lips pouted up, and won't look at me. That's what Zoë does when she doesn't get her way, she crosses her arms, looks away from you, and stays that way. I hate it when Zoë is upset. I lean over to Zoë, whisper in her ear.

"All right," I say, "I'll get magic braids too."

Zoë claps her hands and her mother shakes her head.

"Hold still," Zoë's mom says.

Zoë's mom makes a perfect part down the middle of Zoë's white head and divides her blond hair into three sections.

Their little room is a mattress with a yellow blanket, a table made out of stacked telephone books, and the chairs with the sheets for privacy. All of Zoë's clothes are in a travel bag like they might leave at any time. I wish they had a dresser to unpack their things into.

Zoë's mom puts a rubber band at the end of Zoë's perfect braid, holds her hands up, and Zoë touches behind her head.

"I forgot," I say, "I have to go do something."

"It's your turn," Zoë says.

Standing up, I adjust the green velvet skirt around my legs so it falls right.

"No," I say, "I have to go help Max in the kitchen, plus my hair is really dirty and I should take a bath first."

"It's okay," Zoë's mom says, "I can do your hair quick, Max will wait."

Zoë's mom pats the edge of the mattress and her sad eyes look up at me. Zoë stands up, three layer ruffles around her feet, and she puts her hands on my hands, small fingers around my fingers, and her hands are soft and warm.

"You promised," Zoë says.

Zoë pulls me down and I bite my lip. I turn so my back is to Zoë's mom and I try to see her over my shoulder.

"Well," I say, "it's just that I have a bad tangle back there."

"I get tangles all the time," Zoë says, "I hate tangles."

"Let's take a look," Zoë's mom says.

Zoë's mom moves my hair up, cool air on the back of my neck, and she moves her hand on the tangle. It's tender back there and I bite my lip harder, the taste of blood in my mouth. Zoë holds her skirt in her hands, drops on her knees, and blows against the skin on the back of my neck.

"It's all red," Zoë says, "your neck is mad."

My hand touches the back of my neck and it's hot skin.

"This has been here for a while," Zoë's mom says.

Zoë's mom combs around the back of my neck, little pulls around the tangled part. It's nice to have someone comb my hair and I close my eyes. I wipe my fingers on my face like the tears aren't there at all. Zoë puts her face right in my face and she smells like toothpaste and milk.

"It's okay," Zoë says, "my mom will fix it."

"Zoë, honey," Zoë's mom says, "why don't you get me a glass of water from the kitchen."

"Why?" Zoë says.

"Because I'm thirsty, hurry now."

Zoë stands, feet wide for balance, and then she bends down and pulls up the blue layer of her three-layer skirt. She runs around the wall of sheets and her feet down the hall make a flap-flap sound.

Zoë's mom leans to my ear, her breath warm on my skin.

"It's okay," she says, "you have the kind of hair that tangles easy."

There's a pull at the back of my neck and I put my head straight again, push the sides of my hands against my eyes, push hard, white and black dots in front of my eyes.

"How did it get so bad?" Zoë's mom says.

"Someone stole my comb," I say.

Zoë's mom stops moving her hands.

"Here at the house?" she says. "When, when did that happen?"

My shoulders shrug and I sniff, wipe my nose with the back of my hands.

"Before you and Zoë," I say, "I don't know."

At the back of my neck, Zoë's mom combs and combs and it's the best thing to be untangled.

"There," Zoë's mom says.

My hand feels the back of my neck, the hair straight and soft. I move my fingers through, all the way to the ends. I touch that place on my neck again and it's tender and warm. Turning around, I look at Zoë's mom, her sad eyes.

"Don't tell anyone," I say.

"What?" she says.

"About my hair," I say. "About my comb getting stolen."

Zoë's mom tilts her head and looks at me. Zoë runs back around the magic fort, the sound of her feet, flap-flap, and the glass of water she brought is half-full.

"It's time," Zoë says, "Max says it's time."

"Time?" Zoë's mom says.

Zoë drops her three-layer skirt, reaches the glass of water to her mom.

"The baby," Zoë yells, "the baby is coming."

Zoë and me sit on the floor outside Max and Karen's room, my knees under my long skirt. People go in and come out and when the door is open their room is all sunlight from a circle of windows. Karen hung up squares of see-through purple and white material on the window and the light that comes in is yellow and purple on the wood floor. There's Beatles music on the record player, "Sgt. Pepper's Lonely Hearts Club Band," and there is the smell of incense burning. Karen breathes hard and fast, and walks back and forth in front of the windows. She has her hands on her back and you can see the shape of her round tummy through her paisley dress. Karen's tummy is so big, it's like half her body.

When the door is closed, a bright line of sunlight is under the door and we can still hear "Sgt. Pepper's Lonely Hearts Club Band," can still hear Karen breathe hard and fast.

Zoë's mom is in there, Max is in there, and some lady called a midwife is in there too. Karen says we can come in when the baby is on its way out. Karen says Zoë and me are the welcome committee.

Zoë knows all about babies and says they come out where you pee. No way a whole baby can come out where I pee, but Zoë says it's true, says all women push their babies out that way.

"How do you know that?" I say.

"Momma told me," Zoë says, "Momma helps women have their babies all the time, she knows."

That's when I know why Zoë and her mom are here and I get this bad feeling all over.

The music stops in the room and Max opens the door. Max looks happy and scared and something else, I don't know what, just different.

"Okay," Max whispers, "this is it. Go wash up and come in."

Zoë and me get up off the floor, wash our hands with stinky soap and hot water. Zoë runs up the hall and I follow behind. Zoë isn't afraid of anything, and she runs right to her mother and Karen. I stand by the door, my back against the doorknob.

There is a fold-out wood table in front of the big windows and Karen is on top with a baby blue sheet around her stomach and legs. The midwife is at the end of the table by Karen's feet, and her whole face is calm and full of knowing.

Zoë's mom touches Karen's forehead and they whisper to each other.

The whole room is full of wait and magic and no one has to tell me that this is the most important thing in the world.

Max takes the *Sgt. Pepper* album off the turntable, tips a new record out of an all-white cover, and puts it on. There is the click, click sound and then it's more Beatles music.

Karen turns her head, green-brown eyes on Max.

"'Blackbird,'" Karen says.

"Okay," Max says.

Max picks up the needle on the record and sets it down again.

Zoë waves her hand at me like I should come over too and I push off the door and walk slow steps. Karen looks at me and smiles, her beautiful green-brown eyes shiny with tears.

Zoë's mom stands up where she is and looks at the midwife. Max stands on the other side of Karen's head, looks at the midwife too. It's so quiet, just Beatles music and Karen breathing, hard and fast, and then the midwife nods her head.

Zoë's mom and Max lift Karen, push her up closer to the midwife, who watches between Karen's legs. Karen's eyes are tight closed and her face is all red. She lets her breath out loud like wind while Max and Zoë's mom let her lie back again.

Zoë is right at the end of the table, looking at everything, and she waves at me, waves and points. I come over to where she stands behind the midwife, my back to the sun, all of Karen wide open there. It's not like what I thought, not terrible or scary or anything, just a tiny head of dark hair pushing out, and it's like Karen was made for pushing the baby out just the way Zoë said.

Karen is lifted up again, face all wet, curly hair stuck

around her forehead and cheeks. The midwife lady says, "This is it now," and Karen takes a deep breath like she is going to hold her breath under water. Zoë takes a deep breath too and holds her hands over her mouth.

The music is "blackbird singing in the dead of night," and a baby girl comes right out of Karen, a tiny perfect person.

The midwife gives the baby to Zoë's mom. She holds the baby up in the sunlight and it's impossible anyone could be so small. She lays her carefully on Karen's chest and Karen puts her arms around her like she is made of glass. The baby doesn't cry, just makes this little coo noise, almost not a noise at all.

The music is "take these broken wings and learn to fly," and the midwife says, "There's another baby, Karen."

Max looks at the midwife and Zoë's mom starts to laugh. Another head of dark hair is there, and the midwife tells Karen to push just a little more and then, just like that, another baby girl.

Laughing and crying, everyone is together shaking their heads and touching hands and wiping tears out of their eyes.

The music is just the sound of blackbirds calling and Karen has two tiny babies on her chest. Max kisses Karen's sweaty face, says I love you against her nose. Zoë's mom wipes tears off her face and shakes her head at the two babies.

"Perfect twins," the midwife says, "just perfect."

Zoë wiggles between her mother and Karen, and she's so big compared to the new babies. Max smiles and puts his hand on my shoulder and I move up to look at the babies too.

Zoë puts her finger out and touches one pink hand like she knows all about new life. I hold my finger out too, touch the other baby's little pink hand, and her fingers wrap around and hold on tight.

Just like that, everything in the world is different, even though I don't know how. It's all mixed up with Momma gone, Daddy gone, me all alone, but not really alone the way I thought I was. It's the babies and Karen and Max and Zoë and somehow, right now, we are all the same. Tears sting my eyes and I move my thumb over the top of the baby's soft hand.

Zoë stands on her tiptoes and leans close to the new babies. "Welcome," Zoë whispers, "welcome to the world."

eighteen

Three days after the twins, there's a note on my bed with Deb's writing on the outside. Inside it says *Family Meeting* and the name of a Chinese restaurant, just the name and nothing else, like I go there all the time.

I look around, but Deb's not here. I go to the window and look out, but she's not there either.

Max says the restaurant is on the street that smells like Chinese food, says I'll know it by the red flag in front. I put on a pair of jeans and a loose purple paisley shirt I got out of the lost and found. The shirt has ruffles around the neck, and around the wrists, and when you move the arms, they are like bird wings.

All my clothes are lost-and-found clothes now, Jerry Garcia's face on one gray shirt, a big peace symbol on a tie-dyed sunburst T-shirt, the purple paisley shirt. I found a pair of too-big orange overalls and cut-off baggy shorts too. Every time I find something in the lost and found, I put some of my old clothes in there, just so it's even.

I brush my hair and put it into a ponytail with a leather ponytail holder and wood stick that Zoë's mom gave me.

The Chinese restaurant is red flag out front, lots of people inside. I stand outside and look in and it's Deb, Christopher, Kenny, Ronny, and Bryan at a round table eating bowls of food.

I pull open the door and a little bell rings. No one looks at me and I walk toward the table. Ronny's hair is in her face, Kenny has on a baseball cap, and Christopher's smooth pretty face is broken out with red pimples. Bryan looks like he grew or something and he sees me first, just looks at me with his dark eyes, and the way he looks, I know he's mad at me. I look mad right back at him.

Fuck you, Bryan.

Deb spoons rice with two spoons, the sound of her voice over restaurant sounds.

"You have to try the moo shoo," Deb says. "The plum sauce is so good."

Deb looks at Bryan, looks past me around the restaurant, stops, and then looks right at me.

"Well, there you are," Deb says. "Don't you look . . . interesting."

Everyone stops eating, all their eyes on me. I stand up straight, shoulders back, chin tucked.

"You look weird," Ronny says.

"Totally weird," Kenny says.

"Screw you, Veronica," I say. "And screw you too, Kendall."

Deb laughs a little, hand flipping her hair back, and looks around at the table.

"Why don't you just sit down," Deb says.

Deb points to an empty chair between Kenny and Christopher, Bryan and Ronny across. I sit down and Deb looks around again, laughs a nothing of a laugh.

All the sound comes back around the table, arms reach, forks move, and everyone eats without talking. In the middle of the table is one of those turntables with a bottle of soy sauce, some red sauce, and some yellow mustard. There is a bowl of rice, a bowl of vegetables and nuts, a bowl of brown noodley stuff, and something else with pineapple chunks in it.

Deb says something about how I should have some tea, try the sweet-and-sour pork since it's just the best.

Bryan holds his fork like a weapon and a red stain is up his neck like a rash.

Deb pours a cup of tea in a white cup with a little red line around the inside and sends the cup around. I watch the cup go right by and stop in front of Bryan.

"That's for you, Jenny," Deb says.

"I don't want any tea," I say. "I don't want sweet-and-sour pork either."

Deb touches her hair and puts her hand down again.

"Well," Deb says, "we're all here so let's get this thing going."

Deb moves her body around in her chair and puts both elbows on the table.

"We are leaving the Freedom Community Church," Deb says.

She lets out a long breath, both hands over her heart, and moves her face into a big smile.

"Wow," she says, "that felt great. I am just so overwhelmed right now. What a relief to say this to all of you, all of us together again."

Deb picks up a white paper napkin and dabs at the edges of her eyes. Christopher reaches his hand to Deb, touches fingers to Deb's wrist. Deb looks at Christopher for a long time and takes a deep breath, shoulders up, shoulders down.

"Okay," Deb says.

Deb holds the edges of the table, fingers squeezed white, looks like she might stand up and try to lift the table.

"The Freedom Community is evil with a capital *E*," Deb says, "I only just discovered how evil."

Deb lets go of the table, hands over her heart.

"I gave the Church everything," Deb says, "I sacrificed. Everything."

Deb takes her hands off her heart, points to me, then to Bryan.

"I had to sacrifice my family," she says, "separate my children to show my devotion."

Deb puts her hands over her heart again, shakes her head side to side, eyes on a plate of moo shoo pancakes.

"How could I have known?" Deb says.

I look at Bryan and Bryan looks at me. I don't know what to think now, don't know if Bryan was with Deb this whole time or not. I don't know anything.

Deb takes her napkin, holds it in her long fingers while her eyes tear up.

"You kids," Deb says, "you are all I have left in this world now. The evil Church has taken everything, every dime."

Deb presses the napkin over her face and Christopher puts his arms around her shaking shoulders.

"It's okay, Mom," Christopher says, "it's going to be okay."

I want to laugh and I want to cry and I want to walk out of here like the whole thing is a dream. I can see it too, I can see me stand up, walk out the door with the little bell, and then it will be wind in my face and city noise in my ears.

Daddy will walk right up to me and put his hand out. He will laugh and say, *"That was just a bad dream, wasn't it, Juniper?"* and we'll walk down the beach and look at the sunset. Just like that.

Deb says we have to move to some house across town, near Figueroa Street, says we're now in hiding from the evil Church. Deb says she is going to get enough money together to start her own restaurant since she's always loved to cook. Christopher and Ronny and Kenny nod their heads up and down like everything is fine. Bryan's face is all red to his ears and he looks at his bowl of rice.

"Move?" I say.

Deb stops dabbing her eyes and looks at me.

"Immediately," Deb says.

"I'm not moving," I say.

"I don't think you understand," Deb says, "we are all in grave danger. You absolutely cannot stay there."

"But Zoë," I say, "Karen and Max and the babies."

"What are you talking about?" Christopher says.

Everyone looks at me like I'm crazy. I stand up from the table and shake my head.

"I'm not moving," I say, "you can't make me."

Deb laughs a little laugh.

"I can," Deb says, "and I will. As of right now, you are out of that house. Do you understand me?"

"No," I yell.

"You are making a scene," Deb says, "sit down and control yourself."

The restaurant is quiet and I can feel everyone look at me. I sit down and hold on to my chair. I want to pick up the bowl of sweet-and-sour pork and throw it at Deb, tell her how it's just the best. I see me screaming and throwing food and going crazy, but that's just on the inside. Everything is fine on the outside.

Armanita lives in a big yellow house with her little boy named Sam. Sam and Armanita are milk chocolate brown with curly milk chocolate hair.

The house is front door, living room, stairs up, and lots of rooms upstairs. Downstairs, past the living room, is a kitchen, a hallway, and off the back of the house is the room where I'm supposed to be. Armanita says the room is an add-on.

It's cold in the add-on and the floor angles a little so you walk on a slope when you walk from one wall to the other. The only heat for the add-on is a small white radiator in the corner that turns on and off with a little black turn handle.

The best part of the add-on is how it's private. The worst part is how it's cold and how the big windows face into a backyard full of dark shadowy trees and bushes where someone could hide and look in.

Outside Armanita's house are other big houses and apartment buildings with lots of cars parked along the street. Most of the cars are low-rider cars, some without tires and seats, like they were abandoned here. Big trees shade the sidewalks and the tree roots grow up and make the sidewalks all cracked and uneven.

The people here just hang around, sit on their steps, and lean on the low-rider cars. I can feel their eyes watch me walk by and I know it's because I'm not from here. I walk slow even steps, walk past a bunch of guys who stand around a stereo that plays loud music.

"Yosup," says a guy.

"Hey, sister," says another guy, "little sis-ter."

I put my hands into my pockets and smile, but I don't stop. I walk to the intersection, look both ways, and cross against the DON'T WALK sign.

Deb says the big house is ten blocks away, fifteen maybe. Deb says just follow Figueroa to the number streets. When I hit the number streets, there's the park and then the big house.

Zoë and her mom are gone right now, gone for two whole days to see Zoë's dad or something, and how did I know I would suddenly have to move and not say good-bye.

Behind the wall of sheets, Zoë's bed is all made up with the yellow blanket and I just stand there and look. Upstairs, Karen's door is closed and I lean my head against the wood. Max says never knock since the babies and Karen are always sleeping, so I walk back down the steps, go into the kitchen, and it's the same thing, no one is here.

In the big room, in my room, I look at everything. There's my canopy bed, my furniture, the pink trunk under my bed. I sit at the princess desk and take out a piece of paper and a pencil. I write in careful letters, big so Zoë can understand, and I try to explain about Deb's danger, about Armanita's house, about how I have to go and never come back except I don't understand why. I can't see the paper, can't think of more words to write, and tears fall on the words. I wipe my nose with a purple bird wing sleeve and hold the pencil tight between my thumb and finger.

Then I write how Zoë can't *have* my Barbie but she can watch over her and take her on adventures. I write how keeping Barbie here will mean I can come back and play someday. My letters are all messy and I look at the paper for a long time. I fold the paper in half, half again, half again, and write ZOE on the outside.

I take off my shoe, unlock the pink trunk, and put it back on.

The Barbie suitcase is just like I left it. Malibu Suntan Barbie, clothes, shoes, plastic hangers.

I take the drawer of Barbie shoes all the way out, dump everything on the floor. The black velvet bag is a tight ball and there are wrinkles in the material. I take the black velvet bag and put it back in the trunk under the Our Wedding book.

No one loves Barbie more than Zoë and it's the right thing to do. I put the case back together, slide the note inside, and put the case and the note in the middle of their bed.

Deb says these are desperate times and we must be extra self-sufficient. That means I have to move my bedroom set all alone since Deb is too busy and we have no money for moving men.

It's twelve blocks, eight stoplights, and people look at me like I'm crazy. Anyone looking at me can go screw themselves. I pretend they aren't looking at me at all, just keep my eyes straight ahead on the sidewalk. Go screw yourself.

Over my shoulder, I carry two metal bars that hold my mattress up. I carry them twelve blocks, eight stoplights, and into the add-on room.

I slide the box spring with my fingers curled under the wood frame, one end dragging over city cement. I drag my box spring twelve blocks, eight stoplights, and into the add-on room.

I hug my arms around my bookcase and carry it twelve blocks, eight stoplights, and into the add-on room.

That's the way it is all day. It's bookcase top, desk chair with the gold seat, the princess mirror, three drawers stacked together, three more drawers, and then the pink trunk.

The last thing is my princess dresser and I stand there and look at it. My arms and legs tingle from being tired and the waistband of my baggy jeans is soaked with sweat. The drawers are all gone and you can see how it's put together with wood and screws and glue. I could ask Max to help me and I know he would, except it's time for dinner.

I go to the kitchen and Max is in there with some guy I don't know wearing an apron. They both look at me when I walk in and Max wipes his hand on his apron half folded down.

"Hey, you," Max says.

"I have to leave," I say.

"I know," Max says.

"How do you know?" I say.

Max puts his hand around the back of his neck, scratches.

"Your old lady came by a couple days ago." Max says.

He stops scratching, hands on his hips.

"Pretty strange chick," Max says.

"You can say that again," I say.

Max laughs and I laugh and it's nice. The guy just stands there and looks at us.

"She says I can't come back here," I say, "not ever."

It's one of those times when you want to say more, but you don't know how. I look at my feet and my shoes have little holes where my toes are wearing through.

"Go say good-bye to Karen too," Max says.

My chest hurts, a deep hurt, and I rub my hand over. Max holds his hand out for a regular handshake and I put my hand in his.

"You're cool," Max says, "you'll be fine."

Max lets go of my fingers and it's warm where he touched.

Upstairs, there is light under the door and I tap with my fingers. Karen opens the door, looks out, looks down, and then opens her door all the way.

"Hi, Jenny," Karen says. "Come on in."

Inside her room is warm lamplight, scarves over the lamps so the light is blue and red. Music plays on the record player, something sad and sweet, no singing.

"I have to leave," I say.

Karen steps back, arms wide, and she kneels down to me.

"I know, honey," she says, "I know already."

Karen smells like baby powder, sweet milk, incense. My face is in her soft curly hair and she is warm and skinny and different.

Karen leans back, looks at me, soft mother eyes, green and brown.

"You're going to be okay," Karen says, "it's better you're with your family."

I wipe my face with both hands.

"I'm not supposed to come back," I say, "not ever."

Karen frowns, presses her hands on my shoulders, fingers squeezing.

"You are always welcome here," Karen says. "Okay?"

"Okay," I say.

Baby noise comes out of the bassinet and little hands reach up. Karen puts her hand over one baby body wrapped tight in a pink blanket. The other baby is asleep, eyes closed, tiny eyelashes. The baby Karen touches stops fussing, just blinks its eyes and watches everything.

Karen says she named her babies after flowers since they are so sweet: one is Rose and the other is Daisy. I don't know how but I know I'll never see the babies again and I will never see Karen either. I hug my arms around Karen then, my face against her stomach so I can remember how she smells like flowers and tea.

My Barbie suitcase is right where I put it this afternoon and I open the case, take out the note with *ZOE* on the outside. I put the note into my pocket, close the case, and lock it again. She'll know when she sees Barbie here and my stuff gone, she won't need any stupid note.

I drag my dresser out of my circle of windows, through the big room, and into the entryway.

No one is in the big room and that's weird, seems like there is always someone new here. I look around the room, back at my circle of windows, and then I look at my dresser. I pull the door open and push down the doorstop so it stays that way.

Backward, I lift the dresser over the doorway and angle it down on the top step. I go around to the other side and push the dresser out the door.

The princess dresser is balanced at an angle down the steps. I hold the down end against my chest and pull it down each step with a bang. At the bottom of the steps, the dresser sits on the sidewalk and I bend over to catch my breath.

The only way to carry it is to drag it backward so I drag it over the sidewalk, bump up and down curbs and hurry through intersections for eleven blocks. If anyone looks at me, I make my eyes narrow like "Go screw yourself," and they look away.

At the last light, I wait for the light to change and when it's green, I drag the dresser over the curb and into the intersection. The street is a wide street with lots of lanes and I'm only halfway through when the light changes to green and cars start to roll forward like they might run me over. My arms hurt and legs hurt and I pull as hard as I can.

A man I don't know runs into the crosswalk and puts his hands on my dresser. Cars honk and I look at the man, my eyes "Go screw yourself," but he doesn't care. The man lifts his side and nods at me. I lift my side and we carry the dresser together. On the other side of the street, I put my end of the dresser down on the sidewalk.

"Thank you," I say, "thanks a lot."

The man nods up and down, up and down.

"Go, go," he says.

"That's okay," I say, "I've got it from here."

"No, no," he says. "Go, go."

It is easier with help. I pick up my end of the dresser, walk backward and let him walk the other end. The man watches me and his face never stops with the smile. He has black hair, dark eyes, and his skin is scarred deep around his chin and his cheeks.

It's quiet in front of Armanita's house and I put my dresser down on a lumpy root crack in the sidewalk.

"Thank you," I say. "That's all."

The man smiles and shakes his head.

"More help," he says. "Go, go."

"No," I say. "That's okay."

The man comes around and lifts from the middle of the dresser. He balances it on his head and goes up the steps to Armanita's yellow house. It's funny how he's so small and strong at the same time, funny how my dresser looks up in the air over his head. I run up the steps and open the door. The man carries the dresser into the house.

I point to the add-on and the man carries it in there too. When he puts the dresser down, his face is wet with sweat and his scars are shiny. He looks around my room, looks out the window, and looks at me again. The way he stands there, it's like he's never going to leave, and I get a bad feeling up the back of my neck and over the top of my head.

I clap my hands and the sound is loud in the quiet.

"Thanks, thanks a lot," I say. "See you now, bye-bye."

The man stands with his feet wide and puts his hands on his hips. He has on a yellow jacket, black pants, black shoes.

"You pay?" the man says.

Money, he wants money, and I put my hand over my eyes. Of course, he wants money and I have money saved from working in the kitchen. I wave my arms in the air and point down the hall.

"You wait outside," I say, "I'll get some money."

The man shakes his head and steps closer to me.

"No money," he says, "little kiss."

It's a terrible, trapped, get the hell out of here feeling all the way to my feet. The little man puts his hand on my arm, fingers tight, and I try to pull away. He holds on, not hard, just holds my arm at the elbow.

In between is how he helped me and if all he wants is a kiss, I guess it's not so bad. If I just give him a quick little kiss and that's it, he'll leave. I move like I'm going to kiss his cheek, but he puts his hand on my face and kisses me on the mouth, a full mouth kiss.

My voice is a scream and I scream loud. I pull back fast, but he holds my arm. I kick him in the leg as hard as I can kick and then he lets go. I run up the hall and up the stairs two at a time. No one is here, no Deb, Christopher, Kenny, Ronny, Bryan, Armanita and Sam, no one.

Moody music plays down the hall and then I know Bryan's

in there. I push the door open and Bryan sits cross-legged in front of the turntable.

"There's a man in my room," I yell.

"Bullshit," Bryan says.

"I'm not kidding," I yell, "he helped me with my dresser and then he tried kissing me with his tongue and now he's in there."

"You let some stranger in the house?" Bryan says.

"Go screw yourself," I yell.

Bryan looks at me, really looks, and then he pushes up off the floor.

"Fine," Bryan says, "let's go see."

Outside it's almost dark, the sky dark blue, shadows of bushes and trees out the windows. The ceiling light in the add-on is bright on the window, bright on the princess furniture. There's my desk, bed, dresser, bookcases.

Bryan has on a green T-shirt, cut-off shorts, and his feet are bare, long toes, dirty outline of his flip-flops.

"So?" Bryan says.

"Check the closet," I say.

Bryan slides the closet doors open and shakes his head.

"Nothing," he says.

The add-on is just Bryan and me and I know the little man is really gone. I shake from the top down, have to hold my arm over my stomach, put my other hand on my dresser.

"Maybe he's in the house somewhere," I say, "maybe he's hiding."

"Yeah, right," Bryan says.

I point to the floor, to the carpet, to where I stand.

"He was here," I say, "right here, I swear."

Bryan puts his arms out to his sides, lets them fall down again. He goes to the door, opens it fast, and looks behind like someone might be there. Then he laughs and shakes his head.

"That's not funny," I say.

"Screw you," Bryan says, "liar."

"I'm not a liar," I yell.

"Don't bother me again," Bryan says. He walks out of the add-on and I can hear him down the hall.

"Don't worry," I yell, "I won't, you big jerk."

It's like there never was Zoë, Karen, Max, the twins, even the Freedom Community Church, now the Evil Church, according to Deb.

Just like before, it's rules and family meetings and chores. Christopher, Kenny, Ronny, Bryan, and me fight about what to watch on television, about getting into the bathroom, about who eats what.

There's also Armanita and Sam, except I don't see them very much since Armanita works all the time and Sam goes to a daycare place. I don't think Armanita likes me very much since she always has a look on her face like I stink.

The other thing that's different is how there's no money. Deb is broke and she says the only thing that keeps us going is her job at the shoe store and the monthly check from the government, "Thank god for Social Security," she says.

I don't care about money, I just think of ways to sneak over to the big house and see Zoë, but I know I can't.

I try not to think about Zoë anymore, but it's hard. I miss her. I miss how she's never afraid, how she has fun, how there's magic in everything she sees. Without Zoë, it's like I'm just me again and there is nothing special. Inside is a want for her that's deeper than wanting food, and I know wanting anything that bad is crazy, weak, maybe even means I'm a bad person.

nineteen

It's a month, maybe two months, and it's the hottest part of summer. No one knows how Saturday is official long skirt day but me, and even though there's no magic without Zoë, I do it anyway. I have on my long green skirt with the yellow trim, my yellow T-shirt, and my flip-flops. Flip-flops don't have laces, so I have my silver key inside the pocket of my yellow shirt.

On long skirt Saturday, I always go for a walk and I always end up across the street from the big house, just in case Zoë comes out. Zoë never comes out. She doesn't come out today either and after a while, I give up.

Down the sidewalk, a lady sits on a bench and throws bird-seed for the pigeons. I walk a wide circle around the birds and the birdseed and go up to the corner where I can cross the street. Lots of people are out today, most people in tank tops and shorts since it's so hot. No one has on a long skirt but me.

DON'T WALK turns to WALK and I cross with a bunch of other people. I have to walk on the outside of the crosswalk so I don't get stepped on.

At the other side of the street is a telephone booth. I stop, stick my finger in the coin return, but the slot is empty.

Down the sidewalk is a black guy in front of a theater who passes out bright pink slips of paper and he yells, "All naked, all day. All naked, all day."

I don't look at the guy, don't take a piece of paper. I look at my flip-flop feet pop out from under my skirt as I walk down the sidewalk. Pop out, go under, pop out.

"Jenny," a voice yells.

All around me are grown-up faces, but their eyes don't look down at me. I press my hands over my ears, but the voice isn't inside, not this time. I move my fingers around the waistband of my green skirt and it's all sweaty. I press my hand over the pocket of my yellow T-shirt, the key just past the fabric. I stand up straight, shoulders back, chin tucked, and walk down the sidewalk again.

My feet are pop out, go under, pop out, and then it's a sideways crack and I walk up to the crack so my whole foot is over.

Fuck you, Deb.

"Jenny," a woman yells. "Jenny, stop."

The sound of my name is on my skin and prickles lift up the back of my neck. I stand tiptoe and turn a full circle. It's busy sidewalk, parking meters, strangers, "all naked, all day," but then I see a lady with tan arms, tan legs, and hair cut neat and tidy around her head. I squint my eyes like that will make me see better.

"Jenny," she yells, "wait, wait."

The woman holds a white purse against her side and she wears a blue and white striped shirt and matching white shorts. It's sportswear mix-and-match and just like that I know.

"Oh, my god," Aunt Georgia yells.

Thin, thin, bird thin, Aunt Georgia puts her brown arms

wide, hugs me against her chest, and rocks me back and forth. Her arms are so tight it's like she will never let me go and I try to push back.

Aunt Georgia holds the tops of my arms in her strong fingers and looks me full in the face. I remember her and I don't remember her and it's like being in the deep part of sleep and someone wakes you up.

"It's you," Aunt Georgia says, "I can't believe it's really you."

She turns me side to side and looks me up and down.

"Look how big you are," she says, "you're so tall."

Aunt Georgia's voice is a laugh and a cry all at the same time and she hugs me again with her whole hand pressed against my back. She smells like coffee and mint and I don't know what to do, hug her back, or run away, or just stand there without doing anything.

"Oh my," Aunt Georgia says, "I just left your Uncle Charles back on the street."

Aunt Georgia stands up and holds my hand. She holds her other hand up over her eyes and looks up the sidewalk, looks at me, looks around again.

"Chuck," Aunt Georgia yells, "over here."

I look the way she looks and in the middle of all the strangers in Los Angeles is Uncle Charles with white knee socks, crazy plaid shorts, and a light green shirt. Uncle Charles has sunglasses on his face and he run-walks and waves his arm.

"Well, I'll be dammed," Uncle Charles says, "it is Jennifer."

Uncle Charles takes his sunglasses off his face and his eyes are that baby blue color that is so light they look like a light shines behind them. Uncle Charles bends over, puts his arms down low around my behind, and lifts me up off my feet. I put my hands on his shoulders so I don't fall and I can't help smiling, it's so nice to see people I know, people who know me.

"You are a sight for sore eyes," Uncle Charles says. "We've been looking all over for you."

"Looking for me?" I say.

"I told you," Aunt Georgia says, "I knew it was her."

Uncle Charles holds me against his chest even though I'm way too big for holding that way. He pushes his finger around my tummy like a tickle and laughs a deep laugh.

"We have been looking all over the city for you," Uncle Charles says, "like a needle in a haystack."

I hold my hand over Uncle Charles's finger, hold off his tickle, and he laughs at that. Aunt Georgia laughs too and she pats my back with her hand.

"It's a miracle," Aunt Georgia says, "just a miracle."

Aunt Georgia and Uncle Charles's car is a couple blocks away. Both of them hold my hand like I might disappear or something and when they get to the car, they open the back door and tell me to get inside. In the back seat are blond-haired, blue-eyed Carrie Sue and Jeff. Carrie Sue is little-girl perfect ponytails, pink shorts, and a matching pink T-shirt. Jeff is short hair cut in a perfect line, blue shorts, and a blue and white striped T-shirt. They both have on white-white tennis shoes and white socks.

I let go of Aunt Georgia's hand, let go of Uncle Charles's hand, and step back from the car and the kids in the back seat.

My green skirt has street dirt around the bottom, my faded yellow T-shirt has a circle stain from spilled cola, and my hair is all tangled up again.

"What's the matter, honey?" Aunt Georgia says. "It's just your cousins, they won't bite."

I press my hand over the pocket of my yellow T-shirt, the silver key shape under my fingers. I can't get into the car, no way, not with Carrie Sue and Jeff so clean and perfect. Everyone's eyes are on me and the only thing left to do is cry.

Uncle Charles kneels down and his arms are all around my shoulders.

"It's okay to be scared," Uncle Charles says. "No one is going to hurt you, I promise. In fact, you can sit up front if you want, would you like that? Do you want to sit up front?"

The sound of his voice is deep and warm and full of things I only dream about. I look at my feet, just my feet, and I rub my nose with the back of my hand, rub my arm across my T-shirt.

"Better now?" Uncle Charles says.

My throat can't make words and I just nod my head and sniff hard. Even though I'm not really crying, the tears still come out of my eyes like the faucet is broken.

Aunt Georgia hands me a little travel box of tissue and on the outside of the box is a map of the United States. I hold the box in my hands and laugh at the perfect tiny little box of tissue. Travel tissue.

Aunt Georgia and Uncle Charles look at me, just look, and then they laugh too. The sound of us laughing is one sound, all of us together like that's the way it's supposed to be.

I sit between Aunt Georgia and Uncle Charles and point the directions. After Figueroa Street, it's a couple of turns and I point to the big yellow house.

"That's it," I say. "Armanita's house."

Aunt Georgia looks out the window and puts her hand over her chest like pledging allegiance.

"This is where you *live?*" Aunt Georgia says.

"George," Uncle Charles says.

Uncle Charles parks between two low-rider cars and turns off the engine. He pulls out a pack of cigarettes and lights one with a silver lighter, the smell of lighter fluid and smoke in the car.

"Well," Uncle Charles says, "what now?"

He unrolls the window and Aunt Georgia looks at him like he's crazy. Uncle Charles rolls the window back up so it's just a crack. Aunt Georgia looks down at me and clears her throat.

"Is Bryan home?" Aunt Georgia says.

"I don't know," I say.

"What do you mean you don't know?" Aunt Georgia says.

"I don't know," I say, "it's not like we hang out together or anything."

Aunt Georgia and Uncle Charles look at each other and Uncle Charles blows his smoke up to the little crack of the window.

"I'll stay with the kids," Uncle Charles says, "you both go on up, get B.J., and we'll go out to dinner. Would you like that, Jenny?"

"I want to get out," Jeff says.

Aunt Georgia twists around, arm over the seat, the sound of the lock pushed down.

"Absolutely not," Aunt Georgia says.

I touch my fingers to Uncle Charles's green shirt, just the fabric of his sleeve.

"Not B.J.," I say.

Uncle Charles looks down at me.

"Not B.J.?" Uncle Charles says.

"He hates to be called B.J. now," I say, "it's just Bryan. Don't ask me why."

Uncle Charles squints out the windshield like looking at something far away and he puts his cigarette between his lips. Aunt Georgia moves her hair behind her ears and holds her purse with both hands.

"Hurry, George," Uncle Charles says. "Get Bryan and let's go."

You never bug Bryan when he's in his room with the GO AWAY sign on the door. Aunt Georgia and me stand outside his room and I lean my head to the door. The moody music is on in there so I nod my head. She holds her purse in one hand and reaches for the door.

"You better knock," I say.

Aunt Georgia pulls her hand back and then she clears her throat and stands up straight. She opens the door and the GO AWAY sign falls on the floor. Blankets are tacked to the window so there's no light and Bryan wears a pair of headphones. I stay in the hall and kick my foot over the GO AWAY sign.

In Bryan's room, Aunt Georgia's voice is all high and happy and she says, "You've grown into a young man," and "Let's go see Uncle Charles, we're going out to dinner."

Bryan sits on the floor and puts on a pair of old tennis shoes without any laces. He looks at me and I put my hands wide and it's the first time we have even looked at each other since the day we moved in.

Aunt Georgia holds my hand and Bryan's hand like we're little kids. We're all going down the steps and out the front door when Armanita shows up and says, "Who the hell are you and where are you going with those kids?"

Armanita is big, not fat, just tall and wide. Armanita is the kind of woman you don't want to mess around with. Aunt Georgia doesn't look scared or surprised or anything, just stands tall and holds my hand tight.

"The children's mother is my husband's sister," Aunt Georgia says, "was my husband's sister, my sister-in-law. We are here to see Disneyland, my goodness what a trip, all the way over the Sierras here to Los Angeles, and we stopped to take the kids out to dinner."

Aunt Georgia talks and talks and that's when I remember how Aunt Georgia can talk on and on without even taking a breath. Aunt Georgia explains and Armanita goes from mad to surprised to a look like she wished she never asked anything about Aunt Georgia.

Aunt Georgia tells Bryan and me to go to the car to see the kids, says she is going to leave a note for Deb with a telephone number of some hotel where they will stay tonight and Deb can call and leave a message if she has any questions.

Aunt Georgia and Uncle Charles drive to a hotel where they have two rooms that connect with a door in the middle. Each room has two beds and a bathroom. There's a television in each room too.

Carrie Sue, Jeff, Bryan, and me are in one room and the television is tuned to some program on how to catch a fish. Carrie Sue and Jeff are on one bed and they watch this guy put a worm on his hook and cast out his line. Bryan looks out the window at a swimming pool that is all lit up and he says he should go back to Armanita's house to get his bathing suit since we aren't that far away.

I sit on the bed opposite Carrie Sue and Jeff and lean against the headboard so I can hear in the other room. The

TV in there is on too and it's some news program. Aunt Georgia and Uncle Charles talk on the telephone.

Something is going on, something big. I look at Bryan, but he just looks at the stupid pool. Aunt Georgia comes into our room, but I can see Uncle Charles talk on the telephone with his hand against his forehead.

"Everything okey-dokey in here?" Aunt Georgia says.

"I should have brought my swim trunks," Bryan says, "I could go get them."

"No, no," Aunt Georgia says, "we're going to have some dinner first and then we'll buy you new trunks. How about that?"

"I'm hungry, Momma," Jeff says.

"Me too," Carrie Sue says.

Bryan bites his lip and looks out the window again. Aunt Georgia touches Jeff's blond hair, moves it around.

"I know you're hungry, honey," Aunt Georgia says, "we'll get cleaned up and then we'll go."

Aunt Georgia tells Carrie Sue and Jeff to wash their faces and they jump up quick. Aunt Georgia opens a suitcase and moves some clothes around. She takes out a pair of shorts and a shirt.

"Why don't you come with me," Aunt Georgia says, "and we'll get you cleaned up."

"Cleaned up?" I say.

"Just a little cleaned up," she says, "okay?"

She holds my hand and we go into the other hotel room. Uncle Charles sits on the bed with the telephone to his ear. He looks up at us and smiles.

"What's happening?" I say.

Aunt Georgia tugs me into their bathroom and closes the door.

"Nothing to worry about," Aunt Georgia says, "we just have to make a couple of quick calls."

The bathroom is brown tile on the floor and walls and there is a big mirror over the sink. Aunt Georgia kneels down on the brown tile floor and moves to take off my clothes. I put my hands on her hands.

"I can do it," I say, "just give me a second."

Aunt Georgia drops her hands and holds them on her knees.

"I'm sorry," she says. "I'm just so used to helping Carrie Sue. But you're all grown up now, aren't you? Do you want me to leave you alone for a second?"

Aunt Georgia's voice is all around the bathroom, off the walls, the ceiling, and I don't know what to do. I don't want her to leave, but I don't want her to take my clothes off. The shirt and shorts on the counter are white and pink and clean and I guess it's not so bad if she stays as long as I get undressed myself.

"You don't have to leave," I say.

Aunt Georgia stands up and looks away like she's giving me some privacy. She runs water in the sink and puts a wash-cloth under the water. I pull my skirt down fast, hold it against my chest, and fold it into a small square. I put it on top of the toilet and it's tired and dirty. Aunt Georgia doesn't look at me, but her hand holds the shorts out and I take them out of her hand. I pull on the pink shorts and a little tag scratches against my side. Aunt Georgia bends over, yanks the tag off, and throws it in the trash.

"How do those feel?" she says. "Just right?"

I move the waistband around and the shorts are brand-new perfect.

"Whose are they?" I say.

"We got them for you," she says.

"Me?" I say.

"You," she says. "I remember how much you loved dressing in nice things."

Aunt Georgia talks and while she talks she pulls my T-shirt off just like that. It's cool air on my stomach and the silver key bounces over the brown tile. I reach down and pick it up quick, hold it in my palm with my fist closed over.

"What's that?" she says.

"Nothing," I say, "just a key, my key."

I cross my arms over my chest like I'm cold, but I'm not cold, just embarrassed. She looks at me and tilts her head to the side. This close and I remember Aunt Georgia, really remember her. She is pretty and serious and inside her eyes is a look like something hurts from a long, long time ago.

She makes a small smile like she understands about the key, and tosses my old shirt on the counter and shakes open the new one.

She pulls the new shirt over my head. It's white with pink material around the sleeves and the collar, and there is a little pink pocket with white birds in the design. I put my key into the pocket and Aunt Georgia smiles.

"Now you look like a little girl," Aunt Georgia says.

She turns me in a circle but stops when I face the wall.

"Oh, my god," Aunt Georgia says.

She touches my leg, down by the ankle, and it tickles there. Over my shoulder, I look where she touches and it's a brown crusty scab. I try to turn around, but Aunt Georgia holds her hand around my ankle.

"That's nothing," I say, "just an old burn."

"A burn?" Aunt Georgia says. "What the hell burned you?"

"It was my fault, I just got too close to the radiator," I say. "Deb said it was my fault."

There is a knock on the door and Uncle Charles looks in.

"We've got trouble," he says.

"Trouble?" I say.

"What have you done with my children," Deb yells.

Just like that everything is crazy in the hotel room.

Deb yells at Uncle Charles, Aunt Georgia yells at Deb, Deb yells at Bryan and me, and then she pulls my arm until I am out of the hotel room and next to her side. Carrie Sue cries and Aunt Georgia hugs Carrie Sue against her side and yells at Deb some more. Uncle Charles has his arms in the air and he says, "Let's calm down, let's just calm down now," over and over. Deb yells, "Shut the fuck up," at Uncle Charles and says she is going to call the cops for kidnapping.

Deb shakes me, says I have to go get my own clothes, and pushes me back into the hotel room. I run to the bathroom, grab my skirt and T-shirt, and run back to Deb. Bryan is already outside and he looks at Deb, looks at Uncle Charles, looks at me. He looks like he might start to cry and I know I am already crying.

Deb yanks me out of the room and puts her arm over my shoulders.

Aunt Georgia and Uncle Charles are in there, we are out here, and Deb is in the space between.

"I don't know what you are trying to pull here," Deb yells.

"We're not trying to pull anything," Uncle Charles says. "If you just calm down we can talk."

"Fuck you. I'm calm," Deb yells. "Let's go."

White light from the hotel sign is the only light outside and it's the sound of our feet on the sidewalk. Deb holds her arms tight around my shoulders and Bryan's shoulders and we walk like that in the dark.

"You're my kids," Deb says, "we're a family."

I can barely see Deb's face, her hair all around, flicking in my eyes, and I look at the sidewalk so I can see where the concrete is cracked and lifted by tree roots.

"They can't take you kids from me," she says, "not ever."

Something is wrong, way wrong. Deb doesn't even like me and she barely knows where I am most of the time. Like Bryan says, if it wasn't for the money that came every month, she would have ditched us a long time ago. Still, it's nice to hear someone say they want me, even if it's just for a little while. It's nice even if it's a lie.

twenty

Two weeks later, Bryan is gone. There's no good-bye and no reason. That's just the way it is.

Two weeks after that, Deb says I have to leave too. She says I'm a liability to her family dynamic and it's my punishment to be sent away.

Deb gives me an old duffel bag and says I can pack it and my pink trunk. She says she'll send the rest later.

I don't even know where I'm going, maybe to Uncle Charles and Aunt Georgia, maybe not. Deb just says I'm going to Reno and then she won't say anything after that.

All alone in the add-on, I take off my shoe and open my pink trunk. There is *Snow White and the Seven Dwarfs,* the painting by Keith, the Our Wedding book, the black velvet bag with Momma's pearls and her wedding ring.

It seems like a million years ago and still all my stuff is here like a road you can go back home on. I know when I got everything and I know what it all means and I know it's safe. Maybe that's the way it is, you just keep things safe since people come and go and you need bits and pieces to remember them by.

I don't know what's going to happen to me, but I know I am going to take as many of my things as I can.

I stand up, rub my hands together, take everything off my princess desk, my dresser, and my bookcases, and I put my stuff in the trunk. There's my books, my jewelry box, the sleeping beauty lamp, and my clock radio. I strip my bed down and fold up my pink bedspread, my blanket, my sheets, and the pink canopy that hangs over my bed. I even take out the knobs that hold the canopy fabric in place.

I take everything that will fit and there's so much stuff in my pink trunk, I have to sit on top and bounce up and down to make it close.

When I'm done, the add-on is bare mattress and bare shelves and it looks naked like that. Maybe Deb will send my stuff, maybe she won't. One thing I know about Deb, you can't figure her out. I stand there and look at my stuff like this is the last time and it was nice to have a princess bedroom set, even if I'm not a princess, not really.

There are no good-byes with Christopher, Kenny, or Ronny either. They don't care about me, never did.

Deb borrows someone's car, drives me to the bus station, and she holds the steering wheel with both hands, eyes ahead the whole time. I look at LA through the window and it's always the same, gray and dirty.

Deb parks in the bus terminal full of silver buses. She gets out of the car, opens the back, and lifts out my trunk with both hands. She can barely lift it and I have to hold one side so she doesn't drop it.

"What the hell do you have in here?" she says.

"Everything," I say.

Deb takes a deep breath and crosses her arms.

"I told you I would send the rest later," she says.

I look at Deb and she looks at me. I look away from her face and shift the duffel bag so it rests between my shoulders. She throws her arms up and walks away, opens the door to the main office and goes inside.

I push my pink trunk to the curb and lift it to the sidewalk. Deb is at the ticket counter so I sit down on the pink trunk and watch her. She looks at me through the glass doors, takes her wallet out of her purse, and turns her back to me again. The bus terminal is the smell of oil and gas and the sound is brakes and big engines.

Deb comes out of the doors and she holds a white rectangle of paper in her hand. She has on her short suede coat with the belt around the waist and a pair of black slacks. She is long and skinny, angles and edges, and her green eyes have dark circles like she is sick or tired.

"All right," Deb says, "here's your ticket and here's twenty bucks for the road."

I stand up and take the ticket and the twenty-dollar bill. I fold the money in half, in half again, and in half again until it's a tiny square. I push the square into my jeans pocket.

Deb tugs her belt tighter around her waist, flips her hair, and looks side to side.

"Your bus is over there," Deb says, "just wait in line and they'll load you up."

I look where she points and there is a silver bus at the curb. A man loads luggage under the bus and there is a line at the door.

No one has to tell me I'm never going to see Deb again, I just know that's the way it's going to be. When you know you're never going to see someone again, all the bad feelings aren't so bad anymore, and when I look at Deb, I wish it could have been different.

"Where am I going?" I say.

Deb bites her lip and maybe she wishes things were different too. She flips her hair back over her shoulder one more time.

"You are going to Reno," Deb says. "I think your grandparents will meet you."

"You think?" I say.

Deb bites her lip again and shrugs her shoulder.

"Maybe Georgia and Chuck," Deb says, "I don't know."

I look at the bus, at the man who loads luggage, and I look at Deb's face again.

"Is that where Bryan is?" I say. "With Aunt Georgia and Uncle Charles?"

Deb rubs her eye and nods her head.

"Yes," Deb says, "he's with Charles, for now anyway."

I stand so my leg is against my pink trunk and I look at my bus ticket, *one way* stamped in red.

"Why did he go first?" I say. "Why did I get left behind?"

Deb takes a deep breath in and looks right at my face.

"You always ask too many questions," Deb says. "Why do you ask so many questions?"

I adjust the duffel bag around my back and put the bus ticket in the pocket of my sweatshirt jacket. The only thing I have left is questions and the way Deb looks at me with her creepy cat eyes, I know she isn't going to give me any more answers.

I look at the pink trunk and I look at Deb.

"You need a hand with that?" Deb says.

"I got it," I say.

Deb crosses her arms and steps one foot back, the mannequin pose. I put both hands on the black handle of my pink trunk and lift hard. The trunk isn't too heavy for me. I look at Deb and smile.

"See ya," I say.

Inside the bus is a man behind the steering wheel with a blue hat and a blue jacket. He checks tickets to make sure all the people go to the right place.

When it's my turn, he looks at me and then he looks behind me.

"You all alone, little girl?" the bus driver says.

He has a nice smile, white hair, and old man eyes.

I stand up straight, shoulders back, chin tucked, and hold my ticket so it's right in his face.

"All alone," I say.

The bus driver looks at my ticket, looks at me again and he nods one quick nod so I can go.

Inside, the bus smells like cigarettes and old coffee. I go down three rows and sit in an aisle seat. I put my bag into the seat next to the window, no way I'm sitting next to anyone, not unless I have to.

Ten people go by, eleven, twelve. No one stops to share my seat.

My pink trunk is loaded under the bus and I have a ticket to claim it when I get to Reno. I put the *one-way* bus ticket and the claim ticket into my sweatshirt pocket and I look out the bus window. Deb's car is already gone and it figures.

All around people talk and someone laughs a low laugh. No one else gets on the bus for a long time and the bus driver looks in the long mirror attached over the windshield.

"Last call," the driver yells.

I watch the door and it's a wide-open space. Anyone could come on the bus, anyone.

I look at the open door and I can see him in full color.

Daddy is boy-next-door drop-dead handsome with cinnamon-colored eyes and his squared-up jaw. He's too tall for the bus and he has to bend over a little so he doesn't bump his head on the ceiling. Daddy talks to the driver and then looks around like he lost something.

I stand up so he can see me and his eyes stop on my face. He smiles the best smile and holds his hand out.

"This is a big mistake, Juniper," Daddy says.

My hand is small in his hand and he smells like That Man and cigarettes. Daddy lifts me so I am against his chest and he carries me off the bus and out to the beach, where we can walk along the sand and I can tell him everything.

"Next stop, Sacramento," the driver yells.

I blink my eyes and just like that, I can't see Daddy anymore.

The door closes with the scream of metal on metal and the bus moves out of the terminal. On the street, it's bright daylight and I move my bag to the outside seat so I can sit and look out the window.

twenty-one

The silver bus pulls into the Reno terminal and I hold the dirty gray duffel bag in my lap. People stand on the sidewalk and all the faces are just faces with eyes that don't look for me.

Inside my chest is that heavy alone feeling like maybe no one will be here for me. I get off the bus and look around and that's when my eyes stop on Grandpa Ed, Daddy's daddy.

"There she is," Grandpa yells.

I squeeze my fingers around the strap of the dirty gray duffel bag and walk until we are face to face, me small and him tall. Grandpa has his hands fisted on his hips like he has something to say but he just looks at me and then shakes his head.

"Well, give your old Grandpa a big hug," he says.

I drop my dirty gray duffel bag and hug around his neck, the smell of coffee and mint all around. Grandpa laughs his deep, warm laugh against my face and he stops hugging first.

"My goodness." Grandpa says, "you are a young lady now."

My arms and face and body still feel Grandpa's hug and I just smile and nod since I don't know what else to do.

Grandpa is just like always, round cheeks, wide nose, white hair and bushy white eyebrows. And he's here.

BASIL STREET BLUES

Michael Holroyd

Michael Holroyd is one of the finest biographers of the century.
And yet he was never interested in exploring his own family's
history. His parents' death in the 1980s, however, left an
unexpected vacuum which he gradually felt the need
to fill with their stories, his narrative.

This, in his fashion, is Michael Holroyd's autobiography, a
biography of a biographer and a continuation of his never-
ending love affair with human nature. Part detective story, part
family saga and part oblique voyage of self-discovery, *Basil Street
Blues* is an entrancing and elegiac story, startlingly funny,
profoundly moving: a very English tragi-comedy.

'Holroyd will at last be recognised in full for the great gifts
that he undoubtedly has . . . a perfect book: finely
produced, full of humour and pathos'
Hugh Massingberd, *Mail on Sunday*

'*Basil Street Blues* is an extraordinary piece of work, which takes its
place alongside John Gale's *Clean Young Englishmen*, Richard Cobb's
Still Life and Anthony Powell's *To Keep The Ball Rolling* as a classic
of English autobiography'
D. J. Taylor, *Times Literary Supplement*

'Beautifully crafted, moving in places, a pleasure to read'
The Economist

'Fine, funny and touching . . . an original, unforgettable book'
Victoria Glendinning, *Daily Telegraph*

Abacus
0 349 11134 0

FATHER AND I

Carlo Gébler

'You cannot change the past but, with understanding, you
can sometimes draw the poison out of it.' *Father and I* is Carlo
Gébler's powerful personal testimony to that: the memoir of his
almost impossible relationship with his father Ernest, a man in
later life he would learn to love and understand.

'The literary world has hardly been short of writers'
recollections of their parents in recent years, but they don't come
much better than Carlo Gébler's account of his relationship with his
father . . . This is a marvellous book, beautifully capturing the
bewilderment and betrayals of childhood, as well as the
shifting perspectives of adulthood. At times unbearably
sad, at others ludicrously funny, it is written with
great honesty and charm'
Sunday Telegraph

'A spare, lean, haunting account . . . Written with Gébler's
trademark no-frills prose, and relentless attention to the detail of a
child's life as it is lived, this memoir also provides a vivid evocation
of Britain and Ireland in the 1960s and 1970s'
Will Self, *New Statesmen Books of the Year*

'*Father and I* is more than worthy to share shelf space with such
acknowledged masterpieces of the genre as Edmond Gosse's *Father
and Son* and J. R. Ackerley's *My Father and Myself*'
Times Literary Supplement

'A book of great merit . . . Gébler's is a strong authorial voice,
unsentimental and unabashed. The humanity of the author comes
through and we begin to share his compassion for his father . . .
highly recommendable'
Literary Review

Abacus
0 349 11293 2

Now you can order superb titles directly from Abacus

☐ Basil Street Blues   Michael Holroyd   £7.99
☐ Father and I   Carlo Gébler   £7.99

Please allow for postage and packing: **Free UK delivery.**
Europe; add 25% of retail price; Rest of World; 45% of retail price.

To order any of the above or any other Abacus titles, please call our credit card orderline or fill in this coupon and send/fax it to:

Abacus, P.O. Box 121, Kettering, Northants NN14 4ZQ
Tel: 01832 737527   Fax: 01832 733076
Email: aspenhouse@FSBDial.co.uk

☐ I enclose a UK bank cheque made payable to Abacus for £ ....
☐ Please charge £.............. to my Access, Visa, Delta, Switch Card No.

☐☐☐☐☐☐☐☐☐☐☐☐☐☐☐☐☐☐

Expiry Date ☐☐☐☐   Switch Issue No. ☐☐

NAME (Block letters please) ....

ADDRESS ....

....

....

Postcode ....Telephone ....

Signature ....

Please allow 28 days for delivery within the UK. Offer subject to price and availability.

Please do not send any further mailings from companies carefully selected by Abacus ☐